"TASTY AS WELL AS HEALTHY . . . A VALUABLE AID TO THOSE ON SALT-REDUCED DIETS."
—LESLIE BAER, M.D.,
hypertension specialist,
Columbia Presbyterian Hospital

This unparalleled collection of authentic recipes from every region also has these helpful features:

- Taste-alike substitutes for soy sauce, black bean sauce, and many other seasonings

- Sodium, calorie, fat, and carbohydrate counts for every recipe

- Information on adapting recipes to your own needs

- A two-week diet plan based on 1200 calories and no more than 500 mg. of sodium a day

- Tables of nutritional values for ingredients used

- Complete party menus for brunches, lunches, dinners, and buffets

"Tasty Chinese meals, sure to please the whole family . . . with scores of practical aids to add a flavorful accent to restricted cooking."
—ALMEDA O. DIXON,
Research Dietician,
Department of Medicine,
Columbia University

MERLE SCHELL is the author of *Tasting Good: The International Salt-Free Diet Cookbook* (also available in a Plume edition), winner of a Tastemaker citation, and *The Mexican Salt-Free Diet Cookbook* (an NAL Books hardcover). She lives in New York City, where she counsels individuals who have salt-related health and diet problems.

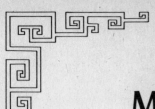
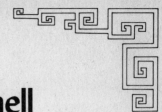

Merle Schell

THE CHINESE
SALT-FREE DIET
COOKBOOK

A PLUME BOOK

NEW AMERICAN LIBRARY

NEW YORK AND SCARBOROUGH, ONTARIO

A hardcover edition was published by New American Library
and simultaneously in Canada by
The New American Library of Canada Limited.

 PLUME TRADEMARK REG. U.S. PAT. OFF. AND FOREIGN COUNTRIES
REGISTERED TRADEMARK—MARCA REGISTRADA
HECHO EN HARRISONBURG, VA., U.S.A.

SIGNET, SIGNET CLASSIC, MENTOR, ONYX, PLUME, MERIDIAN,
and NAL BOOKS are published in the United States by
New American Library, 1633 Broadway, New York, New York 10019,
in Canada by The New American Library of Canada Limited,
81 Mack Avenue, Scarborough, Ontario M1L 1M8.

Designed by Julian Hamer

Library of Congress Cataloging in Publication Data
Schell, Merle.
    The Chinese salt-free diet cookbook.
    Includes index.
    1. Salt-free diet—Recipes.   2. Low-calorie diet—
Recipes.   3. Cookery, Chinese.   I. Title.
RM237.8.S28   1985   641.5'632   85–2992
ISBN 0–453–00491–1
ISBN 0–452–25835–9 (pbk.)

First Plume Printing, August, 1986

1 2 3 4 5 6 7 8 9

PRINTED IN THE UNITED STATES OF AMERICA

For my darling Joey...
Now and always

Acknowledgments

Since the publication of my first book, *Tasting Good*, I have received continued encouragement and support from many people, including those who were most helpful in the preparation of this book. To them, my sincere thanks: Amy Shouse and Christine Merz for their never-wavering friendship, and hours of work checking and rechecking the recipes; Carol Wilson for typing a beautifully clean manuscript; Marie Simmons for her meticulous and very knowledgeable editorial proofreading; Almeda Dixon for giving of her valuable time to evaluate the nutritional elements of the book; my agent, Peter Ginsberg, for being there when I need him; my editor Irene Pink for her guidance, caring, and expertise; and my editor Molly Allen for her patience, humor, enthusiasm, friendship, and complete professionalism. Lastly, to my readers for their kind, warm letters, which make all my efforts worthwhile.

Contents

Foreword

I am very pleased to write an introduction for Merle Schell's new book, dedicated to the many people on restricted diets. This task is simple since I believe so strongly in the book's underlying premise that excess salt is detrimental to health. Many medical studies have clearly shown the relationship between systemic diseases and excessive intake of salt. Nutritional research has further pointed out the huge amount of salt consumed in this country, far more than our dietary needs. Many apparently healthy people are stressing their bodies with too much salt and will eventually manifest a variety of medical problems including cardiovascular disease; salt, water, and metabolic imbalances; and certain endocrine disorders.

Recent research, for example, has shown that patients with high blood pressure can significantly lower their blood pressure with a combination of salt restriction and exercise. These patients were able to reduce the dosage of their antihypertensive medication or, in many cases, to entirely stop their drugs. However, they had to continue salt restriction and regular exercise on a continuing basis.

Patients intellectually understand their doctors' orders to reduce salt and caloric intake, but find it very difficult to follow these recommendations in the real world. Ms. Schell addressed these issues admirably in her first book, *Tasting Good*. Now she has expanded her artful presentation with a carefully documented explanation of Chinese salt-free cooking. The detailed recipes and skillful diets, complete with helpful hints, will bring not only better health but delightful eating to a great many people.

—JEROME W. FISCHBEIN, M.D.
Lecturer on Medicine at Harvard Medical School
Associate Clinical Professor of Medicine at
Boston University School of Medicine

Foreword

Cooking low-sodium Chinese food is not easy because soy sauce, salt, and MSG are so intrinsic to the cuisine, but when our customers request dishes without these ingredients, we do everything we can to give them a Chinese flavor that is as close to the original as possible.

Merle Schell takes the same approach in *The Chinese Salt-Free Diet Cookbook*. The results are admirable. Her recipes deliver the fresh, crisp texture that trademarks much of Chinese cooking. In addition, they capture the essence of the sometimes contrasting, sometimes complementary flavors that spark and heighten the Chinese taste experience.

In short, this book proves that Chinese food, which relies on many and varied ingredients to give it its distinctive flavor, can be enjoyed even without salt.

—BILL LIN
General Manager, HSF Restaurants,
New York, New York;
a former Restaurant Director
for the Culinary Institute of America,
Hyde Park, New York.

Author's Note

Living salt-free is easier than it was a short five years ago. Not perfect, mind you—just easier.

When I wrote my first book, *Tasting Good*, in 1981, I had already been living salt-free for several years and wanted to make life better, easier, tastier for others like me, for I was keenly aware of the problems we salt-free dieters faced. Namely, the physical and emotional difficulties of adjusting to a new life-style, new eating habits, new tastes plus dealing with the anger and, to some degree, the embarrassment at being different from "normal" people—a difference sharply noticed in restaurants or even at family dinners.

How many of you remember feeling waves of envy when everyone around you was gorging on barbecued spareribs while you stared down at a plate of lettuce? I know. I felt the same way.

Matters were not helped by the lack of salt-free products—or rather the difficulty in locating those that did exist (and the poor taste of some of them). I used to order by the case products I could not find at home. Wherever I traveled, I would seek out health stores and survey supermarkets, searching for salt-free foods. When I found something new, I would buy it by the dozen.

Other people would come home from trips with clothes, jewelry, souvenirs. Me? I'd come home with salt-free pickles, or barbecue sauce, or salad dressing.

But today things are much better. Today if you want cookies or pretzels, tomato sauce or mayonnaise, bread or cheese, or anything at all, you can find it salt-free, prominently displayed at your local supermarket.

In fact, salt-free living has touched every industry. Airlines are now happy to serve you a low-sodium meal (on 48 hours' notice). Restaurants no longer find it odd or uncommon for a customer to request a meal without salt. Even Chinese restaurants have a selection of dishes prepared without salt, soy sauce, or MSG.

The supply has obviously risen to meet the demand because everyone's salt consciousness has been raised. Today people are very aware of salt's potential dangers and of the specific medical problems, including hypertension, cardiovascular and kidney disease, emphysema, diabetes, and gout, associated with the consumption of too much salt. Those of us who must live salt-free are finding it more convenient and more acceptable to do so, especially since we need not sacrifice either flavor or variety. Others who choose to reduce their salt intake to safeguard their health are also finding salt-free alternatives more than satisfactory and often very good.

Happily, things have changed considerably over the last five years. Everyone is jumping on the salt-free wagon. Salt-free living and eating have become part of the fiber of our American life-style. They are here to stay, and, as the song goes, I want to shout "hooray," because, selfishly speaking, the more people look for savory, salt-free additions to their kitchen repertoire, the more opportunity for me to share my recipe secrets. After all, what good is a secret if you can't tell it to anyone?

Tasting Good was the beginning: offerings from ten ethnic cuisines with salt-free living tips galore. However, there is still much more to do and explore. Even though salt-free products are now in plentiful supply, information on what to do with them and how to combine them into imaginative, tasty dishes is still scarce.

Cookbooks in particular have not kept pace with consumer interest and enthusiasm nearly as vigorously as manufacturers have. For example, you can buy low-salt soy sauce and low-sodium plum sauce, but try to find a salt-free Chinese cookbook.

That is why I wrote *The Chinese Salt-Free Diet Cookbook*. Where better to begin to discover the wonderful world of salt-free possibilities than with Chinese food. To paraphrase a well-known advertising campaign: You don't have to be Chinese to love egg rolls.

I know I do. And if you do, too, then I hope you will enjoy the tantalizing, authentic-tasting, delicious temptations that follow, brought to you from every region of that mystical, magical heart of the Orient—China.

Note: If you are on a special diet, check with your doctor for eating do's and don'ts before using the recipes in this—or any other cookbook.

THE CHINESE SALT-FREE DIET COOKBOOK

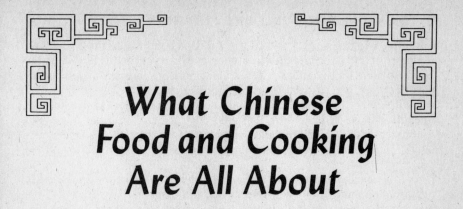

What Chinese Food and Cooking Are All About

The Regional Cuisines and Their Differences

There are four distinct cooking styles in China—each one indigenous, singular and separate from the rest.

China's rough, unyielding, often violent terrain does much to explain why these styles have not meshed more completely through the centuries. In whatever direction you travel, you are confronted by startling, frightening, forbidding beauty. On the North's border, the bleak hopelessness of the Gobi Desert and the imposing grandeur of the Great Wall stretch into seeming infinity. The East is both nurtured and shackled by the relentless, sweeping might of the Yangtze River, which also splits the South from the North. The West is surrounded by the towering Himalayan Mountains—so rugged that they are virtually impenetrable except by fording the treacherous rapids of the Yangtze Gorge.

The majestic expanse of this mystically awesome landscape is crisscrossed by stormy peaks and raging rivers, which conspire to cut off each region and its people from every other. In its dramatic terrain lies the power and the magic of the land.

The East

Of the four directions, the Chinese always place East first—perhaps because the rising sun is one of the positive, warm symbols of the life force, yang—so we, too, will begin here.

The Yangtze River—sometimes called the heart or main street of China—dominates the eastern region. Spreading itself like a benevolent hand, it stretches its many fingers throughout the eastern province to create fertile farmlands and numerous shallow lakes and swamplands where rice grows in abundance.

But the Yangtze is cruel as well as kind. It is bountiful in providing food —a most precious commodity in a country where only 10 percent of the land is suitable for agriculture. Yet, it also imprisons the very people it protects, for they cling to its life-giving shores, never venturing more than a few miles from their birthplace, thus never experiencing any influences other than those in their own cloistered environment. Indeed, if they did want to leave, they would find the swamplands formed by the river treacherous to cross and the steep hills almost impossible to traverse except on foot.

As one travels farther south along the eastern coast, the terrain becomes increasingly mountainous with sheer rock cliffs making passage out of the question. Impenetrable, dense forests dot the coastline. These natural barriers enclose the few habitable oases in this eerily beautiful wasteland.

By sea, however, one can reach Shanghai—the largest and most famous port in China, through which pass some of the finest teas and silks the country has to offer. This bustling city enjoys temperate weather and an abundance of riches from the sea. Unfortunately, the advantages nature provides are neither fully nor artfully exploited in the local cuisine.

With the exception of the red-cooked dishes for which it is famous, Shanghai cooking can best be described as heavy-handed—an anomaly in a country where subtlety is the common denominator. Soy sauce and sugar are the dominant seasonings, and all too often they are used to such excess that they mask and smother the fresh flavor of the sea's delicacies.

Still farther south (after a stop at Yangchow to sample the internationally famous pork dish, Lion's Head), in the modest province of Fukien, the cooking style of the region achieves memorable heights. Here one can savor how wonderful, how high an art the blending of soy sauce and sugar can be. These seasonings, along with other herbs and spices, are used with a delicate, loving hand—not so much to add their own flavors as to heighten and enhance the natural goodness of the food being prepared. See for yourself when you sample Salmon with Zucchini in Soy Sauce (page 118) or Braised Pork with Orange Rings (page 172).

Finally, there are two major qualities—one bad, one good—that distinguish the cuisine of the eastern region from that of the rest of China. First, it lacks the imaginative combinations of tastes and textures found elsewhere, so that, unless the chef is inspired, the food can be disappointing and boring. However, simmering—the cooking method most often used here—is exactly right for the harmonious intermingling of the salt and sugar flavors. It is especially perfect for enhancing the fragile freshness of seafood, producing exquisite results indeed.

As we explore the remaining regions, it is worth noting that the soft, sensuous texture and slightly sweet taste typical of eastern cooking can add a lovely balance to the stir-fried dishes—be they hot or mild—found in the rest of China.

The South

Throughout China, the symbols of yin and yang—the negative and positive life forces that keep the world in harmonious balance—are ever present. The South, surely a symbol of yang, is a lush, tropical paradise, sheltered by the Nan Ling (Southern Mountains) from the cold winds and blustery climate immediately to the north.

Before men settled there, the South was completely blanketed under a tropical rain forest. Today, as in the rest of China, fertile land is scarce and is maximized by terracing and irrigation, but the mild weather of the South encourages abundant vegetation year round, resulting in three harvests a year.

In the thriving Pearl River Delta just south of Canton, rice is the primary crop, along with sugar. Sweet potatoes spring like wildflowers on the hillsides, and throughout the region bananas, pineapples, and lychees flourish.

Because so much of the available land is used for agriculture, many people of the South live on boats and earn their livelihood from the sea. Indeed, the fishing industry of southern China provides 25 percent of the seafood consumed throughout the country.

If the land of southern China seems unique, different, and more exotic compared to the rest of the country, her people are even more so. In many ways, they are strangers in their own land, for they are physically, philosophically, emotionally, and intellectually unlike their countrymen. As a nation, the Chinese revere family and honor above all, even sacrificing precious farmland so that they can bury their dead nearby. This fierce sense of loyalty has kept them close to the areas in which they were born, each community developing and raising to perfection its particular talents. The breathtaking beauty of Ming china is one positive result, but this same introspective pride has also made them unable, indeed, unwilling, to acknowledge and accept anyone or anything outside their own sphere. So, in the end, they have tended to reject progress. All, that is, except the Chinese of the South.

As long ago as 1514, the Portuguese visited Canton, and this city became the international contact point for all visitors to China. In 1842, Canton became the first port officially open to foreign residents.

The Cantonese not only welcomed but readily adopted foods (including tomatoes, ketchup, and Worcestershire sauce), technology, and even the attitudes of their Western friends. As a result, they are more outgoing and adventuresome and more receptive to change and new ideas than are their reserved countrymen.

Thus, it was natural for the Cantonese to be the first Chinese to emigrate —first to Southeast Asia, and later to Europe, Australia, and the Americas. Consequently, it is the cooking of the southern region with which we are the most familiar and which many consider the finest in China.

The cuisine offers innumerable variations in its use of herbs and spices and its blending of tastes and textures. Indeed, the six basic flavors generic to Chinese cuisine—sweet, sour, bitter, spicy, pungent, and, yes, salty—are all found in the cooking of the South. But whether a dish calls for pineapple or oranges, garlic or ginger, curry powder or black bean sauce, seasonings are used only to highlight the main ingredients. These are usually stir-fried—a technique the Cantonese have superbly refined—and then lightly bound in a delicate sauce. Vegetables and meats or fish are often cooked together, with no rules or restrictions, so the food of the South is as unfettered by tradition as the people themselves—and just as delightful.

The West

The Himalayas scrape the skies along the western border. Sheer cliffs, over 1,000 feet high, plunge into the dangerous turbulence of the Yangtze Gorge rapids. Is it any wonder, then, that for centuries the Szechwan province was cut off from the rest of the world.

Yet these same forces of nature created an environment in which the people of the Red Basin could thrive. The mountains, aided by an ever-present cloud cover, trap and focus the sun's rays on the valley below, creating hot, humid summers, heavy rainfall, and winters always above freezing.

In short, Szechwan has perfect weather conditions for food production. In fact, anything and everything that can be grown in the rest of China can be grown here, including sugarcane, bamboo shoots, wheat, corn, citrus fruits, and the well-known Szechwan peppercorn. And, of course, rice paddies are everywhere, thanks to the rich bedlands along the Yangtze. So it is that this province, which has the minimum amount of land for cultivation, is called the Land of Abundance.

Considerable credit for this bounty must be given to the people themselves. More than 2,200 years ago, they devised an irrigation system—still in use today—which redirects the water channel each year and removes the accumulated refuse. Accordingly, land erosion is kept to a minimum and fertile soil is maximized. They also developed a method of terracing that literally carves food shelves into the steeply graded and otherwise unusable hills.

Their ingenuity and efficiency are perhaps best exhibited in the rice paddies. After the rice is harvested, the paddies are turned into reservoirs and stocked with freshwater fish, providing both an off-season food supply and a guaranteed source of water for the next planting cycle. Thus, from very little land, the most populous province in China is able to set an excellent table for its 75 million people.

The culinary center is the ancient walled city of Chengtu, the capital of Szechwan. The cooking skill found here can be savored in city after city throughout the province.

To most of us, Szechwan food is synonymous with hot. Indeed, the hot pepper does have a unique place in the food of this region. Its fire is said to clear the palate and sensitize it to the many flavors in a given dish. But although some dishes are hotter than others, true Szechwan cooking is an artful combination and balance of contrasting flavors: hot and sour, pungent and sweet. To add to the variety, the provinces of Yunnan and Kweichou contribute curry adopted from Indian cuisine.

Multiple contrasting tastes in a single recipe is an earmark of Szechwan cuisine. Multiple cooking methods is another. For example, meat or vegetables may be deep-fried, then added to stir-fried ingredients, all of which are then simmered in the final cooking stage. The result is a burst of textures as well as tastes. Once you experience the different sensations you get with every bite of Szechwan Pork with Vegetables (page 173) or Crispy Spiced Duck (page 157), you will know exactly what I mean.

The North

The North is a bigger-than-life region known as the Land of Extremes. At its northern borders, the Great Wall and, beyond it, the searing Gobi Desert barricade the province, while on its western front, the Tsin Ling Mountains blow freezing, dry winds and dust storms in winter and enclose the oppressive heat of summer.

It is here in this wild, unpredictable region that one of the oldest and most sophisticated civilizations of the world was born. In the thirteenth century, Kublai Khan designed Peking—then and now the capital of China, and its gourmet heartland as well.

Peking is really four cities in one: the Tartar City, within which is the Manchu City, within which lies a small jewel—the Forbidden City, for centuries the sanctuary of the Imperial Family. Outside these walled enclaves is the fourth city, known as the Chinese City. For, ironically, Peking, the center of all things Chinese, was once denied to the Chinese people by the Mongolians and Manchurians who first ruled there.

As the seat of government, Peking was exposed to many peoples and cultures, and their cosmopolitan styles are reflected in the eclectic cuisine. These "new" influences date back more than 2,000 years when caravans traveled the Kansu passageway, carrying goods out of China and returning with new products and new ideas. However, these new ideas were primarily the preserve of the royal court.

The majority of the people, like those in other regions, centered their lives on the river, in this case, the Yellow River (or Hwang Ho), so called because it gathers a yellowish sediment as it spills downward from Tibet. This river is also known as China's sorrow, for instead of nourishing, it often overflows, flooding hundreds of acres within its sphere.

The North, alone among the regions of China, does not produce rice. Not only can the Yellow River not be harnessed to create the necessary swamplands, but the weather extremes and dry air are the antitheses of the moderate, humid conditions needed to grow this food.

Instead, wheat is the staple, and thankfully so since it is the foundation for some of the most popular dishes in China, including crisp spring rolls, feathery won tons, and delectably light pancakes.

Wheat products, seasoned with strong and distinct vegetables and condiments, such as onions, garlic, leeks, vinegar, and soy sauce, are the bulk of the daily fare for the masses. By contrast, food at upper-class tables is both more luxurious and more subtle, relying heavily on wine and slow cooking. Thus, the poor eat filled won tons—like the Won Ton Filling II (page 52), whereas the rich eat Duck in Citrus Sauce (page 161).

There is, however, one area in all of the North where the climate is moist and balmy—Shantung. Perched on a promontory jutting out over the Yellow Sea, it grows most of the wonderful fruits in this region. Shantung is more than a physical paradox in this tempestuous land. It is a peaceful spiritual haven as well, for here rests the holy mountain, T'ai Shan, believed to be the source of life in this world and the next. At its base, Confucius lived and taught, and wrote the commonsense wisdom still relevant today.

If Shantung seems incongruous compared to the rest of the North, its westernmost territory, the Loessland, is even more so. In many areas, there is sufficient rain for farming; in others, so little that the land can only be used for grazing. Yet the diversity of life-styles the weather conditions dictate cannot compare to the different backgrounds of the people themselves.

In the Loessland, Muslims, Mongols, Manchus, Tibetans, Chinese, and Jews live peaceably side by side. It is fitting, therefore, that the melting pot of China should be most renowned for its stew, a random and often varied assortment of meat and vegetables simmered to perfection—the Mongolian Hot Pot.

Such is the splendid variety of the North that some people believe the region has no cooking style of its own but is merely an artful thief, stealing and adapting the best of other regions. Others contend that every Chinese cooking style had its origin here. As in all controversies, the truth may lie somewhere in between, but it does not matter, for the ultimate goodness and truth can be found in the food itself, which is supremely delicious.

The Ingredients and Where to Find Them

Chinese food is so much a part of America's diet that most ingredients generic to Chinese cooking are available in supermarkets throughout the country. Indeed, we have assimilated many Chinese staples, like soy sauce, bamboo shoots, bean sprouts, and snow pea pods, into our own cuisine.

As for the more exotic items such as star anise, black dried mushrooms, and Szechwan peppercorns, many of these, too, are available in local markets and gourmet shops. And, of course, you can always find every conceivable Chinese goody in your local Chinatown.

More like a bazaar than a food market, Chinatown, any Chinatown, is an experience worth having. Amid clamoring, bartering, and squabbling, baskets and bins of foodstuffs intermingled with utensils, toys, and knick-knacks of every kind are piled in seemingly haphazard fashion. Shopping there is colorful and fun, and the foods you take home and enjoy will bring back delightful memories.

What follows is an alphabetical listing of the Chinese and low-sodium ingredients that are used in the recipes in this book. Substitutions and low-sodium options are noted where appropriate. We have not included on our shopping list any of the salted Chinese food items such as dried fish or canned baby corn for which there are neither substitutes nor low-sodium counterparts, but we think you'll find your Chinese pantry very complete without these few things.

A Chinese Pantry

ANISEED (FENNEL SEED)
Both licorice-flavored spices, aniseed and fennel seed are often used to lend a distinct sweetness to meat and poultry and are important ingredients in several spice blends. In cooking, they may be used interchangeably and will keep indefinitely on the shelf, stored in jars or plastic bags. Available in supermarkets.

BAMBOO SHOOTS
A common Chinese vegetable, canned whole or thinly sliced, bamboo shoots are usually packed in water, which is, of course, preferred. Once the can is opened, the shoots should be refrigerated in a jar filled with water. If the water is changed every few days, the shoots will stay fresh and crunchy for several weeks. Available in supermarkets and, of course, in Chinese food stores.

BEAN CURD (TOFU)
Made of pressed soybeans and sold in square cakes, bean curd is white and spongy. Inexpensive, highly nutritious, and low in sodium, bean curd is bland but absorbs the flavors of the foods with which it is cooked. Because it is adaptable to all cooking methods, this humble food is special indeed. Bean curd should be refrigerated in a container filled with water. It will stay fresh about one week if the water is changed every few days. Available packaged in some supermarkets or fresh in Chinese markets.

BEAN SPROUTS

These crispy, crunchy shoots with yellow-green caps are readily available fresh in Chinese markets, vegetable stands, and supermarkets. Do not even consider canned bean sprouts because they are processed in salt and contain 135 milligrams of sodium for a 2-ounce serving versus a trace for the fresh vegetable. Fresh bean sprouts, which are tastier and more healthful than canned, are also easy to grow in a windowbox, so there is no reason to settle for anything less than the best. Just remember: bean sprouts are perishable and will only stay fresh about one week if refrigerated in an airtight container or in a bowl of water changed every few days.

BLACK BEAN SAUCE (BROWN BEAN SAUCE)

Black bean sauce is actually not a sauce at all, but rather the fermented black beans used to flavor a sauce. Fermented black beans are available in cans, jars, or plastic bags and will keep several months, but need no refrigeration. Brown bean sauce (known as miso to the Japanese) is made from either fermented brown beans or a combination of soybeans, salt, flour, and water. It is sold in cans or jars and, if refrigerated after opening, will keep for several months. Both black bean and brown bean sauces taste, and, indeed are salty and pungent. For purposes of this book, we have created our own Black Bean Sauce, which is very close in taste to its Chinese counterparts. Substitute this version (see page 232) whenever you are adapting a recipe calling for either fermented black beans or brown bean sauce. Low-sodium Black Bean Sauce will keep indefinitely if refrigerated in a tightly sealed jar.

BLACK MUSHROOMS

Black mushrooms have a nutty flavor and are a bit chewy, quite unlike the American variety. They come dried and must be soaked in boiling water up to ½ hour to bring out their full flavor. (Discard the stems, which are inedible.) They will keep indefinitely if stored in a tightly covered container. Although the taste won't be the same, you may substitute fresh mushrooms for these or any other Chinese mushroom. Available in Chinese markets and many supermarkets and health food stores.

BOK CHOY (CHINESE CABBAGE)

This vegetable is a tender plant with long white stalks and dark green leaves. Because it wilts fast, it is added to dishes at the last minute of cooking. Readily found in Chinese markets, it also appears more and more frequently in supermarket produce sections. Bok choy is low in sodium. When not available, it is often replaced with celery, which is so high in sodium, at 36 milligrams per ounce, that it is banned from most salt-free diets. For the recipes in this book, go for the crunch rather than the exact taste, and substitute celery cabbage for bok choy. Store in your refrigerator to keep crisp.

CELERY CABBAGE
Americans often refer to this broad, flat-leafed vegetable, which looks like celery, as Chinese cabbage or bok choy. In truth, it resembles regular celery in its crunchy, fibrous texture and is more adaptable than its easily bruised Chinese cousin to all cooking methods. However, as noted above, in this book (or when you want to adapt a recipe), celery cabbage and bok choy can be used as substitutes for each other. Available in Chinese markets and in most supermarkets, it will stay fresh for a week in your refrigerator.

CELLOPHANE NOODLES
Deserving of their name, cellophane noodles, which are sold dried, become transparent when soaked in warm water in preparation for cooking. Although they have no taste of their own, like bean curd the noodles take on the flavors around them. Cellophane noodles, which, appropriately enough, usually come in a cellophane wrapper, can be stored indefinitely on the shelf. However, because they are generally found only in Chinese markets, we suggest vermicelli as a substitute. The taste and texture will be different, but the results are equally enjoyable.

CHILI OIL
Commonly used in Szechwan cooking, this ingredient is exactly what its name implies: salad oil spiced with dried chili peppers. Because it cannot easily be found outside Chinese markets, a recipe is included in this book (page 230). Chili oil can be used to spark sauces, dips, and salad dressings, as well as for cooking. It will keep indefinitely on the shelf.

CHILI PASTE
Made with chili peppers, soybean oil, and garlic, this zingy bottled paste is very hot. It, too, is used primarily in Szechwan cooking and is sold almost exclusively in Chinese markets. For this reason and because commercial chili paste usually contains salt, we've included a version in this book as zippy as the original (see page 230). Bottled and refrigerated, our Chili Paste will stay fresh two to three months.

CHILI POWDER
A reddish combination of garlic powder, paprika, oregano, parsley, cumin, and, most important, dried red "hot" chili peppers ground to a fine powder. Although generic to Mexican cuisine, this blend of hot and sweet flavors perfectly fits the culinary style and taste of Szechwan and Hunan. Many brands of chili powder are commercially available in supermarkets everywhere, but because most of these contain salt, we have included our own version in the Sauces and Seasonings section of this book (page 231). If stored in a tightly closed bottle or jar and kept in a cool, dry place, our Chili Powder will keep its zesty flavor indefinitely.

CHILI SAUCE
Chili sauce is spicy but less hot than chili paste because, in addition to chili peppers, it contains lemon juice, onions, sweet potatoes, and vinegar. It's not only good in cooking sweet and sour dishes, but makes wonderful sauce for meat and poultry. Like chili paste, Chinese chili sauce usually contains salt, so we've provided our own recipe in this book (see page 231). Bottled and refrigerated, it will keep two to three months.

CHINESE BROCCOLI
In this book, we have relied on regular broccoli because, although Chinese broccoli is a little sweeter, it is not readily available even in Chinese food stores, and the slight difference in taste is not worth a delay in trying out a good recipe.

CHINESE EGG NOODLES
Sold fresh in Chinese markets, Chinese egg noodles are used primarily in lo mein. Fresh noodles, if wrapped tightly in plastic bags and refrigerated, will keep for about a week; if frozen, for one month. For convenience, vermicelli is a good substitute, and it is used consistently in this book.

CHINESE MUSTARD
Although Chinese mustard can be purchased in paste form, it is always salted, averaging approximately 62 milligrams per teaspoon. A do-it-yourself mixture of English mustard powder and water is just as easy to come by, virtually sodium-free, and better tasting to boot. You can also control the strength and consistency simply by adding more or less water. Mustard powder will keep indefinitely on the shelf.

CILANTRO (OR CHINESE PARSLEY)
See Coriander.

CINNAMON
True Chinese cinnamon is not cinnamon as we know it, but the dried bark of the cassia tree. However, it is indistinguishable from the Indian cinnamon with which we are so familiar and which is the form used throughout this book.

CLOUD EARS (TREE EARS)
This delicate-tasting food is actually a black, irregularly shaped fungus, sold in dry chip form. Before use, they should be soaked in warm water for ½ hour, during which time they will expand four to five times their size. Although their taste is so subtle it is almost nonexistent, cloud ears are incomparable for their crunchy quality. Stored in a sealed plastic bag, they will keep indefinitely on the shelf.

CORIANDER
Known as Chinese parsley or Spanish parsley under the name cilantro, coriander resembles Italian (flat-leaf) parsley in appearance but has a sharper flavor. It is available fresh only in Chinese or Spanish markets and will last about one week if refrigerated. Dried, it is generally sold under the name cilantro, and can be found on spice racks in food stores throughout the country. Ground, it is usually sold under the name coriander, and also is widely available in food stores everywhere. Both dried and ground forms will keep indefinitely on the shelf. To avoid confusion, we have chosen the most frequently used designations for this book: namely, coriander when the ground form is to be used; cilantro or parsley, which is a viable substitute, when the dried or fresh forms are called for. American parsley—fresh or dried—is an acceptable substitute.

CURRY POWDER
Curry powder, often found in Szechwan cooking, was introduced from India. It is a spicy blend of flavors, including cumin, fenugreek, cinnamon, turmeric, and aniseed. Since most commercial blends also contain salt, we have provided one of our favorite curry combinations in this book (see page 232). Curry powder will keep indefinitely on the shelf.

DRIED ORANGE PEEL
Many Chinese dishes (especially those with poultry) call for dried orange or tangerine peel, which, for our purposes, can be used interchangeably. Although sold in Chinese markets, dried orange peel is far easier to make yourself by air-drying the rind of an orange or tangerine at room temperature. Once dried, the peel will keep indefinitely on the shelf if stored in a tightly closed plastic bag.

DRIED RED PEPPERS (HOT PEPPER FLAKES)
Used frequently to add the fire to Szechwan food, dried peppers are available, whole or crushed, in most markets. Cayenne pepper is a reasonable substitute. Dried peppers will keep indefinitely on the shelf and should be stored in a tightly closed plastic bag. In this book, recipes calling for their use identify them as hot pepper flakes.

DUCK SAUCE (PLUM SAUCE)
This sauce of plums, chili, and spices, at once both tart and sweet, is known as plum sauce to the Chinese who use it in cooking. To Americans, however, this condiment is principally used as a dip and probably comes by the name duck sauce since it is often an accompaniment to poultry. We have supplied our own recipe since the commercial variety contains salt (see page 234). Refrigerated in jars, it will keep indefinitely.

EGG ROLL SKINS
Egg roll skins are sold in a two-pound package in Chinese markets, but we offer a salt-free recipe here (see page 64). Their use is delectably self-explanatory. Egg roll skins should be stored, individually separated by waxed paper and wrapped securely in aluminum foil. As such, they may be frozen indefinitely or refrigerated up to five days.

FIVE-SPICE POWDER
A pungent combination of ground aniseed, fennel seed, ginger, cinnamon, and cloves (see page 228), this brown-powdered blend is most often used to flavor poultry and fish. Since its aroma is as strong as its taste, it should be used sparingly. Our variation is offered in this book (see page 228). Stored in a jar, it will keep indefinitely on the shelf.

GINGER ROOT
This gnarled, knobby, oddly shaped root is a key ingredient in Chinese cooking. It is variously used to flavor the oil for stir-frying, to neutralize the odor of fish, and to add its own unique spiciness to the foods of the western region. It is readily available in Chinese markets, gourmet shops, and most supermarkets, but if you do not have it on hand, you can substitute ginger powder, but *not* crystallized ginger. Ginger root will keep several months in the refrigerator. To guarantee long-term freshness, peel the root and refrigerate it in a jar of dry sherry.

HOISIN SAUCE
Both spicy and sweet, hoisin sauce is a most unusual and delectable condiment. A combination of chili, garlic, spices, and soybeans, it is used both in cooking and as a dip, and adds a wonderful flavor to roast duck and pork in particular. We developed our own special Hoisin Sauce recipe for this book (page 228), so you can savor its unique taste without the salt found in the commercial varieties. Refrigerated in a jar, Hoisin Sauce will stay fresh several months.

KUMQUATS
A tiny, oval, smooth-skinned citrus fruit, the orange kumquat makes a tangy dessert and is often used to cleanse the palate between courses at a Chinese banquet. Kumquats grow as abundantly in warm, sunny regions of the United States as they do in China. They are commonly available in cans or jars packed in water or heavy syrup. Once opened, kumquats can be kept in a glass container in the refrigerator for up to one month.

LOQUATS
Somewhat like the apricot in taste, the loquat is a small, round, orange-colored fruit which grows best in tropical climates like the southern region of China. It is wonderful prepared with poultry, but is most often served

for dessert. Loquats are available, canned in water or heavy syrup, in Chinese markets. Once opened, loquats should be transferred to a bottle and will keep refrigerated up to one month.

LYCHEES
Lychees are among the most popular fruits from China. Protected by a reddish brown, nutlike shell, the fruit itself is a tender, sweet white oval. Lychees are a pleasant, if mild, dessert food and are sometimes found in sweet and sour dishes. They are available canned in water or heavy syrup in Chinese food stores, but are best known in this country in the dried state we call lychee nuts, which will keep indefinitely on the shelf.

OYSTER MUSHROOMS
So called because in their commonly available dried state, they are shaped like oysters, these mushrooms have a mildly pungent flavor that makes any dish special. Before use, they must be soaked in hot water for at least 15 minutes. Available in Chinese markets and gourmet shops, oyster mushrooms will keep indefinitely on the shelf if bottled or protected in a plastic wrapping. There is no substitute for this tender delicacy.

OYSTER SAUCE
A thick brown sauce made of oysters cooked in soy sauce and salt, then pureed, oyster sauce is used to add a meaty taste to poultry, seafood, and beef. We offer a greatly simplified salt-free version (page 234) which, though of a much thinner consistency, has the same distinct flavor. Stored bottled in the refrigerator, it will keep fresh for three or four days.

PEANUT OIL
Peanut oil is the most popular cooking oil in China because it has the rich flavor of lard, which the Chinese love, but does not congeal or taste rancid in reheating. It is commonly available everywhere and will keep indefinitely on the shelf.

RICE FLOUR
Ground rice is used primarily for dessert dough. It is readily available in Chinese markets in one-pound bags. Store it as you would regular flour.

RICE VINEGAR
Made from rice wine, rice vinegar has three forms: red, generally used for dipping; white, stronger in flavor and used in cooking; and black, slightly milder than white and used in braised and red-cooked dishes. Like other vinegars, rice vinegar, if bottled, will keep indefinitely on the shelf. However, because many brands contain salt, we recommend substituting regular red and white vinegars plus cider vinegar as we have done throughout this book.

SESAME SEEDS
The appeal of sesame seeds is as much their fragrant aroma as their exotic flavor. They add a special quality to any dish and can be used raw or toasted. Available in Chinese markets and health food stores, sesame seeds come in cans or bottles and will keep indefinitely on the shelf.

SESAME SEED OIL
Golden brown in color, sesame seed oil tastes as rich as it looks. It is made from toasted sesame seeds. It is rarely used in cooking since it burns easily, but instead is added to a dish right before serving. Sesame seed oil is available in Chinese and American supermarkets, but only the Chinese version has the authentic taste and texture. It will keep indefinitely on the shelf.

SESAME SEED PASTE
Sold in jars in Chinese markets, sesame seed paste looks, at first glance, like creamy peanut butter. Indeed, low-sodium peanut butter blended with a few drops of sesame seed oil is a reasonable substitute. Used as a seasoning for vegetables and meats, sesame seed paste is deliciously rich and flavorful. To ensure its thorough mixing with other ingredients, it must be diluted with hot water. If refrigerated, it will stay fresh two or three months.

SHERRY
Dry sherry is often used to lend a subtle yet lingering sweetness to Chinese dishes. It is important to note that cooking sherry (or any cooking wine so labeled) contains salt and is, therefore, not acceptable. On the other hand, any regular sherry or wine will do very nicely and will keep indefinitely on the shelf.

SHRIMP PASTE
Traditionally, shrimp paste is a preserve of pureed shrimp in brine, similar in taste to anchovy paste. Our version (page 240) more closely replicates its name in flavor, and can be used to add a delicate nuance to fish and meat dishes. Refrigerated in jars, it will keep two to three weeks.

SNOW PEA PODS
Broad, flat pods, with a hint of the peas underneath, snow pea pods are eaten whole. Although they are sweeter than their American relations, fresh peas can be substituted, and are, indeed, a better alternative than frozen pea pods, which seem stringy. Snow pea pods add an elegant, out-of-the-ordinary crunchiness and appealing color to any dish. They are available at Chinese markets and many vegetable stands and supermarkets throughout the country. To enjoy their succulent goodness to the fullest, eat them within two weeks of purchase.

SOY SAUCE
A key staple in a Chinese kitchen, soy sauce, which is made of fermented soybeans and salt, is the most commonly used seasoning in Chinese cuisine. It is also one of the saltiest, containing 1,047 milligrams of sodium per tablespoon. Even the low-salt soy sauce, with 620 milligrams of sodium per tablespoon, is much too salty for the low-salt dieter. Regular soy sauce has both a light and dark blend. The former is used in soups and as a dip; the latter, with molasses added to temper the salty taste, in general cooking. It is the dark blend on which we have based our own salt-free Soy Sauce (page 227). Refrigerated in bottles, it will keep indefinitely, and is a delectable 4 milligrams of sodium per tablespoon.

SPRING ROLL SKINS
Though often confused with egg roll skins, spring roll skins are more delicate in flavor, more pastrylike and flaky in texture. And unlike egg rolls, spring rolls do not keep well and should be used immediately.

STAR ANISE
This licorice-flavored, eight-pointed star is an important spice in Szechwan cooking. In its powdered state, it is a key ingredient in such blends as curry powder and five-spice powder. Because it mingles so well with soy sauce and other spices, it is used, albeit sparingly, to add its refreshing taste to dishes throughout China. Stored in a bottle or plastic bag, star anise will keep indefinitely on the shelf.

SZECHWAN PEPPERCORNS
Reddish brown and highly aromatic, Szechwan peppercorns are sold whole and bottled. When crushed to release their full flavor, they taste mildly hot, numbing rather than burning the palate. Used primarily in their province of origin, Szechwan peppercorns lend their unique flavor to a wide variety of dishes—marinated, pickled, cured, hot and cold. They will keep indefinitely on the shelf.

SZECHWAN PEPPER SPICE
Made by dry-roasting and then grinding Szechwan peppercorns, this spice adds a zesty spark to foods without the hot sting of black peppercorns. Stored in bottles, Szechwan pepper spice will keep indefinitely on the shelf. For our version see page 229.

TIGER LILY BUDS (GOLDEN NEEDLES)
Literally dried buds of the tiger lily flower, these very thin tan-colored strips add an unusual and faintly sweet flavor to dishes. Slightly chewy, they are especially good in soups. They should be soaked in hot water for at least 20 minutes before use. Available in Chinese markets and gourmet stores, tiger lily buds will keep indefinitely on the shelf when stored either in a bottle or plastic container.

WATER CHESTNUTS
Covered by a dark brown skin, water chestnuts are usually simmered in sugar and eaten as candy in China. In the United States, however, we rarely see fresh water chestnuts. Rather, we are better acquainted with them, stripped of their chestnut-like skins, canned whole or sliced in water. Water chestnuts are the number one choice if a dish requires a sweetly crisp texture. If kept in a jar of water (which should be changed every few days), they will stay fresh for about one week.

WON TON SKINS
See Egg Roll Skins. Although the ingredients are the same, egg rolls are always fried, while won tons are often steamed, boiled in soups or deep-fried. In addition, won tons are generally filled with minced meat, poultry, or seafood. Egg rolls may contain these as well, but their primary stuffing is a vegetable mixture.

YELLOW BEAN SAUCE
Made with yellow beans, this sauce is a slightly sweeter version of brown bean sauce. An unsalted version is supplied here (page 236), and, if bottled and refrigerated, will keep up to two months.

A Low-Sodium Pantry

BOUILLON, BEEF AND CHICKEN
Bouillon mixed with boiling water is a commonly used shortcut when a recipe calls for soup or stock. But there's a big difference between salted and unsalted bouillon. One teaspoon of salted beef or chicken bouillon contains 1,143 milligrams of sodium—more than some of us are allowed all day. Compare that to unsalted beef bouillon, which has only 10 milligrams of sodium per teaspoon, or unsalted chicken bouillon, which has only 5 milligrams of sodium per teaspoon—an amazingly healthy difference.

These low-sodium seasonings are widely available today in health food stores and supermarkets throughout the country. Although some come in powdered form, the most common are granulated, packed in small jars. Chicken bouillon is an instant, "salty" pick-me-up for poultry, fish and shellfish, and vegetables. Beef bouillon has the same taste effect on all meats. Low-sodium bouillon has the added benefits of being low in fat, carbohydrates, and calories, and high in potassium. It will keep indefinitely on the shelf.

CORN
Corn, plain or creamed style, and, for that matter, a garden variety of other vegetables are widely available today canned in water for low-sodium

consumption. You can find these items in the diet section of most super-markets, as well as health food stores. So popular have they become that, like their salty counterparts, they usually come in two sizes (8 and 15 ounces), often produced by leading brand-name manufacturers. Because they are vacuum-packed, they have an indefinite shelf life. In addition, there is a bonus: because salt drains off the flavorful moisture of any food, the low-sodium products taste fresher and richer than the salty ones.

Note: Although frozen vegetables are also acceptable, they often have added salt, so before using them, read the labels carefully.

KETCHUP
Ketchup was introduced to China via Canton. Its combination of sweet and pungent flavors was a familiar concept to the Chinese people, and they readily adopted this tomato-based condiment. Used in dishes from every region, ketchup has become a staple in the Chinese kitchen. Several low-sodium options are widely available in stores across the country. One variation is low-sodium chili ketchup, which contains chopped onion, and sometimes chopped pickle, in the ketchup base. They are delicious and have only 5 to 10 milligrams of sodium per tablespoon compared to 298 milligrams for the salted variety. If they are refrigerated after opening, they will keep indefinitely.

LEMON PEEL POWDER
Ground from dried lemon peel, this spice concentrate adds zip to any dish. It is available in the spice sections of food stores throughout the country. If bottled or tightly sealed in a plastic bag and stored in a cool, dry cup-board, it will keep its full pungent flavor indefinitely.

ORANGE PEEL POWDER
Ground from dried orange peel. See Lemon Peel Powder.

PEANUT BUTTER
Low-sodium peanut butter is by far better than any other because it con-tains no preservatives, no additives like sugar, nothing but ground, fresh-roasted peanuts. Whether your preference is creamy or chunky, you will find whichever low-sodium brand you buy to be richer and thicker than the popular salted commercial varieties. The fact is, low-sodium peanut butter tastes like homemade. It is available in health food stores and in the diet section of most supermarkets from coast to coast. If stored in a dry, cool place, it will keep indefinitely.

Note: If kept for a long time, the peanut oil will eventually separate and rise to the top of the jar, but there is nothing wrong with the product. Just stir to blend before use.

SUGAR SUBSTITUTES
Natural sugar—whether raw or processed—is a simple carbohydrate. Dia-betics, of course, should avoid it altogether, and too much of it is un-

healthy for all of us. The sugar substitutes on the market come in packets, containing one- or two-teaspoon equivalents, and are sold in boxes. They will keep indefinitely on the shelf. We recommend using only those made with calcium saccharin since it is low-sodium as well as sugar-free.

TOMATO PASTE
This condiment is used sparingly but regularly in many Chinese dishes. Low-sodium tomato paste, with only 3 milligrams of sodium per ounce, is widely available in supermarkets and health food stores across the country. It is rich and better tasting than its salty counterpart, containing 57 milligrams of sodium per ounce. Although tomato paste is sold in cans to preserve its freshness, once opened, it should be transferred to glass or plastic containers, leaving ½ inch of headspace; it can be stored up to two months in the refrigerator, or indefinitely in the freezer.

VINEGAR
Red, white, or cider vinegars, commonly available in all food stores, are consistently used throughout this book in place of Chinese rice vinegar, which sometimes contains salt.

WORCESTERSHIRE SAUCE
The British brought Worcestershire sauce to China. Because two of its key ingredients are soy sauce and vinegar, Worcestershire sauce found a welcome home among the Chinese and is today used to season a wide variety of foods in every region. A low-sodium version can now be found in health food stores and many supermarkets. It will keep indefinitely on the shelf.

For Ease of Preparation

Chinese food is easy to prepare for many reasons. First, so many dishes are stir-fried that you can often get a meal on the table in just a few minutes. Second, many dishes are meals-in-one, that is, they contain meat plus vegetables and so cut down on time in the kitchen, as well as the cleanup time afterwards. Even the utensils used in a Chinese kitchen are designed to maximize efficiency. In fact, most of the effort that goes into a Chinese meal is in the assembling and preparation of ingredients.

Utensils

You do not have to buy Chinese utensils to cook good Chinese food. Indeed, such items as strainers, spatulas, and steamers have American counterparts that will serve quite well. Even a specific implement like the wok can be replaced by a skillet, Dutch oven, saucepan, or poacher, depending on recipe requirements.

But the fact is, Chinese utensils are designed and shaped to produce results with maximum speed, efficiency, and ease. For all these reasons, they are well worth knowing.

Bamboo Steamer. Steaming is an important method in Chinese cooking. It is quick, seals in flavor and nutrients, and delivers a finished product as pleasing to look at as it is delicious to eat. Thus, bamboo steamers are a must for Chinese chefs.

The steamers come in several diameters, single or multi-leveled. Wooden slats form the sides, and the bottoms are open-weave bamboo through which steam can easily circulate. A multi-level steamer can cook several dishes at once. Those ingredients requiring the longest cooking time (chicken or fish, for example) are placed on the bottom tray, vegetables on the second, and buns or dumplings on top.

Generally, before being placed in the steamer, foods are protected against too much moisture by a heatproof dish or wet cloth. The solid wooden cover locks in the steam so that the foods quite literally cook in their own juices.

The bamboo steamer is the next best thing to your own personal cook.

Skimmer and Strainer. Actually, both of these items are sieves made of wire mesh. The former is a tight-weave mesh, so that the perforations are small. It is used primarily to catch and skim off excess oil. The latter, which is shaped like an oversized shallow ladle, is made of open-weave mesh, so the holes are large. It is excellent for turning deep-fried foods and for scooping ingredients and holding them while unwanted drippings escape. An ordinary strainer and a colander are adequate substitutions for each.

Spatula and Ladle. These are long-handled metal utensils. The spatula is used primarily for stir-frying. It is physically different from its American counterpart in two ways: it is broader at the base and has slightly turned-up sides. Both features give the cook maximum control in turning and flipping food.

The ladle, however, is not much different in configuration and no different in function from the American variety. Practically speaking, you can use your own spatula and ladle with equal success.

The Wok. Probably the best known of all Chinese utensils, the wok is an all-purpose cooking pan. It can be used for stir-frying, deep-frying, braising, poaching, and steaming. A large skillet is a reasonable substitute for the first three techniques; a large saucepan or Dutch oven for the last two.

There are several versions: flat-bottomed (often with a copper base); electric; and the traditional round-bottomed tempered-iron pan. While all woks are generally sold with a metal cover, the round-bottomed one also comes with a metal ring which fits over the gas burner and on which the wok rests.

The round-bottomed iron wok was so constructed for several reasons:

Most Chinese homes, even today, do not have stoves, and the round-bottomed wok can easily be moved about over a fire to make sure food cooks evenly.

Tempered iron conducts heat quickly and evenly over the entire surface, so that even when food is pushed to the sides, it continues to cook.

The round bottom requires less oil than does a flat-bottomed utensil.

Although the round-bottomed original is generally preferred, it is neither always necessary nor always the best choice. For an electric range, for example, a flat-bottomed wok can come in direct contact with the heat and can, therefore, help disperse it evenly, approximating the intensity of a gas stove. An electric wok, with heat control, is also a reasonable alternative to the electric range.

While it is still new, a wok should be properly seasoned. First, brush the entire surface with oil and wipe dry or heat dry over low heat. Then, wash, rinse, and towel-dry it. The seasoning, which helps to prevent rust and keeps food from sticking, is usually required for iron- and copper-bottomed woks but not for steel ones.

That's it. The wok is a near-perfect cooking utensil—it is adaptable and easy to use for any number of cooking methods.

Preparation and Assembly

Uniformity is the single most important element in the preparation of Chinese ingredients. Very simply, when items are the same size and shape, they cook evenly, in the same amount of time.

How ingredients are cut is of equal importance. There are several techniques:

Chopping uses a sharp, quick, firm motion, coming straight down to split soft foods, including poultry, fish, and spareribs.

Cubing and Dicing mean chopping ingredients into small ½- to 1-inch cubes or, for dicing, into even smaller (¼-inch) bits.

Mincing reduces ingredients that are already chopped, sliced, cubed, or diced to a superfine, almost grainy texture.

Slicing has three variations:

Straight slicing is just what it says: cutting fish, meats, or vegetables straight up and down. (*Note:* Fish and meats, including poultry, are easier to slice if partially frozen.)

Diagonal slicing is used to expose the broadest surface of meats and vegetables because foods cut on a slant cook quickly and absorb the flavors around them. It is most often used for tough cuts like London broil or fibrous vegetables like asparagus and carrots.

Rolled slicing is diagonally slicing from many different angles, resulting in multiple exposed surfaces. Even more than diagonal slicing, rolled slicing enables ingredients to cook quickly and evenly while capturing the seasonings around them. It is a technique reserved primarily for fibrous vegetables like asparagus, carrots, eggplant, and zucchini.

Shredding is straight slicing ingredients into thin strips.

Julienne is cutting already shredded ingredients into matchstick-thin strips.

As you can see, the preparation of food in the Chinese kitchen is very specific, but for a good reason: good preparation makes the cooking faster and easier.

Since timing is everything, ingredients in a Chinese dish are usually added one at a time, starting with the one requiring the longest cooking time. To help keep the many ingredients organized and the cooking process smooth, you'll find small dessert bowls come in handy—one bowl per ingredient, lined up in order of use.

When you stop to think about it, the preparation for Chinese cooking is designed not only to minimize your efforts but to make the finished product beautiful.

Cooking Methods

The respect the Chinese have for food is nowhere better expressed than in the cooking itself. They are scrupulous about using the exact technique that will best enhance a particular dish. These precision-oriented cooking methods are described below:

Deep-Frying produces the best results with foods that require minimum cooking time such as shrimp or vegetables. To deep-fry properly, you need at least two inches of oil (one to four cups depending on the size of your utensil), heated to 375°. The oil is hot enough when a piece of scallion or bread cube sizzles upon immersion.

Before deep-frying, ingredients are sometimes marinated but are often coated in cornstarch, flour, or breading to keep them from drying out during cooking. Once coated, the food is lowered gently into the piping-hot oil to fry until golden brown.

Note: Because too much fat in the diet isn't good for any of us, there are very few deep-fried foods in this book.

Stir-Frying is the most popular and widespread cooking technique in China. The wok is usually heated first over high heat, which is then reduced to medium. Just enough oil is added to cover the bottom of the wok; the heat is returned to high and the ingredients are added, one by one, to be stir-fried constantly until done. In this book, the stir-frying technique used is somewhat unorthodox. Foods are started over low or medium heat (so that they cook partially in their own juices) and finished over high heat. This modification reduces the amount of fat required.

In any event, stir-frying is quick, locking in nutrients and leaving foods a tasty tender-crisp.

Shallow-Frying is very much like sautéeing and generally requires more oil than does stir-frying. This method, during which food is slowly fried over medium heat until browned on both sides, is often the final stage for food that has already been partially cooked by another method. It is especially good for meats.

Steaming, to the Chinese, specifically means wet steaming, that is, when the steam freely circulates around the food through a rack or the traditional open-weave bamboo steamer. Food is placed in a steaming unit above boiling water. The unit is then tightly covered and the food is left to cook until tender. Like stir-frying, steaming locks in both nutrients and flavor, and foods prepared this way are easy to digest.

Simmering or Poaching refers to foods barely covered with liquid and cooked at low heat just below the boiling point. Chicken and whole fish are especially tender, tasty, and moist when prepared this way.

Red Cooking resembles American stewing except that foods are generally prepared whole rather than cut in chunks. In addition, soy sauce is always added to the cooking liquid, which gives the ingredients a rich flavor and the reddish brown color for which the technique is named. Red cooking is a leisurely, unhurried process. In fact, with this method, there is no risk of overcooking, for the longer the time, the richer the taste and the more tender the ingredients. What's more, food prepared this way often tastes better a day—or even a week—later. A stew by any other name is still a stew.

Boiling in Chinese cuisine generally means either parboiling or a boil which is immediately reduced to a simmer. In the former instance, primarily used for vegetables, foods are cooked just below boiling, then immediately plunged into cold water to prevent overcooking. Foods prepared this way are commonly added to a dish already in process or are chilled for salads.

The latter variation of boiling is generally reserved for soups, whereby a broth is brought to a slow but full boil, then reduced to low heat and simmered per recipe directions.

Blanching is similar to parboiling. But for blanching, foods are plunged into already boiling water, allowed to cook briefly, then drained and rinsed with cold water. Although this method is used mainly for vegetables, blanched foods, like parboiled, are most often served hot so their full, tender, crisp flavor can be enjoyed instantly.

Roasting in the orthodox Chinese manner means cooking in an open-pit oven over a charcoal fire. However, a western stove will produce equally delicious results.

Braising is actually slow cooking with moist heat. Foods are cooked in a small amount of liquid—on the stove or in the oven—in a tightly covered vessel. Additional liquid is added only to keep foods from sticking.

With so many refined distinctions, you can understand why cooking is an honored profession in China—equal in prestige to teaching, philosophy, and the arts.

How to Adapt Your Favorite Chinese Recipes

Chinese food without soy sauce? Salt? MSG? Impossible? Well, it is not only possible but can taste authentically Chinese whether your preference is Cantonese, Szechwan, Hunan, Fukien, or Peking.

When a recipe calls for salty additives, what do you do? What you do not do is leave out these ingredients and hope for the best. Instead, you replace them with other Chinese spices, herbs, and condiments that will best enhance the flavor of a particular dish yet maintain the integrity of the original.

But, you may ask, can you truly enjoy "real" Chinese food without the salty products that are so much a part of traditional Chinese cooking? The answer is definitely yes.

The fact is, Chinese cuisine offers a plethora of highly distinct spices. Used individually or in combination, they make a dish so uniquely and unmistakably Chinese and so pungent in flavor that salty items become unnecessary, and, indeed, redundant.

For example, garlic and ginger are two of the most frequently used ingredients in Chinese cooking. The sharpness of the former and the snap and bite of the latter will make you forget about salt. What is more, sherry, intensified by vinegar or mustard powder, will play the same trick on your tongue.

So will curry powder, chili oil, or crackling hot dried peppers used on any foods that strike your fancy.

But it is not just the hot or the bitter or the pungent which create that seasoned, salty taste. The milder Chinese herbs and spices do so as well. Try the nutty robustness of sesame seed oil on vegetables, and you will never want to eat them any other way. Licorice-flavored aniseed adds a wonderfully refreshing zip to fish, poultry, or lamb, as well as to vegetables with strong tastes of their own, like cauliflower and eggplant. The memorable flavors of Szechwan peppercorns and coriander produce the same effect.

And there is more. Vinegar, orange peel, or lemon peel added to a sauce or marinade has a magical effect on meat, fish, or poultry, for the acidity in these condiments replicates the taste of salt.

To further assist your Chinese cooking adventure and assure delectable results, refer to the chapter on sauces (page 227). It supplies, for your cooking and eating pleasure, low-sodium versions of such Chinese culinary staples as soy sauce (page 227), duck sauce (page 234), hoisin sauce (page 228), black bean sauce (page 232), and many more.

These low-sodium substitutes do not purport to taste exactly like the real thing straight from the jar, but in cooking, you will be amazed at the resemblance.

One last hint should leave you fully equipped to create authentic-tasting, scrumptious Chinese food: low-sodium bouillon. One dash of the beef- or chicken-flavored granules, added during cooking, will give a lip-smacking zing to any dish.

But, you may ask, how do I know when to use what? Very simply, it does not matter. Whether you are adapting a recipe or experimenting on your own, just remember that Chinese cooking at its best is a medley of very definite flavors, and all the spices, herbs, and condiments generic to the cuisine—the subtle as well as the assertive—are so pronounced and produce such flavorful results that they are guaranteed to preclude the need for salt.

How you blend them is up to you. Which ones you call on to create a salty taste is also your decision. You cannot go wrong, and you will quickly find that salt and salty ingredients are neither important nor relevant.

By now, the point should be made: there are many ways to keep the spice in your life (and in your Chinese food) without a grain of salt.

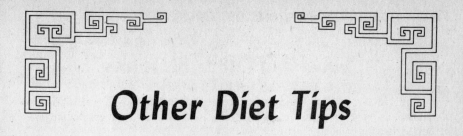

Other Diet Tips

As much as we hope you enjoy this book, it is unlikely that you will eat Chinese food, and only Chinese food, every day. So we would like to discuss how to avoid other salty products and how to get the most pleasure from salt-free living.

Salt Watching

On July 30, 1981, the *Wall Street Journal* published an article which stated ". . . salt watching is becoming as popular as calorie counting."

If that article was true then, it is even more true today. More and more people *are* watching their salt. Manufacturers and retailers are rushing to meet their needs and demands. And thanks to the dedication and hard work of organizations like Center for Science in the Public Interest, more and more food companies are producing new lines of salt-free products and, as important, are providing full-disclosure ingredients listings on the labels of their salted items.

Seldom now are the words "natural ingredients" used as a coverup for salt. Words like "chocolate" are usually followed by a parenthetical detailing of their contents. But salt still masquerades in many disguises.

Following is a guide for salt watchers:

Avoid everything from saccharin to soda that contains salt or a sodium compound, such as sodium benzoate, disodium sulfate, sodium saccharin, brine, sodium bicarbonate (baking soda), etc.

Avoid products that still list "natural ingredients," which is often the deceptive label for, among other things, salt.

Avoid all packaged goods and canned goods that are not labeled "low-sodium."

When eating outside your own home, avoid foods that are prepared in advance. They generally contain salt and include soups, salad dressings, sauces and gravies, bread, cakes, and pastries. When in doubt, ask before you place your order.

The few simple reminders noted above will soon become automatic. Not only will you find it easier and easier to keep your body healthy, but you will be very proud of yourself for being in control.

Travel and Other Pleasures

The travel and hotel industries have always led the salt-free brigade. Indeed, these service businesses have consistently shown the greatest awareness of any special diet problems.

With 48 hours' notice, any airline will provide one of a number of special diet meals, including low-calorie, vegetarian, seafood, kosher, diabetic, and low-sodium. These meals are special in more ways than one, for often they are much tastier than regulation airline fare.

Hotels will also try their best to accommodate your dietary needs. On request, they will install a refrigerator in your room (usually for a modest day rate) so you can have any special foods or medication at hand. What is more, if you explain your problem and requirements to room service, the restaurant maître d', or the hotel manager, they will generally be understanding and helpful. But one word of caution: wherever you are and whatever the circumstances, if the food you get is not the food you ordered, send it back. Never, but never, settle for less than perfection when your health is at stake.

By the way, it is always a good idea to carry a few low-sodium snacks and canned goods when you travel, in case an emergency arises or boredom sets in. A small container of your favorite spices will also come in handy for perking up a meal out.

Closer to home, you will have many more occasions to eat out. Today restaurants are much more sensitive to the special dieter than they were a decade ago. I used to carefully explain to the waiter or captain not only what I needed but why, trying to communicate how important my requests were. They would listen politely but with slightly bemused expressions, and would often reply, "Ah, yes, Madame is watching her figure." Funny to think about now, but maddening and often disastrous then. They did not take me seriously, and my food, when it arrived, was predictably unacceptable.

But times have changed. Today that same waiter in that same restaurant will nod with understanding as you describe your problem. He will also faithfully see that your order is prepared exactly as you like it. Even Chinese restaurants have added special salt-free dishes to their repertoire, or will offer to prepare any dish on the menu without salt, soy sauce, or MSG.

As for visiting, do not be shy. Tell your friends the problem. Chances are they will want to prepare food you can enjoy. If that is not possible, brown-bag your own. It is as easy as that.

Always be aware, however, that even with the best intentions, people can make mistakes. Be glad they are receptive and want to be helpful, but, fortified with the tips outlined above, you should—and must—always be the questioner, the final judge of, and the last word on what is best for you.

Recipes

The recipes in this book were created specifically for the salt-free dieter. Some are adaptations of Chinese classics and are noted as such. Others have a pinch here or a dash there that no cook can resist in making a dish her own. Many are the product of my own imagination.

For all these reasons, none of the dishes can be called completely authentic, but they are totally faithful to the style, spirit, and flavor of Chinese cuisine and its four major regions.

Once you try them, we hope you will also agree that salt-free Chinese food can be both easy and exciting, nutritious and delicious. And, more important, it can taste like the real thing.

You may wonder, however, why a book that emphasizes ease and convenience as well as taste does not take the expedient route of salt substitutes. Quite frankly, to do so would defeat a double purpose.

First, it is just as easy—and much tastier—to enhance the natural goodness of food with imaginatively selected herbs and spices as it is to camouflage that flavor with salt of any kind.

Second, it is healthier. Potassium chloride (salt substitute) and sodium chloride (table salt) are two cuts from the same cloth. Too much of the former can do as much harm as overconsumption of the latter.

Also, in the interest of good health, and in our attempt to accommodate those with diabetes, sugar has been kept to a minimum (except in the Dessert section). We chose not to use sugar substitutes in our recipes because they are not yet adaptable to high heat. Consequently, during cooking, they break down and release a bitter, lingering aftertaste.

However, when sugar is called for, the actual amount per serving in most recipes, including some desserts, is so small it may not be a problem. But do not take maybe as an answer. Check first with your own doctor or nutritionist.

Last, but definitely not least, the recipes in this book are low in calories and fat—two happy facts intrinsic to Chinese cuisine.

So when salt, sugar, calories, and fat are greatly reduced, what is left? Health: healthy eating, healthy living, a beautifully healthy body. And taste: the sweet and sour, hot and mild, spicy and pungent, wonderful tastes of China—tastes so distinct unto themselves that they require no other additives.

There are just two more things you should know before you turn the page and begin what we hope will be a memorable adventure in salt-free Chinese cooking and eating:

    1. The calorie, sodium, carbohydrate, and fat counts given for each recipe include all ingredients called for but do not include any of the suggested accompanying dishes.

    2. For convenience, we have not used fresh herbs and spices in these recipes, unless specifically noted. However, fresh is always best, and we encourage you to substitute accordingly when you can. Just remember: the flavor in dried, ground, or powdered herbs and spices is concentrated, so if you go to fresh, triple the amount called for in the recipe.

Enough said. The recipes will, we hope, speak for themselves. So with an invitation to take chopsticks in hand, to taste, and to enjoy, we will heed the words of the ancient Chinese sage, Lao-tzu:

Others appreciate welcome from the perfect host
Who, barely appearing to exist,
Exists the most.

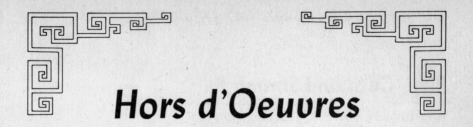

Hors d'Oeuvres

Cocktail parties as we know them, with people chatting and milling about, a drink in one hand, a small plate of finger foods in the other, are virtually unheard-of in China. In the first place, the Chinese would consider it terribly impolite to eat standing up. In the second, hors d'oeuvres per se simply do not exist there.

For the Chinese, appetizers are small portions of what would otherwise be main dishes, very often served as the first three or four courses of a traditional meal. What distinguishes these courses from the rest of the menu is the accompanying wine or tea (the trademark of welcome and conviviality) to whet the appetite for the main attractions to follow.

We Americans have already adopted some of these mini-dishes for our own social gatherings. Egg rolls and baby spareribs, for example, are always sure-fire hits. This chapter offers delicious salt-free variations of both, as well as Coconut Chicken Wings, Steak Slices in Oyster Sauce, Ginger-Sherry Shrimp, and many more—all tantalizing morsels that are sure to please.

Yunnan Curried Mushrooms   SERVES 8

1 tablespoon vegetable oil
16 large fresh mushrooms, halved
1/16 teaspoon ginger powder
1/8 teaspoon lemon peel powder

1 tablespoon dry sherry
1/2 tablespoon Curry Powder (page 232)

1. In wok, heat oil over low heat. Add mushrooms and stir-fry 1 minute.
2. Stir in ginger and lemon peel, blending well.
3. Stir in remaining ingredients. Cover and simmer 2 minutes.

Per serving: 33 calories; 8.7 mg. sodium; 2.6 gm. carbohydrates; 2.0 gm. fat.

Bean Curd and Shrimp Puffs

SERVES 8

A variation of a delicate, light Cantonese dish.

¼ pound medium shrimp, shelled, deveined, and minced
1 egg white
2 tablespoons cornstarch, divided
1 teaspoon low-sodium chicken bouillon
Black pepper to taste
4 tablespoons water
1 teaspoon sesame seed oil
1 leek, chopped, including greens

1 clove garlic, minced
1 slice ginger root, minced, or pinch of ginger powder
4 slices bean curd, halved diagonally
2 tablespoons vegetable oil, divided
½ cup Chicken Stock (page 68), divided

1. In bowl, combine shrimp, egg white, 1 teaspoon cornstarch, bouillon, and black pepper. Cover and refrigerate ½ hour.
2. In second bowl, combine remaining cornstarch and water, blending well. Set aside.
3. In wok, heat sesame seed oil over low heat. Add leek, garlic, and ginger. Stir-fry 1 minute.
4. Add shrimp mixture and stir-fry 1 minute more, or until shrimp turn pink all over.
5. Take each bean curd half and make a slit in the cut edge to form a pocket.
6. Fill each pocket with equal amounts of shrimp mixture. Crimp edges together.
7. Moisten each crimped edge with cornstarch mixture to seal.
8. In skillet, heat 1 tablespoon vegetable oil over low heat. Add half the bean curd puffs. Turn heat to medium and fry 1 minute.
9. With spatula, gently turn puff. Add half the chicken stock and fry 1 minute more. Transfer to platter.
10. Repeat Steps 8 and 9 with remaining oil, puffs, and stock.

Per serving: 82 calories; 23.8 mg. sodium; 6.01 gm. carbohydrates; 4.8 gm. fat.

Pork Balls in Hot Sauce   MAKES 20 CANAPÉS

This is the kind of dish that gives Szechwan cuisine its hot reputation.

½ pound pork, cut in ½-inch cubes
2 scallions, chopped, including
  greens
¼ can (2 ounces) water chestnuts,
  chopped
½ tablespoon Curry Powder (page
  232), divided
½ teaspoon Chili Paste (page 230)
1 egg, lightly beaten
2 cloves garlic, minced

1 tablespoon sesame seed oil
1 cup boiling water
1½ tablespoons low-sodium
  chicken bouillon
3 tablespoons low-sodium peanut
  butter
4 tablespoons dry sherry
1 tablespoon white vinegar

1. In blender or food processor, combine first 7 ingredients. Grind. Transfer to bowl. Form into walnut-sized balls.
2. In wok, heat oil over low heat. Add pork balls and fry, stirring occasionally, until brown all over. Transfer to platter.
3. While pork balls are cooking, in bowl, combine remaining ingredients, blending thoroughly.
4. Pour peanut butter mixture into wok. Turn heat to low and cook 2 minutes, stirring constantly.
5. Return pork balls to wok. Cook 5 minutes more, stirring often.
6. Transfer pork balls and remaining sauce to platter. Skewer balls with toothpicks.

Per canapé: 64 calories; 12.6 mg. sodium; 1.6 gm. carbohydrates; 3.9 gm. fat.

Beef and Shrimp Balls
MAKES 20 CANAPÉS

Sesame seed oil gives a nutty snap to this otherwise Cantonese-style dish.

1 pound ground beef
1 tablespoon low-sodium beef
  bouillon
⅛ teaspoon ginger powder
½ teaspoon garlic powder
Black pepper to taste
2 teaspoons sesame seed oil

¼ pound small shrimp, shelled,
  deveined, and chopped fine
8 scallions, chopped, including
  greens
1 tablespoon dry sherry
1 egg, lightly beaten

1. In bowl, combine first 5 ingredients, blending thoroughly. Set aside.
2. In wok, heat oil over low heat. Add shrimp and scallions. Stir-fry 1 minute, or until shrimp turn pink all over. Stir into beef mixture.
3. Stir sherry and egg into shrimp-beef mixture, blending thoroughly.
4. Form mixture into walnut-sized balls. Place in large skillet. Turn heat to low and let cook in their own juices until browned all over.
5. Transfer beef and shrimp balls to platter. Skewer balls with toothpicks.

Per canapé: 84 calories; 23.3 mg. sodium; 0.9 mg. carbohydrates; 5.6 mg. fat.

Chicken Cubes in Peanut Butter Sauce

SERVES 8

The use of soy sauce and red wine vinegar might suggest a northern influence, but the Szechwan flavor predominates. Serve with cucumber or zucchini slices to balance the hot.

2 whole chicken breasts, skinned, boned, and cubed, bones reserved
2 cups cold water
1 tablespoon low-sodium chicken bouillon
1 tablespoon low-sodium peanut butter
½ teaspoon sesame seed paste
1 tablespoon boiling water
2 tablespoons Soy Sauce Substitute (page 227)

1½ tablespoons red wine vinegar
1 teaspoon dry sherry
Black pepper to taste
1 slice ginger root, minced, or pinch of ginger powder
2 scallions, chopped, including greens
1 tablespoon dried cilantro (or parsley)

1. In bowl, place chicken. Cover and refrigerate.
2. In wok or Dutch oven, combine chicken bones and water. Bring to a boil and continue boiling until liquid is reduced by half. Discard bones.
3. Add chicken and bouillon to broth, stirring to dissolve bouillon. Continue boiling until chicken turns white all over. Remove chicken with slotted spoon to chilled bowl. Cover and refrigerate overnight.
4. Pour broth into second chilled bowl. Cover and refrigerate overnight.
5. Cream together peanut butter and sesame seed paste. Add boiling water and blend until smooth.
6. Stir in remaining ingredients, except broth and chicken.
7. Stir in 2 tablespoons broth (which should have a slightly gelatinous texture). Reserve remaining broth for future use. (It may be frozen up to 6 months.)
8. Pour sauce over chicken and chill 2 hours more.

Per serving: 54 calories; 16.7 mg. sodium; 2.1 gm. carbohydrates; 2.3 gm. fat.

Spiced Beef Cubes

SERVES 16

Fukien can claim the credit for the origin of this delectable adaptation. Steamed carrots cut into 1-inch rounds are a good accompaniment.

2 pounds bottom round, cut in
  1-inch cubes
1 teaspoon sesame seed oil
1 onion, minced
2 slices ginger root, minced, or ⅟₁₆
  teaspoon ginger powder
Water to cover
1 star anise
3 tablespoons dry sherry

4 scallions, minced, including
  greens
2 teaspoons orange peel, minced,
  or ⅟₁₆ teaspoon orange peel
  powder
6 tablespoons Soy Sauce Substitute
  (page 227)
1 tablespoon sugar

1. In wok, over high heat, sear beef on all sides. Transfer to platter.
2. Reduce heat to low. To wok, add sesame seed oil and onion. Cook until onion is limp, stirring occasionally.
3. Add ginger. Return beef to wok. Cover with water.
4. Add star anise. Turn heat to medium and bring to a slow boil. Reduce heat to low. Cover and simmer 1½ hours.
5. Add sherry, scallions, and orange peel. Cover and simmer ½ hour more.
6. Add remaining ingredients and simmer ½ hour more. Discard star anise.
7. Transfer to server. Skewer chunks with toothpicks.

Per serving: 179.1 calories; 29.4 mg. sodium; 3.6 gm. carbohydrates; 12.1 gm. fat.

Sesame Beef Cubes   SERVES 8

A savory beef dish from the Muslim school of the North.

½ pound flank steak, cut in 1-inch
  cubes
1 clove garlic, minced
1 slice ginger root, minced, or
  pinch of ginger powder
2 tablespoons white vinegar

1 egg white
½ tablespoon cornstarch
1 tablespoon sesame seeds
1 tablespoon sesame seed oil

1. In bowl, combine first 4 ingredients. Stir to blend. Cover and refrigerate overnight, turning cubes occasionally.
2. In second bowl, combine, egg white, cornstarch, and sesame seeds. Stir to blend thoroughly.
3. Drain beef cubes and add to egg white mixture, turning to coat cubes thoroughly. Reserve beef marinade.
4. In wok, heat oil over medium-low heat. Add beef cubes and stir-fry until brown on all sides, adding marinade as needed to prevent sticking.
5. Transfer beef cubes to warm platter. Skewer with toothpicks and serve.

Per serving: 87 calories; 19.0 mg. sodium; 1.6 gm. carbohydrates; 4.7 gm. fat.

Hot Ribs   SERVES 12

Hot and good, compliments of Hunan.

4 large spareribs, chopped into
  1-inch pieces
2 cloves garlic, minced
2 slices ginger root, minced, or ¹⁄₁₆
  teaspoon ginger powder
2 teaspoons orange peel, minced,
  or ⅛ teaspoon orange peel
  powder

⅛ teaspoon hot pepper flakes
2 tablespoons Black Bean Sauce
  (page 232)
3 tablespoons dry sherry
2 teaspoons cornstarch
1 teaspoon vegetable oil

1. In bowl, combine all ingredients except oil. Mix to blend thoroughly.
2. Grease a heatproof plate. Place spareribs on plate. Place plate in steamer unit in wok with water boiling ½ inch below steamer.
3. Cover and steam ½ hour.

Per serving (2 pieces): 146.2 calories; 27.5 mg. sodium; 3.4 gm. carbohydrates; 11.9 gm. fat.

Sherry-Vinegar Baby Spareribs   SERVES 8

A mildly spiced offering from the Szechwan school.

4 large spareribs, chopped into
  1½-inch pieces
4 tablespoons dry sherry
2 tablespoons red wine vinegar
⅟₁₆ teaspoon Szechwan Pepper
  Spice (page 229)
1 tablespoon sesame seed oil
1 onion, minced
2 cloves garlic, minced

2 tablespoons low-sodium tomato
  paste
¼ cup water
2 tablespoons Soy Sauce Substitute
  (page 227)
Dash of Five-Spice Powder (page
  228—optional)

1. Preheat oven to broil.
2. In bowl, combine first 4 ingredients. Let stand 15 minutes. Drain, reserving marinade.
3. In broiler pan, place sparerib pieces. Broil 6 inches from heat 4 minutes. Turn ribs and broil 4 minutes more. Remove to bowl.
4. In large saucepan, heat oil over low heat. Add onion and garlic and stir-fry until onion is wilted.
5. Add all remaining ingredients, including marinade (but not spareribs). Simmer over low heat until sauce gets bubbly around the edges.
6. Add spareribs to the mixture and cook until sauce is reduced by half, stirring occasionally.

Per serving: 220 calories; 43.5 mg. sodium; 4.3 gm. carbohydrates; 18.9 gm. fat.

Steak Slices in Oyster Sauce   SERVES 4

This Cantonese-style dish proves once again why this cuisine is so loved.

½ pound flank steak, sliced in thin
  1-inch x 3-inch strips
¼ cup Oyster Sauce (page 234)
1 tablespoon cornstarch
Black pepper to taste

¼ cup dry sherry
2 teaspoons mustard powder
⅛ teaspoon garlic powder
1 teaspoon vegetable oil
1 can (8 ounces) water chestnuts,
  drained

1. In bowl, combine first 4 ingredients. Stir to blend until cornstarch is dissolved. Cover and refrigerate 1 hour. Then drain, reserving marinade.
2. In second bowl, stir together sherry and mustard and garlic powders, stirring until mustard is dissolved.
3. In wok, heat oil over low heat. Add steak slices and stir-fry until slices turn brownish gray.
4. Turn to medium heat. Add sherry mixture and reserved marinade and stir to blend.
5. Transfer steak to platter. Place 1 water chestnut in center of each slice. Roll up and secure with toothpicks.

Per serving: 184 calories; 55.5 mg. sodium; 12.0 gm. carbohydrates; 2.7 gm. fat.

Coconut Chicken Wings   SERVES 8

Although a bit unorthodox, this and other recipes using chicken wings will require an oven rather than a wok, simply to avoid excess oil. The recipe that follows is in the Szechwan style.

1 teaspoon Chili Oil (page 230)
⅓ cup orange juice
3 tablespoons Soy Sauce Substitute
  (page 227)
1/16 teaspoon ginger powder

3 tablespoons grated coconut
2 tablespoons low-sodium chili
  ketchup
16 chicken wings

1. In bowl, combine all ingredients except chicken wings. Stir to blend. Let stand ½ hour.
2. On broiler pan, place chicken wings. Spoon half the sauce over the wings and broil 6 inches from heat 4 minutes.
3. Turn wings. Spoon on remaining sauce and broil 4 minutes more.

Per serving: 170 calories; 45.2 mg. sodium; 4.4 gm. carbohydrates; 9.3 gm. fat.

Sherried Onion Chicken Wings   SERVES 8

From the Chinese capital, Peking, this recipe has a subtle yet distinctly elegant taste.

1 onion, minced
⅔ cup Chicken Stock (page 68)
⅓ cup dry sherry
Black pepper to taste
4 tablespoons Hoisin Sauce
   Substitute (page 228)

16 chicken wings
8 cloves garlic, minced, divided
¼ cup water
1 tablespoon cornstarch
2 teaspoons sugar

1. In bowl, combine first 6 ingredients. Cover and refrigerate 1 hour, stirring occasionally.
2. On broiler pan, place chicken wings, reserving marinade. Sprinkle wings with half the garlic. Broil 6 inches from heat 3 minutes.
3. Turn wings. Sprinkle with remaining garlic. Broil 3 minutes more.
4. While wings are broiling, heat marinade in saucepan over low heat until it starts to simmer.
5. While marinade is heating, in bowl, combine water and cornstarch, stirring to dissolve cornstarch. Stir into marinade.
6. Stir in sugar and continue stirring until sauce starts to thicken.
7. Pour sauce over wings and broil 1 minute more.

Per serving: 175.2 calories; 51.1 mg. sodium; 9.3 gm. carbohydrates; 9.4 gm. fat.

Hot and Sour Chicken Wings   SERVES 8

The skillful balance of soy sauce and sugar is temptingly demonstrated in this dish in the Fukien tradition.

16 chicken wings
4 tablespoons Soy Sauce Substitute
   (page 227)
4 tablespoons lemon juice
¼ cup water
1 teaspoon low-sodium chicken
   bouillon

2 tablespoons red wine vinegar
1 tablespoon dry sherry
1/16 teaspoon hot pepper flakes
2 tablespoons sugar

1. In bowl, combine first 3 ingredients. Stir to blend. Cover and refrigerate ½ hour.

2. On broiler pan, place chicken wings and broil 6 inches from heat, basting occasionally with marinade, until golden brown on both sides.
3. While chicken wings are broiling, in saucepan, combine remaining ingredients. Bring to a slow boil, stirring constantly to dissolve sugar. Continue boiling until sauce bubbles.
4. Onto platter, pour a thin coating of sauce. Place chicken wings on top. Pour remaining sauce over all.

Per serving: 153.3 calories; 45.9 mg. sodium; 5.2 gm. carbohydrates; 6.7 gm. fat.

Sizzling Chicken Wings
SERVES 8

This dish is really a blending of northern and eastern cuisines, and it is quite delicious.

16 chicken wings
2 tablespoons Hoisin Sauce
  Substitute (page 228)
2 tablespoons dry sherry
2 teaspoons Chili Oil (page 230)
1 leek, chopped, including greens
1/16 teaspoon ground coriander
1/16 teaspoon ground Szechwan
  peppercorns

2 teaspoons sugar
1/2 cup Chicken Stock (page 68)
2 tablespoons Soy Sauce Substitute
  (page 227)
1/2 tablespoon cornstarch

1. In bowl, combine first 3 ingredients. Set aside.
2. In wok, heat oil over low heat. Add leek, coriander, and Szechwan pepper. Stir-fry 1 minute.
3. Stir in sugar, blending well. Remove from heat.
4. Preheat oven to broil.
5. On baking sheet, place chicken wings. Broil 6 inches from heat 5 minutes. Turn and broil 5 minutes more. Remove to platter.
6. In bowl, combine last 3 ingredients.
7. Return wok mixture to high heat. Add chicken stock mixture and stir until mixture thickens.
8. Pour sauce over chicken wings.

Per serving: 175.2 calories; 48.1 mg. sodium; 4.8 gm. carbohydrates; 8.1 gm. fat.

Cucumber Stuffed with Chicken Livers

MAKES 24 CANAPÉS

Curry powder indicates the Yunnan influence of this delicious and zesty treat.

2 large cucumbers, scraped, halved, and seeded
2 tablespoons cider vinegar
2 tablespoons dry sherry
1 tablespoon sesame seed oil
2 tablespoons orange peel, minced, or ¼ teaspoon orange peel powder
1 pound chicken livers, washed and drained, cut in half along the membrane

4 scallions, chopped, including greens
Black pepper to taste
1 tablespoon Hoisin Sauce Substitute (page 228)
1 star anise
1½ teaspoons Curry Powder (page 232)

1. In 8-inch square dish, place cucumber halves. Spoon vinegar and sherry over all. Let stand 15 minutes, turning occasionally.
2. In wok, heat oil over low heat. Add all remaining ingredients, except curry powder. Stir-fry until livers lose all pink color. Discard star anise.
3. In food processor or blender, combine liver mixture and curry powder. Grind.
4. Remove cucumber halves from marinade. Cut each half into 6 equal pieces.
5. Spread liver mixture over each cucumber piece. Arrange on platter. Cover and chill ½ hour.

Per canapé: 46 calories; 19.7 mg. sodium; 1.9 gm. carbohydrates; 1.4 gm. fat.

Chicken Livers
Wrapped in Red and Green   MAKES 24 CANAPÉS

Very typically Cantonese in style, blending sweet and hot, pungent and sharp.

1 pound chicken livers, washed and drained, cut in half along the membrane
3 tablespoons dry sherry
1 teaspoon mustard powder
1 tablespoon peanut oil, divided
2 cloves garlic, minced

2 slices ginger root, minced, or $\frac{1}{16}$ teaspoon ginger powder
2 large green peppers, cut in 8 slices
1 large red pepper, cut in 8 slices
½ cup boiling water
2 teaspoons honey

1. In bowl, combine first 3 ingredients, stirring to dissolve mustard. Let stand 20 minutes.
2. In wok, heat 2 teaspoons oil over low heat. Add chicken livers and reserve marinade. Stir-fry livers 3 to 5 minutes, or until all pink color is gone. With slotted spoon, remove to warm platter.
3. To wok, add remaining teaspoon of oil. Add garlic, ginger, and green and red peppers and stir-fry 2 minutes, or until peppers are limp, adding marinade as necessary to prevent sticking. Remove to platter with livers.
4. To wok, add water and honey plus any remaining marinade. Stir to blend well. Pour over livers.
5. Place each liver on a pepper strip. Roll pepper around liver and secure with toothpick.
6. Arrange on a platter, alternating 2 green strips with one red.

Per canapé: 46 calories; 22.1 mg. sodium; 3.9 gm. carbohydrates; 1.4 gm. fat.

Barbecued Chicken Buns   MAKES 24 BUNS

A unique and lovely hors d'oeuvre common to all regions.

1 Basic Buns recipe (page 62)
2 whole chicken breasts, skinned, boned, and diced
2 cloves garlic, blanched and mashed
2 slices ginger root, minced, or ⅟₁₆ teaspoon ginger powder
2 tablespoons lemon juice
1 tablespoon peanut oil
1 onion, minced

½ can (4 ounces) bamboo shoots, chopped
2 tablespoons unsalted peanuts, crushed
2 tablespoons honey
2 tablespoons cider vinegar
1 tablespoon low-sodium ketchup
5 scallions, chopped, including greens

1. Follow Steps 1 through 5 for Basic Buns.
2. In bowl, combine chicken, garlic, ginger, and lemon oil. Cover and refrigerate 1 hour.
3. In blender or food processor, place chicken mixture. Grind briefly. Set aside.
4. In wok, heat oil over low heat. Add onion, bamboo shoots, and peanuts. Stir-fry 2 minutes.
5. To wok mixture, add chicken mixture plus honey, vinegar, ketchup, and scallions. Stir-fry 1 minute. Remove from heat.
6. Turn Basic Buns dough onto floured surface. Knead until springy. Divide into 2 equal parts and shape each into a 12-inch log.
7. Cut each log into 12 equal pieces.
8. Flour each piece and roll into a 3-inch circle.
9. Place ½ teaspoon chicken mixture in center of each circle.
10. Flute edges all around and bring the edges together into a knot.
11. Place buns, knot side down, onto lightly floured board, leaving 2-inch space between each bun. Cover with cloth and let stand in warm place ½ hour.
12. Turn half the buns, knot side up, onto heatproof plate.
13. Place on rack over boiling water. Cover with damp cloth and steam 15 to 20 minutes. Turn off heat. Let buns rest 5 minutes. Set aside.
14. Repeat Step 13 with remaining buns.
15. May be refrigerated up to 4 days. Reheat by steaming 15 to 20 minutes.

Per bun: 146 calories; 10.3 mg. sodium; 24.5 gm. carbohydrates: 2.0 gm. fat.

Sweet Vegetable Buns

MAKES 20 BUNS

Served as an hors d'oeuvre or entrée, this dish, in the northern style, is similar to the filled buns savored throughout China.

6 tablespoons boiling water
1 teaspoon low-sodium chicken
  bouillon
1 tablespoon sesame seed oil
2 zucchini, chopped
4 broccoli stalks, chopped
10 fresh mushrooms, chopped

4 scallions, chopped, including
  greens
3 tablespoons Hoisin Sauce
  Substitute (page 228)
1 Steamed Buns recipe (page 63)

1. In bowl, combine first 2 ingredients. Stir to dissolve bouillon.
2. In wok, heat oil over low heat. Add zucchini, broccoli, and mushrooms. Stir-fry 2 minutes.
3. Add scallions. Stir-fry 30 seconds.
4. Stir in hoisin sauce and remove to dish. Let cool.
5. Follow Steps 1 through 9 for Steamed Buns.
6. Take each piece of bun dough and roll into a thin 3-inch circle.
7. Place 2 teaspoons of vegetable mixture in center of circle. Gather all the edges together and twist at the top so that each bun resembles a small sac.
8. Repeat Step 7 until all bun pieces and filling are gone.
9. Cover buns with a damp towel and let stand 15 minutes.
10. In wok, add enough water to come up to 1 inch below a bamboo steamer. (Any steamer unit will do if it has holes in the bottom. Grease the floor of the steamer.)
11. Bring water to a boil. Place buns ½ inch apart in steamer. Cover and steam 15 minutes.
12. Remove buns while water is still boiling to prevent buns from collapsing.
13. Repeat process until all buns are done. Let cool slightly before serving.

Per bun: 152 calories; 7.6 mg. sodium; 35.6 gm. carbohydrates; 1.4 gm. fat.

Peanutty Vegetable Buns
MAKES 16 BUNS

The taste is western Chinese, but the enjoyment is national. This dish also makes a lovely hors d'oeuvre or brunch selection.

1 Basic Buns recipe (page 62)
2 teaspoons sesame seed oil
½ cup Chinese or American white
  cabbage, shredded
¾ teaspoon sugar
¼ cup bean sprouts, chopped
1 tablespoon dry sherry

Black pepper to taste
2 scallions, chopped, including
  greens
1½ tablespoons sesame seeds
4 tablespoons low-sodium peanut
  butter

1. Follow Steps 1 through 5 for Basic Buns.
2. In wok, heat oil over low heat. Add cabbage. Cover and cook 5 minutes, stirring occasionally.
3. Stir in sugar, blending well.
4. Stir in bean sprouts, sherry, pepper, and scallions. Stir-fry 2 minutes. Transfer mixture to bowl.
5. Stir in sesame seeds and peanut butter and blend thoroughly.
6. Turn Basic Buns dough onto floured surface. Knead until springy. Divide into 2 equal parts and shape each into an 8-inch log.
7. Cut each log into 8 equal pieces.
8. Flour each piece and roll into a 5-inch circle.
9. Place 1 teaspoon of vegetable mixture in center of each circle.
10. Flute edges all around and bring the edges together into a knot.
11. Place buns, knot side down, onto lightly floured board, leaving 2-inch space between each bun. Cover with cloth and let stand in warm place ½ hour.
12. Turn half the buns, knot side up, onto heatproof plate.
13. Place on rack over boiling water. Cover with damp cloth and steam 15 to 20 minutes. Turn off heat. Let buns rest 5 minutes. Set aside.
14. Repeat Step 13 with remaining buns.
15. May be refrigerated up to 4 days. Reheat by steaming 15 to 20 minutes.

Per bun: 177.8 calories; 2.5 mg. sodium; 33.4 gm. carbohydrates; 1.9 gm. fat.

Beef and Spinach Buns

MAKES 16 BUNS

A lovely appetizer, or breakfast, enjoyed throughout China.

1 Basic Buns recipe (page 62)
½ pound ground beef
⅛ teaspoon garlic powder
1 tablespoon low-sodium beef
 bouillon
1 tablespoon sesame seed oil,
 divided
2 slices ginger root, or ⅟₁₆ teaspoon
 ginger powder
4 scallions, chopped, including
 greens

½ can (4 ounces) water chestnuts,
 minced
1 package (10 ounces) frozen
 spinach, squeezed almost dry
2 tablespoons Soy Sauce Substitute
 (page 227)
1 teaspoon orange peel powder
Black pepper to taste

1. Follow Steps 1 through 5 for Basic Buns.
2. In bowl, combine beef, garlic powder, and bouillon, blending thoroughly.
3. In wok, heat 2 teaspoons oil over low heat. Add ginger, scallions, water chestnuts, and meat mixture. Stir-fry 3 minutes. Transfer to large bowl.
4. To vegetables and beef mixture, add spinach, blending thoroughly.
5. Stir in soy sauce, orange peel powder, pepper, and remaining teaspoon oil. Then divide mixture into 16 equal portions.
6. Turn Basic Buns dough onto floured surface. Knead until springy. Divide into 2 equal parts and shape each into an 8-inch log.
7. Cut each log into 8 equal pieces.
8. Flour each piece and roll into a 5-inch circle.
9. Place 1 teaspoon of beef and spinach mixture in center of each circle.
10. Flute edges all around and bring the edges together into a knot.
11. Place buns, knot side down, onto lightly floured board, leaving 2-inch space between each bun. Cover with cloth and let stand in warm place ½ hour.
12. Turn half the buns, knot side up, onto heatproof plate.
13. Place on rack over boiling water. Cover with damp cloth and steam 15 to 20 minutes. Shut off water. Let buns rest 5 minutes. Set aside.
14. Repeat Step 13 with remaining buns.
15. May be refrigerated up to 4 days. Reheat by steaming 15 to 20 minutes.

Per bun: 226 calories; 24.7 mg. sodium; 35.3 gm. carbohydrates; 5.0 gm. fat.

Pork and Scallop Buns

MAKES 16 BUNS

In the northern Chinese tradition, this dish also makes a surprisingly filling light lunch served with Peaches and Pineapple (page 246).

1 Basic Buns recipe (page 62)
1/4 pound ground pork
1/8 teaspoon onion powder
1/4 teaspoon Curry Powder (page 232)
1/4 pound scallops
1 teaspoon lemon juice
4 teaspoons peanut oil, divided
4 scallions, chopped, including greens

1/2 can (4 ounces) bamboo shoots, chopped
1 zucchini, cubed
1 teaspoon dry sherry
Black pepper to taste
1 tablespoon low-sodium beef bouillon
3 tablespoons Hoisin Sauce Substitute (page 228)

1. Follow Steps 1 through 5 for Basic Buns.
2. In bowl, combine pork, onion powder, and curry powder, blending thoroughly.
3. In second bowl, combine scallops and lemon juice.
4. In wok, heat 2 teaspoons oil over low heat. Add scallions, bamboo shoots, and pork mixture. Stir-fry 2 minutes.
5. Add zucchini. Stir-fry 2 minutes more.
6. Add scallop mixture. Stir-fry 1 minute more. Transfer mixture to large bowl.
7. To pork and scallop mixture, add sherry, pepper, bouillon, and hoisin sauce, stirring to blend thoroughly; then divide mixture into 16 equal portions.
8. Turn Basic Buns dough onto floured surface. Knead until springy. Divide into 2 equal parts and shape each into an 8-inch log.
9. Cut each log into 8 equal pieces.
10. Flour each piece and roll into a 5-inch circle.
11. Place 1 teaspoon of pork and scallop mixture in center of each circle.
12. Flute edges all around and bring the edges together into a knot.
13. Place buns, knot side down, onto lightly floured board, leaving 2-inch space between each bun. Cover with cloth and let stand in warm place 1/2 hour.
14. Turn half the buns, knot side up, onto heatproof plate.
15. Place on rack over boiling water. Cover with damp cloth and steam 15 to 20 minutes. Shut off water. Let buns rest 5 minutes. Set aside.
16. Repeat Step 15 with remaining buns.
17. May be refrigerated up to 4 days. Reheat by steaming 15 to 20 minutes.

Per bun: 204.5 calories; 28.2 mg. sodium; 34.4 gm. carbohydrates; 3.1 gm. fat.

Egg Roll Filling I

MAKES 32 CANAPÉS

Egg rolls might have originated in the North, but they are enjoyed throughout China as they are here. The following recipes offer two popular fillings. Serve with Duck Sauce (page 234) or with white vinegar seasoned with garlic cloves.

1 tablespoon vegetable oil
¼ pound small shrimp, shelled, deveined, and chopped
4 scallions, minced, including greens
¼ pound bean sprouts, chopped
½ can (4 ounces) water chestnuts, diced
½ cup Chinese or American white cabbage, shredded and chopped fine

½ teaspoon sugar
⅛ teaspoon garlic powder
Pinch of ginger powder
2 tablespoons Soy Sauce Substitute (page 227)
Black pepper to taste
1 Egg Roll Skins recipe (page 64)
2½ cups peanut oil

1. In wok, heat vegetable oil over low heat. Add shrimp, scallions, bean sprouts, and water chestnuts. Stir-fry 1 minute, or until shrimp turn pink all over. Transfer to platter.
2. To wok, add cabbage, sugar, garlic and ginger powders, soy sauce, and pepper. Stir to blend. Cover and steam 1 minute. Transfer to platter. Blend thoroughly with shrimp mixture.
3. In center of each egg roll skin, place 1½ tablespoons filling and spread in a thin line down center of skin.
4. Fold skin over filling and pinch edges together. Then fold short ends over and pinch together.
5. In wok, heat peanut oil over high heat until crackling. Add egg rolls seam-side down, a few at a time, and fry until golden brown and crispy. Drain on paper towels. Cut each egg roll in half.

Per canapé: 117.3 calories; 9.0 mg. sodium; 12.4 gm. carbohydrates; 6.5 gm. fat.

Egg Roll Filling II

MAKES 32 CANAPÉS

Serve with Duck Sauce (page 234) or with white vinegar seasoned with garlic cloves.

1½ tablespoons sesame seed oil, divided
1 onion, minced
1 half chicken breast, skinned, boned, and cubed
¼ pound pork, shredded
4 fresh mushrooms, chopped
1 can (8 ounces) bamboo shoots, chopped

2 broccoli stalks, diced
1/16 teaspoon ginger powder
1 tablespoon dry sherry
2 tablespoons Soy Sauce Substitute (page 227)
Black pepper to taste
1 Egg Roll Skins recipe (page 64)
2½ cups peanut oil

1. In wok, heat ½ tablespoon sesame seed oil over low heat. Add onion and stir-fry 2 minutes, or until onion is wilted.
2. Add remaining sesame seed oil along with chicken, pork, mushrooms, and bamboo shoots. Stir-fry 2 minutes, or until chicken is white all over.
3. Push mixture to sides of wok. To well formed in center, add broccoli, ginger powder, sherry, soy sauce, and pepper. Stir-fry 1 minute. Transfer mixture to platter.
4. In center of each egg roll skin, place 1½ tablespoons filling and spread in a thin line down center of skin.
5. Fold skin over filling and pinch edges together. Then fold short ends over and pinch together.
6. In wok, heat peanut oil over high heat until crackling. Add egg rolls seam-side down, a few at a time, and fry until golden brown and crispy. Drain on paper towels. Cut each egg roll in half.

Per canapé: 128 calories; 8.2 mg. sodium; 12.3 gm. carbohydrates; 7.3 gm. fat.

Curried Chicken and Shrimp Egg Rolls

MAKES 32 CANAPÉS

A Szechwan version of the classic and popular egg roll. Serve with Duck Sauce (page 234).

1 whole chicken breast, skinned, boned, and diced
½ pound small shrimp, shelled, deveined, and diced
2 teaspoons low-sodium beef bouillon
1 teaspoon Curry Powder (page 232)
1 egg white
1 tablespoon cornstarch
Black pepper to taste
2 tablespoons plus 2 cups vegetable oil, divided

1 slice ginger root, minced, or pinch of ginger powder
¼ pound Chinese or American white cabbage, shredded
½ can (4 ounces) water chestnuts, minced
⅓ pound bean sprouts, chopped
2 tablespoons dry sherry
1 Egg Roll Skins recipe (page 64)

1. In bowl, combine first 7 ingredients, stirring to blend thoroughly. Cover and refrigerate 1 hour.
2. In wok, heat 2 tablespoons vegetable oil over low heat. Add chicken and shrimp mixture plus ginger and cabbage. Stir-fry 1 minute.
3. Add water chestnuts, bean sprouts, and sherry. Stir-fry 1 minute more. Transfer to platter.
4. In center of each egg roll skin, place 1½ tablespoons filling and spread in a thin line down center of skin.
5. Fold skin over filling and pinch edges together. Then fold short ends over and pinch together.
6. In wok, heat peanut oil over high heat until crackling. Add egg rolls seam-side down, a few at a time, and fry until golden brown and crispy. Drain on paper towels. Cut each egg roll in half.

Per canapé: 144 calories; 30.5 mg. sodium; 12.8 gm. carbohydrates; 7.0 gm. fat.

Pork and Oyster Egg Rolls   MAKES 32 CANAPÉS

A light touch from Shantung.

⅓ pound pork, chopped fine
3 tablespoons Soy Sauce Substitute
  (page 227)
4 scallions, minced, including
  greens
2 pints oysters, shucked, liquid
  reserved
2 tablespoons lemon juice
1 tablespoon dry sherry
1 tablespoon sesame seed oil

1 onion, minced
8 fresh mushrooms, chopped
Black pepper to taste
1 red pepper, diced
1 tablespoon crushed pineapple
  (optional)
1 Egg Roll Skins recipe (page 64)
2 cups vegetable oil

1. In blender or food processor, combine first 6 ingredients. Grind briefly.
2. In wok, heat sesame seed oil over medium heat. Add pork mixture, onion, mushrooms, black pepper, and red pepper. Stir-fry 1 minute.
3. Add reserved oyster liquid and pineapple, if desired. Stir-fry 30 seconds more. Transfer to platter.
4. In center of each egg roll skin, place 1½ tablespoons filling and spread in a thin line down center of skin.
5. Fold skin over filling and pinch edges together. Then fold short ends over and pinch together.
6. In wok, heat peanut oil over high heat until crackling. Add egg rolls seam-side down, a few at a time, and fry until golden brown and crispy. Drain on paper towels. Cut each egg roll in half.

Per canapé: 133 calories; 24.3 mg. sodium; 13.1 gm. carbohydrates; 6.7 gm. fat.

Won Ton Filling I

MAKES 24 CANAPÉS

Like egg rolls, won tons are standard fare throughout China. Following are two filling options—the first Cantonese and the second more in the northern tradition. Serve with Duck Sauce (page 234), Six-Fruit Sauce (page 242), Soy Sauce Substitute (page 227), or Sweet and Sour Sauce (page 235).

1½ tablespoons sesame seed oil, divided
½ pound flounder fillet, cubed
2 cloves garlic, minced
½ cup Chinese or American white cabbage, shredded and chopped fine
8 scallions, chopped, including greens
4 fresh mushrooms, chopped
2 teaspoons lemon juice

Black pepper to taste (or dash of hot pepper flakes)
1½ teaspoons low-sodium chicken bouillon
1½ tablespoons cold water
1 teaspoon cornstarch
1 Won Ton Skins recipe (page 65)
2 quarts Chicken Stock (page 68) or water

1. In wok, heat ½ tablespoon oil over low heat. Add flounder and garlic, and simmer 5 minutes, stirring occasionally. Transfer to platter.
2. To wok, add remaining oil. Add cabbage and scallions. Stir-fry 3 minutes.
3. Push cabbage mixture to sides of wok. To well formed in center, add mushrooms and lemon juice. Stir-fry 1 minute.
4. Return flounder mixture to wok. Add pepper and bouillon. Stir to blend thoroughly. Let simmer 2 minutes.
5. While mixture is simmering, in bowl, combine water and cornstarch, stirring until cornstarch is dissolved. Stir into flounder mixture, blending thoroughly. Transfer to platter.
6. In center of each won ton skin, place 2 teaspoons filling. Fold skin in half and pinch edges together. Then fold short ends toward each other and pinch them together.
7. In a saucepan, bring to boil chicken stock or water. Add won tons a few at a time and boil 10 minutes. With slotted spoon, remove to platter.

Per canapé: 136 calories; 10.9 mg. sodium; 1.7 gm. carbohydrates; 11.1 gm. fat.

Won Ton Filling II

MAKES 24 CANAPÉS

Serve with Duck Sauce (page 234), Six-Fruit Sauce (page 242), Soy Sauce Substitute (page 227), or Sweet and Sour Sauce (page 235).

¼ pound flank steak, shredded
1 tablespoon cider vinegar
1 teaspoon mustard powder
2 tablespoons Soy Sauce Substitute (page 227)
¼ pound shrimp, shelled, deveined, and chopped
1 tablespoon lemon juice
½ tablespoon vegetable oil
1 leek, chopped, including greens

1 zucchini, chopped
1 tablespoon dry sherry
4 scallions, chopped, including greens
½ can (4 ounces) water chestnuts, chopped
1 tablespoon dried cilantro (or parsley)
1 Won Ton Skins recipe (page 65)

1. In bowl, combine first 4 ingredients. Cover and refrigerate 1 hour, stirring occasionally. Drain, reserving marinade.
2. In second bowl, combine shrimp and lemon juice. Cover and refrigerate 1 hour.
3. In wok, heat oil over low heat. Add meat mixture and leek. Raise heat to high. Stir-fry 30 seconds.
4. Add zucchini and reserved meat marinade. Stir-fry 1 minute more. Transfer to platter.
5. To wok, add shrimp mixture, sherry, scallions, and water chestnuts. Reduce heat to low and stir-fry 30 seconds, or until shrimp turn pink all over. Transfer to platter.
6. Stir in cilantro.
7. In center of each won ton skin, place 2 teaspoons filling. Fold skin in half and pinch edges together. Then fold short ends toward each other and pinch them together.
8. In saucepan, bring to boil chicken stock or water. Add won tons a few at a time and boil 10 minutes. With slotted spoon, remove to platter.

Per canapé: 141 calories; 12.0 mg. sodium; 3.0 gm. carbohydrates; 0.6 gm. fat.

Minced Oysters

MAKES 2¾ CUPS

Excellent served with unsalted sesame seed crackers or with sliced cucumber.

2 pints shucked oysters, liquid
  reserved
2 tablespoons lemon juice
1 cup cooked rice
1 tablespoon orange peel, minced,
  or 1 teaspoon orange peel
  powder
1 tablespoon low-sodium beef
  bouillon

⅓ cup boiling water
Black pepper to taste
4 scallions, minced, including
  greens
Dash of ginger powder

1. In bowl, marinate oysters in lemon juice 5 minutes.
2. In wok, over high heat, poach oysters in lemon juice 10 seconds. Remove to bowl and mince.
3. Add rice. Stir to blend thoroughly.
4. In second bowl, combine orange peel, bouillon, water, and black pepper. Stir to dissolve bouillon. Add scallions and ginger powder.
5. Pour bouillon mixture over oyster-rice mixture. Stir to blend thoroughly.
6. Stir in reserved oyster liquid.

Per recipe: 783 calories; 128 mg. sodium; 91.5 gm. carbohydrates; 15.7 gm. fat.
Per cup: 285 calories; 46.5 mg. sodium; 33.3 gm. carbohydrates; 5.7 gm. fat.
Per tablespoon: 18 calories; 2.9 mg. sodium; 2.1 gm. carbohydrates; 0.4 gm. fat.

Deep-Fried Oyster Puffs

SERVES 12

The Szechwan pepper spice leaves no doubt that these crackling morsels are adaptations of a Szechwan dish. We prefer our own version to the ground pepper traditionally used.

2 pints shucked oysters, liquid
  reserved or frozen* for future use
10 cups boiling water
8 tablespoons all-purpose flour
4 tablespoons cornstarch
2 teaspoons low-sodium chicken
  bouillon

10 tablespoons cold water
1 tablespoon plus 3 cups vegetable
  oil, divided
1 cup cider vinegar
¼ cup Szechwan Pepper Spice
  (page 229)

1. Place oysters in strainer and rinse under cold water.
2. Lower strainer into boiling water and boil oysters 10 seconds. Drain and turn oysters into a dish. Drain wok.
3. In bowl, sift together flour and cornstarch. Stir in bouillon and water. Then stir in 1 tablespoon oil. Blend thoroughly.
4. Add oysters to batter and blend thoroughly.
5. In wok, heat 3 cups oil over high heat until crackling. Reduce to medium heat.
6. With slotted spoon, scoop one oyster from batter, scraping off excess liquid. Gently slip oyster into oil. Then quickly repeat process with remaining oysters.
7. Fry oysters until golden brown, turning occasionally. Remove oysters and drain on paper towels.
8. Arrange oyster puffs on platter. Serve vinegar and Szechwan pepper spice on the side as seasonings.

Per serving: 153 calories; 42.9 mg. sodium; 13.9 gm. carbohydrates; 8.1 gm. fat.

* May be frozen up to 2 months.

Ginger-Sherry Shrimp

SERVES 16

Simple and simply lovely, this dish is Oriental in flavor, but of no particular origin. Serve Hoisin Sauce Substitute (page 228) as a dip.

½ pound small shrimp
4 tablespoons dry sherry
½ tablespoon low-sodium chicken
 bouillon

2 slices ginger root, minced, or ¹⁄₁₆
 teaspoon ginger powder

1. In bowl, combine first 3 ingredients. Cover and refrigerate ½ hour.
2. In wok, stir-fry ginger over low heat 1 minute. Discard ginger.
3. Turn heat to high. Add shrimp mixture and stir-fry 1 minute, or until shrimp turn pink. Transfer to platter. Skewer with toothpicks.

Per serving: 20 calories; 20.8 mg. sodium; 0.4 gm. carbohydrates; 0.3 gm. fat.

Shrimp in Black Bean Sauce

SERVES 8

The loquats are added in the experimental spirit of the Cantonese in our adaptation of this traditional dish.

1 pound medium shrimp, shelled
 and deveined
4 scallions, chopped, including
 greens
2 tablespoons Black Bean Sauce
 (page 232)
1 tablespoon sesame seed oil

2 teaspoons low-sodium chicken
 bouillon
Dash of ginger powder
1 can (15 ounces) loquats, drained,
 liquid reserved

1. In bowl, combine first 3 ingredients, blending well.
2. In wok, heat oil over low heat. Add shrimp mixture, bouillon, and ginger powder. Stir-fry 1 minute.
3. Add half of the reserved loquat liquid. Raise heat to high and stir-fry 30 seconds, or until shrimp turn pink all over. With slotted spoon, remove shrimp to platter.
4. Skewer 1 loquat between 2 shrimp and arrange on platter.

Per serving: 105 calories; 82.0 mg. sodium; 9.7 gm. carbohydrates; 3.0 gm. fat.

Shrimp in Hot Garlic Sauce SERVES 16

It is hot, and it is Hunan.

1 pound small shrimp
1 tablespoon Soy Sauce Substitute
  (page 227)
2 teaspoons Chili Oil (page 230)

2 teaspoons unsalted peanuts,
  crushed
4 cloves garlic, minced
1 teaspoon cider vinegar

1. In bowl, combine first 2 ingredients. Stir to blend.
2. In wok, heat chili oil over high heat. Add peanuts and garlic. Stir-fry until garlic starts to brown.
3. Add shrimp and soy sauce mixture. Reduce heat to medium and stir-fry until shrimp turn pink.
4. Stir in vinegar and blend.
5. Transfer shrimp to warm platter. Skewer with toothpicks and serve.

Per serving: 40 calories; 40.7 mg. sodium; 1.3 gm. carbohydrates; 1.2 gm. fat.

Lobster Balls MAKES 8 CANAPÉS

Don't worry. Most of the oil will be left in the wok. We have tempered the amount of soy sauce and sherry in this Shanghai adaptation so that the sweet taste of the lobster comes through.

½ pound cooked lobster meat,
  minced
2 tablespoons cornstarch
2 scallions, minced, including
  greens
1 tablespoon Soy Sauce Substitute
  (page 227)

1 egg
1 teaspoon cider vinegar
2 tablespoons dry sherry
1 small carrot, scraped and grated
1 cup vegetable oil
¾ cup white vinegar
4 cloves garlic, sliced

1. In bowl, combine first 8 ingredients. Blend thoroughly. Cover and chill at least 1 hour.
2. Shape lobster mixture into walnut-sized balls.
3. In wok, heat oil over high heat until sizzling. Reduce heat to medium.
4. With slotted spoon, add lobster balls and deep-fry 5 minutes, or until lightly golden. With slotted spoon, remove to platter.
5. In second bowl, combine vinegar and garlic. Let stand 15 minutes. Serve as a dip for the lobster balls.

Per canapé: 88 calories; 72.0 mg. sodium; 6.8 gm. carbohydrates; 4.0 gm. fat.

Lion's Head Miniatures

MAKES 16 CANAPÉS

This is a traditional New Year's dish in the eastern China region of Yang-chow, so called because the four meatballs are so large that when placed on the cabbage they signify a lion's head and mane, and when served on New Year's Day they represent the four blessings: happiness, prosperity, health, and longevity. The recipe that follows is one version of the dish, now national in fame and popularity. We have divided each of the four patties into smaller meatballs more appropriate for hors d'oeuvres.

1 pound finely ground pork, divided
4 scallions, minced, including greens
2 slices ginger root, minced, or ⅟₁₆ teaspoon ginger powder
1 teaspoon sugar
3 tablespoons dry sherry
1 tablespoon cornstarch
2 teaspoons low-sodium beef bouillon

Black pepper to taste
2 tablespoons Soy Sauce Substitute (page 227)
1 tablespoon vegetable oil
2 pounds Chinese or American white cabbage, chopped coarsely
¼ cup water (approx.)
2 cups Chicken Stock (page 68)

1. In blender or food processor, combine 1 tablespoon pork plus scallions and ginger. Grind briefly. Spoon into bowl.
2. Add remaining pork, sugar, sherry, cornstarch, bouillon, pepper, and soy sauce. Mix to blend thoroughly. Separate mixture into 4 equal patties. Then separate each patty into 4 meatballs. Set aside.
3. In wok, heat oil over low heat. Add cabbage and stir-fry 30 seconds, or until cabbage is soft, adding water as necessary to prevent sticking.
4. Spoon half the cabbage into a flameproof 8-inch square casserole. Spoon remaining cabbage into second bowl.
5. To wok, add half the meatballs and over high heat fry briefly in their own juices until lightly browned on all sides. With slotted spoon, re-move meatballs and place on top of the cabbage.
6. Repeat Step 5 with remaining meatballs.
7. Cover meatballs with remaining cabbage.
8. Pour chicken stock over all. Bring mixture to a slow boil over medium heat. Then reduce heat to low. Cover and simmer 45 minutes.
9. Serve in the casserole.

   Note: Lion's Head can be prepared in advance and reheated just before serving.

Per canapé: 111.2 calories; 39.9 mg. sodium; 9.4 gm. carbohydrates; 6.3 gm. fat.

Watercress-Rolled Pork
MAKES 16 CANAPÉS

A tantalizing sample of eastern cooking. Serve with Six-Fruit Sauce (page 242).

1 cup chopped watercress
1 teaspoon sugar
4 tablespoons Soy Sauce Substitute (page 227)
¾ pound ground pork
2 cloves garlic, minced
¹⁄₁₆ teaspoon hot pepper flakes

2 tablespoons dry sherry
2 teaspoons low-sodium beef bouillon
2 scallions, chopped, including greens

1. In bowl, combine first 2 ingredients plus 2 tablespoons soy sauce. Let stand 15 minutes.
2. In wok, combine pork, garlic, and pepper flakes. Stir-fry over medium heat until pork loses its pink color.
3. Stir in remaining ingredients, including watercress mixture. Stir-fry until liquid is absorbed. Spoon mixture into blender or food processor. Grind briefly. Remove to bowl.
4. Shape mixture into 16 balls. Steam over medium heat 15 minutes according to steaming directions (page 22).

Per canapé: 95 calories; 20.5 mg. sodium; 3.9 gm. carbohydrates; 3.4 gm. fat.

Ground Lamb with Walnuts
MAKES 1¼ CUPS

Because of its strong flavor, lamb is not a favorite with the majority of Chinese. However, it is a staple among Muslim sect in the North. The following dish—almost a pâté—enhances this meat's distinctive taste with some Szechwan spices. Serve with low-sodium crackers.

1 onion, minced
½ pound ground lamb
¼ cup unsalted walnuts, blanched and minced
¼ teaspoon Szechwan Pepper Spice (page 229)
¹⁄₁₆ teaspoon Five-Spice Powder (page 228), or coriander

2 tablespoons Soy Sauce Substitute (page 227)
1 tablespoon dry sherry
1 tablespoon cider vinegar
3 scallions, chopped, including greens

1. In wok, over medium heat, stir-fry onion and lamb in lamb's own juices until lamb loses all pink color. Drain off fat.
2. Stir in remaining ingredients, except scallions, and stir-fry 30 seconds. Spoon lamb mixture into bowl. Cover and chill at least 4 hours.
3. Garnish with scallions.

Per recipe: 763 calories; 199.7 mg. sodium; 35.5 gm. carbohydrates; 60.7 gm. fat.
Per cup: 610 calories; 159.8 mg. sodium; 28.4 gm. carbohydrates; 48.6 gm. fat.
Per tablespoon: 38 calories; 10.0 mg. sodium; 1.8 gm. carbohydrates; 3.0 gm. fat.

Lamb-Filled Jao-Tze   SERVES 12

Popular among the Mongolians and Muslims of the North, this zesty offering makes an exotic hors d'oeuvre. Serve with Dipping Sauce (page 233).

¾ pound ground lamb
1 onion, minced
Dash of ground Szechwan
  peppercorns
1 teaspoon Chili Powder (page 231)
¹⁄₁₆ teaspoon ginger powder
2 teaspoons dry sherry
4 scallions, chopped, including
  greens

1 tablespoon low-sodium beef
  bouillon
1 Jao-Tze Wrappers recipe (page
  64)
8 cups water

1. In wok, over low heat, cook lamb in own fat, stir-frying until lamb loses all pink color.
2. Add onion, Szechwan pepper, chili powder, and ginger powder. Stir-fry 2 minutes, or until onion is wilted.
3. Stir in all remaining ingredients except jao-tze and water. Blend thoroughly. Transfer mixture to bowl.
4. Place 1 teaspoon of filling in center of each jao-tze wrapper.
5. Fold wrapper in half to form a half moon. Pinch edges together to seal.
6. In wok, bring water to a slow boil over medium heat. Carefully drop in jao-tze, a few at a time, and boil 10 minutes, or until they float to top.

Per serving: 228 calories; 36.3 mg. sodium; 31.5 gm. carbohydrates; 4.9 gm. fat.

Breads, Wrappers, and Dumplings

Most Chinese families cannot afford the luxury of an oven. In the absence of this modern appliance, they prepare bread in the age-old tradition by steaming dough over an open pit. The resulting fluffy, white, uncrusted mound has many advantages.

For example, the bread's consistency is softer and spongier than oven-baked bread and is beautifully adaptable to all manner of fillings, including meats, fish, vegetables, and sweets. The flexibility of the steamed bun is such that it can be the hors d'oeuvre that starts your meal or the dessert that ends it. What is more, steamed buns can be frozen and resteamed (when first warmed to room temperature) with no loss in flavor or texture. Sometimes the old ways are the best.

Bread and buns are by no means the extent of the Chinese wheat kitchen. Skins, wrappers, and dumplings are also integral parts of daily Chinese fare, and a tempting selection is included in this chapter.

Egg Dumplings   SERVES 8

Delicious in soups or as a side dish alternative to rice.

1 cup all-purpose flour
8½ cups water, divided
1 egg, lightly beaten

Black pepper to taste
1½ tablespoons low-sodium
chicken bouillon

1. In bowl, combine flour plus ½ cup water, blending thoroughly.
2. In second bowl, beat together egg, pepper, and bouillon.
3. Stir egg mixture into flour mixture, blending to form a batter.
4. In wok, bring remaining water to a slow boil over medium heat.
5. Gradually pour batter into boiling water, using a knife to cut off strips as they fall into water. Boil 3 minutes, or until strips curl. Drain.
6. Cover with cold water until ready to use. Then simmer 3 minutes more in 5 cups of broth or water.

Per serving: 124 calories; 10.3 mg. sodium; 22.5 gm. carbohydrates; 1.4 gm. fat.

Basic Buns

MAKES 16 BUNS

This recipe and the one that follows are basic recipes for Chinese buns. See the Hors d'Oeuvres and Desserts sections for a variety of delicious variations that demonstrate the versatility of this soft bread.

1 package dry yeast
1¼ cups warm water, divided
3 cups all-purpose flour
2 tablespoons sugar

1½ teaspoons low-sodium baking
  powder

1. In bowl, combine yeast and ¼ cup water, stirring until yeast is dissolved.
2. In bowl, combine flour, sugar, and baking powder, blending thoroughly.
3. Make a well in center of flour mixture. Pour yeast mixture into well. Add remaining water and stir until dough is formed. (Dough will be somewhat lumpy.)
4. Turn dough onto lightly floured board and knead until smooth and springy to the touch.
5. Place dough in lightly greased bowl. Cover with damp cloth and let stand in warm place 2 hours, or until doubled in size.
6. Turn dough onto lightly floured board and knead again until smooth and springy.
7. Separate dough into 2 equal pieces. Shape each piece into a log 8 inches long.
8. Cut each log into 8 equal pieces.
9. Place buns on lightly floured baking pan, leaving a 2-inch space between each bun. Cover with cloth and let stand in warm place ½ hour.
10. Place 8 buns on heatproof plate lined with damp cloth.
11. Place plate on rack over boiling water. Cover and steam 15 to 20 minutes. Shut off water. Let buns rest 5 minutes. Set aside.
12. Repeat Step 11 with remaining buns.
13. May be refrigerated up to 4 days. Reheat by steaming 15 to 20 minutes. Serve plain or filled. For example, try Beef and Spinach Buns (page 45), Pork and Scallop Buns (page 46), and Apricot-Orange Buns (page 252).

Per bun: 165.1 calories; 1.3 mg. sodium; 34.0 gm. carbohydrates; 0.5 gm. fat.

Steamed Buns

MAKES 20 BUNS

These differ from Basic Buns (page 62) in only two ways: the extra yeast gives these buns a lighter texture, and the greater elasticity of the dough yields more buns.

2 packages active dry yeast
1½ tablespoons sugar
½ tablespoon onion powder
  (optional)

1¼ cups warm water, divided
3 cups all-purpose flour, sifted

1. In large bowl, combine first 3 ingredients plus ⅓ cup of water. Let stand 10 to 15 minutes, or until mixture is bubbly.
2. Gradually add remaining water to the yeast mixture, stirring to blend.
3. Gradually add flour, ½ cup at a time, stirring to completely absorb the flour.
4. Turn dough onto lightly floured board. Knead until dough is smooth and elastic.
5. Place dough in a greased bowl, turning to grease all over. Cover dough with a damp cloth, and leave in a warm place until doubled in size— about 45 minutes.
6. Punch dough down. Turn onto lightly floured board. Knead again.
7. Repeat Step 5.
8. Turn dough onto lightly floured board. With hands, separate into 2 equal halves.
9. Shape each half into a long, thin cylinder (approximately 2 feet long and 2½ inches in diameter). Cut into 10 equal pieces; cover with a damp cloth and let rise 15 minutes.
10. In wok, add enough water to come up to 1 inch below a bamboo steamer. (Any steamer unit will do if it has holes in the bottom. Grease the floor of the steamer.)
11. Bring water to a boil. Place buns ½ inch apart in steamer. Cover and steam 15 minutes.
12. Remove buns while water is still boiling to prevent buns from collapsing.
13. Repeat process until all buns are done. Let cool slightly before serving.

Per bun: 131.7 calories; 1.1 mg. sodium; 26.9 gm. carbohydrates; 0.4 gm. fat.

Jao-Tze Wrappers
MAKES 16 WRAPPERS

A more pastrylike wrapper than Egg Roll Skins (below), indigenous to the North.

2 cups flour
2 eggs

1 tablespoon low-sodium chicken
    bouillon
½ cup plus 2 tablespoons water

1. In bowl, combine first 2 ingredients, blending until eggs are completely absorbed.
2. Add bouillon and water, blending and kneading until smooth dough is formed, adding more water if necessary.
3. On floured board, roll out dough until paper-thin. Cut into 3-inch circles. Stack separated by waxed paper and wrapped in aluminum foil. May be refrigerated up to 1 week. Moisten with water and let come to room temperature before use.

Per wrapper: 117.4 calories; 8.4 mg. sodium; 21.7 gm. carbohydrates; 1.1 gm. fat.

Egg Roll Skins
MAKES 16 SKINS

The Cantonese version which uses an egg, resulting in a lighter, moister skin.

2 cups all-purpose flour, sifted
2¼ cups water
1 egg

1 teaspoon plus 8 tablespoons
    vegetable oil, divided

1. In bowl, combine first 3 ingredients, blending thoroughly. Stir in 1 teaspoon oil. Blend well.
2. Preheat 6-inch frying pan over medium heat. Add ½ tablespoon oil and swirl around pan. Reduce heat to low.
3. Into pan, pour just enough batter to cover bottom. Cook until set, or until edges start to turn up slightly. Then turn and fry a few seconds more. Turn skin onto towel or plate. Cover with waxed paper.
4. Repeat Step 3 until oil and batter are gone. Skins may be individually wrapped in waxed paper and frozen indefinitely at this time. When ready to use, let stand at room temperature 1 hour.
5. See Curried Chicken and Shrimp Egg Rolls (page 49) or Pork and Oyster Egg Rolls (page 50) for filling and frying instructions.

Per skin: 175 calories; 4.0 mg. sodium; 21.3 gm. carbohydrates; 8.3 gm. fat.

Won Ton Skins

MAKES 24 SKINS

1 Egg Roll Skins recipe (page 64)

Follow all directions for Egg Roll Skins with one difference: fry in 4-inch pan.

Per skin: 116.5 calories; 2.7 mg. sodium; 14.2 gm. carbohydrates; 5.5 gm. fat.

Multi-Purpose Batter

MAKES 1¾ CUPS

Common to all regions, this makes enough batter for one pound of meat, fish, poultry, or vegetables.

½ cup flour
¼ cup cornstarch
½ teaspoon garlic powder
¾ teaspoon onion powder
2 tablespoons low-sodium chicken
  bouillon

⅛ teaspoon black pepper
¼ cup low-fat milk
½ cup water
1 egg, lightly beaten

1. In bowl, combine first 6 ingredients, stirring to blend thoroughly.
2. Stir in milk, water, and egg to form a smooth batter, adding more water if necessary. (Batter should be smooth but not runny.)
3. Batter may be covered and refrigerated overnight, but should be brought to room temperature before being used. Food dredged in this batter should be deep-fried.

Per recipe: 831 calories; 117.0 mg. sodium; 150.4 gm. carbohydrates; 11.8 gm. fat.
Per cup: 475.2 calories; 67.2 mg. sodium; 86.4 gm. carbohydrates; 6.4 gm. fat.
Per tablespoon: 29.7 calories; 4.2 mg. sodium; 5.4 gm. carbohydrates; 0.4 gm. fat.

Chinese Sweet Bread

SERVES 24

This is the Chinese substitute for white sandwich bread.

1 package dry yeast
½ cup warm water, divided
⅓ cup sugar, divided
½ cup low-fat milk

¼ cup vegetable oil
2 tablespoons lemon juice
3½ cups cake flour

1. In large bowl, combine yeast, ¼ cup water, and 2 tablespoons sugar, stirring until yeast and sugar are dissolved. Let stand 20 minutes.
2. Stir in remaining water, milk, and oil. Blend thoroughly.
3. Stir in lemon juice.
4. Stir in flour, ½ cup at a time, kneading with fingers until dough is formed.
5. Turn dough into lightly greased bowl, turning dough until greased all over. Cover with damp cloth and let stand in warm place 1½ hours, or until doubled in size.
6. Punch dough down. Cover with cloth and let stand ½ hour more.
7. Divide dough into 2 equal portions. Shape each into a 12-inch loaf. Place loaves on waxed paper. Cover with dry cloth and let stand 1½ hours more.
8. Place loaves on damp cloth on top of rack. Place rack over boiling water. Cover and steam 15 to 20 minutes.
9. May be prepared up to 4 days in advance. Reheat by steaming 15 to 20 minutes.

Per serving: 157.7 calories; 3.3 mg. sodium; 28.4 gm. carbohydrates; 2.8 gm. fat.

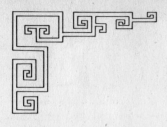
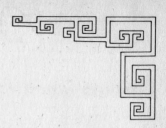

Soups

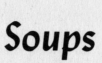

Soup is the most important part of every Chinese meal because, to the Chinese, soup is a beverage that both cleanses and refreshes the palate. Moreover, it is the only beverage served during a meal, replacing the water, soda, or wine that we are accustomed to drinking.

Surrounded by all the other dishes to be savored, soup is the centerpiece at the dining table. Family members help themselves from the huge tureen with an oversize porcelain ladle, spooning the soup into their rice bowls or individual soup bowls, if the latter are provided.

In China, soup is definitely not commonplace fare. Tempting exotica like Sweet and Hot Chicken Mushroom Soup (page 72) or Fish and Seafood Soup (page 78) are the norm. In fact, soups are often the dessert or are the final specialty at a banquet.

But for Western dining, Chinese soups are equally welcome as the introductory promise of the meal to follow.

Fish Stock   SERVES 6 (MAKES 3 CUPS)

Bones, head, and tail of a 1½- to 2-pound whitefish
4 cups Chicken Stock (page 68)
1 onion, minced
2 scallions, chopped, including greens

Black pepper to taste
2 tablespoons cider vinegar
2 tablespoons dried cilantro (or parsley)
2 tablespoons low-sodium chicken bouillon

1. In wok or Dutch oven, combine first 6 ingredients. Over medium heat, bring mixture to a boil.
2. Add cilantro. Reduce heat to low. Cover and simmer ½ hour.
3. Stir in bouillon. Cover and simmer 10 minutes more.
4. Strain soup. Serve as a clear consommé. Use as a base for Fish Sauce (page 238). Use as called for in recipes, or as a substitute for oyster broth or lobster broth.

    Note: When tightly sealed, the stock can be refrigerated for 2 weeks or frozen indefinitely. (If freezing, be sure to leave 1 inch of headspace to allow for swelling.)

Per serving: 112.7 calories; 59.2 mg. sodium; 7.2 gm. carbohydrates; 3.4 gm. fat.
Per cup: 225.4 calories; 118.3 mg. sodium; 14.4 gm. carbohydrates; 6.8 gm. fat.

Chicken Stock
SERVES 14 (MAKES 10 CUPS)

Although Fukien is famous for its rich and flavorful stocks, their preparation is refined throughout China. This chicken stock is one example. For the deluxe version, try adding ¼ pound cooked and cubed pork to the pot after adding the onions in Step 3.

12 cups water
1 3-pound chicken, quartered
3 scallions, cut diagonally in 1-inch pieces
4 slices ginger root, or ⅛ teaspoon ginger powder

Black pepper to taste
2 large onions, minced
1 tablespoon dry sherry
1½ tablespoons low-sodium chicken bouillon

1. In wok or Dutch oven, over medium heat, bring water to a slow boil.
2. Add chicken, scallions, ginger, and black pepper. Bring to a second boil. Skim off foam that rises to the top.
3. Stir in onions. Reduce heat to low. Cover and simmer 2 hours.
4. Stir in sherry. Cover and simmer 1 hour more. Strain stock. Discard chicken. Then stir in bouillon.
5. Serve as clear consommé, or bottle, leaving 1 inch of headspace. May be refrigerated up to 2 weeks or frozen indefinitely. If freezing, it is best to store some of the stock in freezer trays. Each freezer unit holds about 4 tablespoons—perfect when small quantities of stock are called for. Skim fat off top before use.

Per serving: 64.1 calories; 26.6 mg. sodium; 4.6 gm. carbohydrates; 2.4 gm. fat.
Per serving with pork: 85.8 calories; 32.3 mg. sodium; 4.6 gm. carbohydrates; 3.6 gm. fat.
Per cup: 91.4 calories; 37.3 mg. sodium; 6.5 gm. carbohydrates; 3.4 gm. fat.
Per cup with pork: 120.4 calories; 45.3 mg. sodium; 6.5 gm. carbohydrates; 5.0 gm. fat.

Meat Stock

SERVES 12 (MAKES 6 CUPS)

2 pounds pork bones, or any
  2-pound combination of pork,
  beef, and/or chicken bones
1 onion, chopped
4 slices ginger root, or ⅛ teaspoon
  ginger powder
8 scallions, chopped, including
  greens

Black pepper to taste
2 tablespoons dry sherry
12 cups water
4 tablespoons low-sodium beef
  bouillon

1. In wok, combine first 7 ingredients. Turn heat to medium and bring to a slow boil. Continue boiling 5 minutes.
2. Reduce heat to low. Simmer 3 hours, or until stock is reduced by half.
3. Stir in bouillon. Simmer 15 minutes more, stirring often.
4. Strain stock. Let stand 10 minutes.
5. Serve as clear consommé, or bottle, leaving 1 inch of headspace. May be refrigerated up to 2 weeks or frozen indefinitely. If freezing, it is best to store some of the stock in freezer trays. Each freezer unit holds about 4 tablespoons—perfect when small quantities of stock are called for.

Per serving: 27 calories; 11.6 mg. sodium; 4.6 gm. carbohydrates; 1.0 gm. fat.
Per cup: 54 calories; 23.1 mg. sodium; 9.1 gm. carbohydrates; 2.1 gm. fat.

Hot and Sour Soup I   SERVES 8

This dish, which originates in the North, is such a familiar favorite of the Chinese that every family has its own version. The original calls for pork, but fish is equally delicious and we give options for each. By the way, the white or black pepper represents the "hot." Use less or more than called for to satisfy your own taste.

2 large dried black mushrooms*
¼ cup tiger lily buds*
¾ cup boiling water
5 cups Chicken Stock (page 68)
½ can (4 ounces) water chestnuts, sliced
½ can (4 ounces) bamboo shoots, sliced
¼ pound pork, shredded
1 teaspoon low-sodium beef bouillon
½ tablespoon cornstarch
1 cake bean curd, cut in strips

¼ teaspoon white or black pepper
1 tablespoon Soy Sauce Substitute (page 227)
3 tablespoons red wine vinegar
2 egg whites, lightly beaten
3 scallions, cut diagonally in 1-inch pieces
1 tablespoon dried cilantro (or parsley)

1. In bowl, combine first 3 ingredients. Let stand ½ hour.
2. In wok or Dutch oven, bring chicken stock, chestnuts, and bamboo shoots to a slow boil over medium heat.
3. While stock is heating, in second bowl, combine pork, bouillon, and cornstarch, mixing to combine thoroughly.
4. Drain mushrooms and add to stock along with bean curd, pepper, soy sauce, and vinegar. Cook for 2 minutes more.
5. Add egg whites and scallions. Stir quickly to blend.
6. Simmer 2 minutes more.
7. Add pork mixture, stirring to separate pork shreds. Simmer 15 minutes.
8. Pour soup into a large tureen. Garnish with cilantro.

Per serving: 130 calories; 40.7 mg. sodium; 7.1 gm. carbohydrates; 4.5 gm. fat.

* If not available, substitute 4 fresh mushrooms, sliced, and omit boiling water.

Hot and Sour Soup II

SERVES 8

This version is distinctly Szechwan in character. Serve with Chinese Pepper Steak (page 179) for a refreshing taste alternative.

1 pound red snapper, flounder, or cod fillets, cut in 1-inch chunks
2 tablespoons Soy Sauce Substitute (page 227)
1 teaspoon low-sodium chicken bouillon
2 tablespoons dry sherry
2 slices ginger root, or ⅟₁₆ teaspoon ginger powder
1 tablespoon minced orange peel, or ⅛ teaspoon orange peel powder
5 cups Chicken Stock (page 68)
⅛ teaspoon ground Szechwan peppercorns

3 tablespoons red wine vinegar
4 fresh mushrooms, sliced
16 snow pea pods, cut diagonally in half
1 cup water
1 tablespoon cornstarch
4 scallions, cut diagonally in 1-inch pieces
2 egg whites, lightly beaten
1 teaspoon sesame seed oil
1 tablespoon dried cilantro (or parsley)

1. In large bowl, combine first 6 ingredients. Let stand 15 minutes.
2. In wok or Dutch oven, bring chicken stock to a slow boil over medium heat.
3. Stir in pepper, vinegar, mushrooms, and snow pea pods. Cook 2 minutes.
4. While stock is cooking, in small bowl, combine water and cornstarch, stirring until cornstarch is dissolved.
5. Stir cornstarch and scallions into stock. Then add fish mixture.
6. Add egg whites and sesame seed oil. Stir quickly to blend. Simmer 8 minutes more. Discard ginger slices.
7. Pour soup into a large tureen. Garnish with cilantro.

Per serving with snapper: 135 calories; 53.4 mg. sodium; 5.7 gm. carbohydrates; 3.5 gm. fat.
Per serving with flounder: 127 calories; 70.6 mg. sodium; 5.7 gm. carbohydrates; 3.5 gm. fat.
Per serving with cod: 126 calories; 66 mg. sodium; 5.7 gm. carbohydrates; 3.2 gm. fat.

Sweet and Hot
Chicken Mushroom Soup   SERVES 4

Typically Szechwan and unbelievably tasty.

1 half chicken breast, skinned,
  boned, and cubed
1/16 teaspoon ground Szechwan
  peppercorns
1 tablespoon dry sherry
1 teaspoon vegetable oil

8 fresh mushrooms, sliced
Dash of Five-Spice Powder (page
  228)
3 cups Chicken Stock (page 68)
Dash of Curry Powder (page 232)
1 cup watercress, chopped

1. In bowl, combine first 3 ingredients. Stir to blend. Cover and refrigerate
   ½ hour.
2. In wok, heat oil over low heat. Add mushrooms and stir-fry 1 minute.
3. Add chicken and stir-fry until chicken is white all over. Stir in five-spice
   powder.
4. Add chicken stock. Turn heat to high and bring to a rapid boil.
5. Stir in curry powder and watercress. Cook 1 minute more, stirring
   occasionally.

Per serving: 114 calories; 55.7 mg. sodium; 2.5 gm. carbohydrates; 4.5 gm. fat.

Puffed Chicken and Tomato Soup   SERVES 4

This northern dish can be varied by substituting 3½ ounces of pork for
the chicken. For a totally satisfying meal, follow with Mixed Seafood in
Hoisin Sauce (page 126) and boiled white rice.

1 half chicken breast, skinned,
  boned, and chopped
1 clove garlic
2 scallions, chopped, including
  greens
1 egg white
1½ tablespoons cornstarch, divided
2 tomatoes, cubed
¼ teaspoon Szechwan Pepper Spice
  (page 229)

3 cups Chicken Stock (page 68)
  divided
1 teaspoon low-sodium beef
  bouillon
1 teaspoon dry red wine
1 teaspoon sesame seed oil
1 tablespoon unsalted slivered
  almonds

1. In food processor or blender, combine first 3 ingredients. Mince.

2. In bowl, combine minced chicken mixture, egg white, and ½ tablespoon cornstarch. Blend thoroughly. Set aside.
3. In wok, combine tomatoes, Szechwan pepper spice, and 2¾ cups chicken stock. Turn heat to medium and bring to a slow boil. Remove soup from heat.
4. Drop chicken mixture into soup, ¹⁄₁₆ teaspoon at a time.
5. Return wok to medium heat and bring to a second boil. Reduce heat to low and simmer 10 minutes.
6. While soup is cooking, in bowl, combine remaining cornstarch and remaining chicken stock. Stir into soup.
7. Stir in bouillon, wine, sesame seed oil, and almonds. Simmer 5 minutes more.

Per serving with chicken: 175 calories; 47.7 mg. sodium; 12.9 gm. carbohydrates; 6.9 gm. fat.
Per serving with pork: 211 calories; 52.7 mg. sodium; 12.9 gm. carbohydrates; 9.9 gm. fat.

Duck and Cabbage Soup   SERVES 8

In this adaptation of a traditional Peking dish, we have added the tingle of vinegar and the moist texture of noodles to complement the cabbage.

Carcass from 3- to 4-pound duck
10 cups water
1 teaspoon cider vinegar
Black or ground Szechwan peppercorns to taste
1 slice ginger root, or pinch of ginger powder
3 tablespoons low-sodium chicken bouillon

2 ounces cellophane noodles, or vermicelli, boiled al dente*
4 cups Chinese or American white cabbage, chopped
¼ teaspoon ground coriander

1. In wok, combine first 5 ingredients. Turn heat to medium and bring to a slow boil. Skim off foam. Reduce heat to low. Cover and simmer 1½ hours.
2. Stir in bouillon. Cover and simmer 1 hour more.
3. Stir in noodles and cabbage. Simmer, uncovered, 20 minutes more.
4. Stir in coriander. Discard ginger.

Per serving: 69 calories; 31.2 mg. sodium; 10.6 gm. carbohydrates; 8.3 gm. fat.

* Do not add salt to boiling water.

Beef, Oyster, and Cucumber Soup   SERVES 8

When served with Chicken and Snow Pea Pod Salad (page 93), this generic soup becomes a wonderful main course.

½ pound sirloin steak, shredded
1 tablespoon red wine vinegar
1 teaspoon cornstarch
Dash of Szechwan Pepper Spice
  (page 229)
1 teaspoon vegetable oil
8 cups Chicken Stock (page 68)

2 tablespoons Soy Sauce
  Substitute (page 227)
1 cucumber, scraped, halved,
  seeded, and cut in ½-inch pieces
1 pint shucked oysters, chopped,
  including liquid
Black pepper to taste
1 teaspoon lemon juice

1. In bowl, combine first 5 ingredients. Mix to blend thoroughly. Cover and refrigerate ½ hour.
2. Heat wok over medium heat. Add meat mixture. Stir quickly to separate shreds and stir-fry until meat loses all pink color, adding teaspoons of stock as necessary to keep from sticking. Transfer to warm platter.
3. To wok, add chicken stock. Over medium heat, bring to a slow boil. Continue boiling 5 minutes.
4. Stir in soy sauce and cucumber. Cook 2 minutes more, stirring occasionally.
5. Stir in meat mixture. Cook 2 minutes more, stirring occasionally.
6. Stir in oysters, pepper, and lemon juice. Cook 1 minute more.

Per serving: 240 calories; 94.1 mg. sodium; 5.2 gm. carbohydrates; 12.7 gm. fat.

Chili Beef Soup   SERVES 8

This Szechwan soup will surely warm you on a chilly winter day.

4 cups Meat Stock (page 69)
5 tablespoons lemon juice
2 tablespoons Oyster Sauce (page
  234)
1 teaspoon Chili Powder (page 231)
½ pound flank steak, sliced in
  matchstick strips

1 tablespoon dried cilantro (or
  parsley)
Black pepper to taste
1 cup cauliflowerettes
Dash of Five-Spice Powder (page
  228—optional)
2 scallions, chopped, including
  greens

1. In wok, combine first 2 ingredients. Turn heat to medium and bring to a slow boil.

2. Reduce heat to low. Stir in oyster sauce, chili powder, and meat. Cover and simmer ½ hour.
3. Stir in all remaining ingredients except scallions. Raise heat to medium and bring to a boil. Continue boiling 3 minutes.
4. Add scallions and boil 2 minutes more.

Per serving: 92 calories; 34.6 mg. sodium; 6.5 gm. carbohydrates; 3.2 gm. fat.

Cauliflower with Pork Soup   SERVES 4

Adapting from a Cantonese favorite, we have substituted the rich-tasting meat stock for the pork broth generally used. This soup will whet your appetite for any dish that follows.

2 tablespoons cold water	1 leek, chopped, including greens
1 tablespoon cornstarch	Black pepper to taste
1½ cups boiling water, divided	¼ pound pork, shredded
¼ cup tiger lily buds*	1 tablespoon low-sodium beef
1½ cup cauliflowerettes, divided	bouillon
3 cups Meat Stock (page 69)	1 tablespoon dry sherry
6 fresh mushrooms, sliced	

1. In bowl, combine first 2 ingredients, stirring to dissolve cornstarch. Set aside.
2. In second bowl, combine ½ cup boiling water and tiger lily buds. Let stand ½ hour. Drain. Set aside.
3. In saucepan, combine remaining cup boiling water and ½ cup cauliflowerettes. Boil 5 minutes. Then, in blender or food processor, puree cauliflowerettes. Set aside.
4. In wok, combine meat stock, mushrooms, leek, pepper, tiger lily buds, and pureed cauliflower. Turn heat to low and simmer 20 minutes, stirring occasionally.
5. Add remaining cauliflower, pork, bouillon, and sherry. Simmer 20 minutes more.
6. Stir in cornstarch mixture and simmer 2 minutes more, or until mixture thickens, stirring occasionally.

Per serving: 183 calories; 57.7 mg. sodium; 17.7 gm. carbohydrates; 6.4 gm. fat.

* If not available, substitute 4 fresh mushrooms, sliced, and omit ½ cup boiling water.

Hot and Vinegar Pork Soup SERVES 4

Another heart-warmer from Szechwan.

1 teaspoon sesame seed oil
¼ pound ground pork
4 scallions, chopped, including
  greens
1 slice ginger root, minced, or ¹⁄₁₆
  teaspoon ginger powder
2¾ cups Chicken Stock (page 68)
¹⁄₁₆ teaspoon white or black pepper

2 tablespoons cider vinegar
1 leek, cut in ½-inch rounds,
  including greens
¾ cup boiling water
2 teaspoons low-sodium chicken
  bouillon

1. In wok, heat oil over low heat. Add pork, scallions, and ginger. Stir-fry
   constantly until pork loses all pink color.
2. Add chicken stock, pepper, and vinegar. Turn heat to medium and
   bring to a slow boil.
3. Add leek and water. Reduce heat to low and simmer 5 minutes, stirring
   occasionally.
4. Stir in bouillon and cook 2 minutes more.

Per serving: 172 calories; 49.0 mg. sodium; 7.5 gm. carbohydrates; 8.2 gm. fat.

Shrimp and Pork Go Ba SERVES 8

Go Ba technically means "pot sticking" and refers to the rice patties often
used in soups. Such soups have numerous variations and are popular
throughout China.

¼ pound small shrimp, shelled,
  deveined, and halved lengthwise
2 tablespoons lemon juice
2 teaspoons cornstarch, divided
¼ pound pork, sliced in matchstick
  strips
2 tablespoons Soy Sauce Substitute
  (page 227)
2 teaspoons dry sherry, divided
4 cups Chicken Stock (page 68)

1 teaspoon peanut oil
4 fresh mushrooms, sliced
½ can (4 ounces) water chestnuts,
  sliced
1 zucchini, chopped
8 Rice Patties (page 209)
Black pepper to taste
4 scallions, chopped, including
  greens

1. In bowl, combine first 2 ingredients plus 1 teaspoon cornstarch. Blend
   well. Set aside.

2. In second bowl, combine pork, soy sauce, 1 teaspoon sherry, and remaining cornstarch. Blend well. Set aside.
3. In wok, over medium heat, bring chicken stock to a slow boil. Add pork mixture. Reduce heat to low and simmer 10 minutes.
4. While soup is simmering, in small pan, heat oil over low heat. Add mushrooms, water chestnuts, and zucchini and stir-fry 2 minutes. Set aside.
5. Place rice patties on lightly oiled baking sheet. Heat in 375° oven 5 minutes. Set aside.
6. Add vegetables to soup, along with shrimp mixture. Simmer 5 minutes. Stir in pepper.
7. Place 1 rice patty in each of 8 soup bowls. Pour soup over patties.
8. Garnish with scallions.

Per serving: 279 calories; 55.0 mg. sodium; 41.5 gm. carbohydrates; 4.7 gm. fat.

Curried Fish Soup
SERVES 8

The Yunnan influence is at work here. Serve as a light lunch, accompanied by Sugar Beef Salad (page 95), or as a first course to a meal featuring Roast Duck with Eggplant (page 158).

½ pound flounder fillet, cut in 1-inch chunks
1 teaspoon lemon juice
1 tablespoon Soy Sauce Substitute (page 227)
4 cups Chicken Stock (page 68)
1 leek, chopped, including greens
2 carrots, scraped and cubed (optional)
1 slice ginger root, or pinch of ginger powder

1 small cucumber, scraped, seeded, and cubed
1½ teaspoons Curry Powder (page 232)
1 square bean curd, sliced
4 tablespoons Oyster Sauce (page 234)
1 teaspoon dry sherry
¼ pound cleaned squid, chopped

1. In bowl, combine first 3 ingredients. Stir to blend. Let stand 15 minutes.
2. In wok, combine chicken stock, leek, carrots, if desired, and ginger. Turn heat to medium. Bring to a slow boil.
3. Add cucumber, curry powder, and bean curd. Stir to blend. Reduce heat and simmer, uncovered, 10 minutes.
4. Stir in oyster sauce and sherry. Add fish mixture and simmer 10 minutes more.
5. Add squid and simmer 5 minutes more. Discard ginger.

Per serving with carrots: 98 calories; 60.1 mg. sodium; 6.5 gm. carbohydrates; 2.4 gm. fat.
Per serving without carrots: 83 calories; 44.7 mg. sodium; 5.7 gm. carbohydrates; 1.96 gm. fat.

Fish and Seafood Soup
SERVES 8

In this dish of Fukien origin, the more varied the fish and shellfish, the more interesting and savory the end result. This one is worth the time required, and is a meal unto itself. Serve with Szechwan Fried Rice (page 208).

1 pint shucked oysters, liquid reserved
½ pound flounder fillets, cut into 1-inch chunks
½ pound red snapper fillets, cut into 1-inch chunks
2 egg whites
Black pepper to taste
3½ tablespoons dry sherry, divided
2 tablespoons Soy Sauce Substitute (page 227)
3½ tablespoons cornstarch, divided
4 cups water
2 teaspoons vegetable oil
1 clove garlic, minced

2 leeks, chopped, including greens
Dash of ginger powder
4 fresh mushrooms, sliced
1 pound green beans, sliced diagonally in 1-inch pieces
1 teaspoon sugar
6 cups Chicken Stock (page 68), divided
1 1-pound lobster, steamed and cut into bite-size pieces
2 teaspoons low-sodium beef bouillon
½ tablespoon dry vermouth
2 teaspoons sesame seed oil

1. In large bowl, combine first 5 ingredients. Add 2 tablespoons sherry, soy sauce, and 2 tablespoons cornstarch. Mix to blend thoroughly. Cover and refrigerate at least 2 hours.
2. In wok, bring 4 cups of water to a boil. Reduce heat to simmer. Add fish and oyster mixture, stirring gently to separate pieces.
3. Turn heat to medium and bring to a second boil. Continue boiling 30 seconds.
4. With slotted spoon, remove fish and oysters to warm platter. Drain wok.
5. In small bowl, combine oyster liquid plus remaining sherry and cornstarch. Set aside.
6. In wok, heat vegetable oil over low heat. Add garlic and stir-fry 1 minute. Then add leeks, ginger, and mushrooms and stir-fry 1 minute more.
7. Push vegetables to sides of wok. Add green beans and sugar. Stir to blend. Add 4 tablespoons chicken stock and stir-fry 1 minute, or until liquid is absorbed.
8. Add lobster pieces, remaining chicken stock, bouillon, and vermouth. Cover. Turn heat to medium and cook 5 minutes.
9. Add fish and oysters. Stir in sherry mixture and sesame seed oil. Cook 3 minutes more.

Per serving: 253 calories; 139.3 mg. sodium; 54.9 gm. carbohydrates; 7.1 gm. fat.

Scallop and Corn Soup

SERVES 8

Plan the rest of your meal carefully, or this Cantonese course will be the runaway star of the show. May we suggest Crispy Spiced Duck (page 157) or Red Pork Roast (page 166).

1 teaspoon sesame seed oil
2 slices ginger root, minced, or
 ⅟₁₆ teaspoon ginger powder
1 leek, minced, including greens
½ pound large scallops, sliced
8 snow pea pods, cut diagonally
 in half
1 teaspoon sugar
1 tablespoon dry sherry
6 cups Chicken Stock (page 68)
2 cans (8 ounces each) low-sodium
 creamed corn

1½ tablespoons cider vinegar
2 egg whites, lightly beaten
2 scallions, chopped, including
 greens
1 tablespoon low-sodium beef
 bouillon
Black pepper to taste
1 tablespoon dried cilantro (or
 parsley)

1. In wok, heat oil over low heat. Add ginger and stir-fry 30 seconds.
2. Add leek and scallops and stir-fry 30 seconds more.
3. Push scallop mixture to sides of wok. Add snow pea pods and sugar. Stir-fry 30 seconds. Remove mixture to bowl. Add sherry. Set aside.
4. To wok, add chicken stock. Over medium heat, bring stock to a slow boil.
5. Stir in corn and vinegar. Reduce heat to low and simmer 10 minutes.
6. Stir in scallop mixture. Gradually stir in egg whites and all remaining ingredients except cilantro. Simmer 5 minutes more.
7. Garnish with cilantro and serve.

Per serving: 163.5 calories; 107.9 mg. sodium; 17.0 gm. carbohydrates; 4.4 gm. fat.

Seafood and Noodle Soup   SERVES 4

A lovely light Cantonese lunch accompanied by Piquant Tomatoes and
Cucumber (page 201) or Zucchini and Walnuts (page 204).

½ pound shrimp, shelled, deveined,
   and halved lengthwise
½ pound large scallops, sliced
1 teaspoon sesame seed oil
1 tablespoon Soy Sauce Substitute
   (page 227)
4 large dried black mushrooms*
½ cup boiling water

2 teaspoons low-sodium beef
   bouillon
3 cups Chicken Stock (page 68)
4 asparagus spears, cut diagonally
   in 1½-inch pieces
4 ounces cellophane noodles or
   vermicelli, boiled al dente†

1. In bowl, combine first 4 ingredients. Stir to blend. Set aside.
2. In second bowl, combine mushrooms, boiling water, and bouillon. Let
   stand 15 minutes.
3. In wok, turn heat to low. Add seafood mixture and stir-fry until shrimp
   turn pink—about 30 seconds. With slotted spoon, remove seafood to
   warm platter.
4. To wok, add mushrooms plus liquid and chicken stock. Raise heat to
   medium and bring to a boil. Continue boiling 2 minutes.
5. Add asparagus and boil 5 minutes more.
6. Add noodles and seafood. Stir to blend and cook 1 minute more.

Per serving: 316 calories; 208.1 mg. sodium; 28.7 gm. carbohydrates; 7.0 gm. fat.

* If not available, substitute 4 large fresh mushrooms, sliced ½ inch thick, and replace boiling water with cold water.
† Do not add salt to boiling water.

Chinese Cabbage Soup   SERVES 4

Every Chinese region has its own version of cabbage soup. The recipe
below is our own.

1 teaspoon vegetable oil
1 onion, minced
3½ cups Chicken Stock (page 68)
2 ounces vermicelli

½ head Chinese or American
   white cabbage, shredded
1 teaspoon dry sherry

1. In wok, heat oil over low heat. Add onion and cook 1 minute, or until
   onion is wilted, stirring occasionally.

2. Add chicken stock and vermicelli. Raise heat to medium and bring mixture to a slow boil. Continue boiling 5 minutes.
3. Reduce heat to low. Add cabbage and simmer 5 minutes more.
4. Stir in sherry.

Per serving: 165 calories; 47.8 mg. sodium; 21.6 gm. carbohydrates; 4.5 gm. fat.

Ginger Carrot and Peanut Soup   SERVES 8

Straight from the spicy heart of the western region.

2 large carrots, scraped, cut in
  ½-inch rounds and steamed,
  divided
1 fresh chili pepper, seeded and
  chopped
2 slices ginger root, chopped, or
  ¹⁄₁₆ teaspoon ginger powder

¼ cup unsalted peanuts
3 cups Chicken Stock (page 68)
¹⁄₁₆ teaspoon ground coriander
2 scallions, chopped, including
  greens
1 tablespoon dried cilantro (or
  parsley)

1. In blender, combine half the carrots plus the chili pepper, ginger, and peanuts. Puree until smooth. Set aside.
2. In wok, combine chicken stock and coriander. Turn heat to medium and bring to a slow boil.
3. Stir in puree mixture. Reduce heat to low and simmer 5 minutes, stirring occasionally.
4. Add remaining carrots and cook 10 minutes more.
5. In tureen, place scallions. Pour soup on top. Garnish with cilantro.

Per serving: 95 calories; 36.2 mg. sodium; 2.9 gm. carbohydrates; 4.9 gm. fat.

Mushroom and Corn Soup   SERVES 4

A soul-satisfying soup from Canton.

4 dried black mushrooms*
¼ cup tiger lily buds*
¾ cup boiling water
2 tablespoons Soy Sauce Substitute
  (page 227)
3½ cups Meat Stock (page 69)
⅛ teaspoon garlic powder
1 teaspoon sugar

4 large fresh mushrooms, sliced
2 teaspoons low-sodium chicken
  bouillon
1 can (8 ounces) low-sodium corn
  niblets
1 cup bean sprouts
⅛ teaspoon mustard powder

1. In bowl, combine first 4 ingredients. Let stand ½ hour.
2. In wok, over medium heat, bring meat stock to a slow boil.
3. Reduce heat to low. Stir in garlic powder, sugar, and fresh mushrooms. Turn heat to medium and bring to a second boil.
4. Reduce heat to low. Stir in dried mushrooms (including liquid) plus bouillon and corn. Stir to blend. Cover and simmer 5 minutes.
5. Add bean sprouts and mustard powder. Simmer, uncovered, 5 minutes more, stirring often.

Per serving: 159 calories; 36.0 mg. sodium; 24.1 gm. carbohydrates; 46.0 gm. fat.

* If not available, substitute 4 fresh mushrooms, sliced, and omit boiling water.

Three-Color Soup   SERVES 8

In this adaptation of a Peking dish, we have eliminated the original ingredients (chicken, peas, and tomatoes) to substitute our own three-color choices (bamboo shoots, broccoli, snow pea pods, and bean curd).

1 teaspoon vegetable oil
1 slice ginger root, or pinch of
  ginger powder
1 clove garlic, minced
1 onion, minced
4 cups Chicken Stock (page 68)
2 teaspoons dry sherry

¼ teaspoon mustard powder
Black pepper to taste
½ can (4 ounces) bamboo shoots,
  sliced
1 cup broccoli flowerettes
½ square bean curd, cubed
16 snow pea pods, halved diagonally

1. In wok, heat oil over low heat. Add ginger, garlic, and onion. Stir-fry until onion is golden.
2. Add chicken stock and simmer 5 minutes.

3. While soup is simmering, in bowl, combine sherry and mustard, stirring until mustard is dissolved. Stir into soup. Add pepper.
4. Raise heat to medium and bring to a slow boil. Add bamboo shoots, broccoli, and bean curd, and bring to a second boil.
5. Add snow pea pods and cook 1 minute more.

Per serving: 91 calories; 21.5 mg. sodium; 5.3 gm. carbohydrates; 2.4 gm. fat.

Sugar and Spice Tomato Soup   SERVES 4

A wonderful new tomato soup for your repertoire, originating in northern China.

5 cups Chicken Stock (page 68)
2 large tomatoes, chopped
2 slices ginger root, or ¹⁄₁₆ teaspoon ginger powder
¹⁄₁₆ teaspoon ground coriander
1 teaspoon sugar
1 star anise

Black pepper to taste
2 scallions, chopped, including greens
2 tablespoons dried cilantro (or parsley)

1. In wok, combine all but last 2 ingredients. Turn heat to low and simmer ½ hour, stirring occasionally.
2. Add scallions and simmer 10 minutes more. Discard ginger root and star anise.
3. Garnish with cilantro.

Per serving: 129 calories; 49.5 mg. sodium; 8.0 gm. carbohydrates; 4.6 gm. fat.

Vegetable Hot Soup
SERVES 8

Kweichou brings us one version of the renowned Chinese hot pot. Serve with Chinese Chicken and Rice (page 215) to complete your dining pleasure.

1 cup boiling water
8 dried black mushrooms*
6 cups Chicken Stock (page 68)
1 large onion, sliced thin
1 tablespoon dry sherry
2 tablespoons red wine vinegar
1 teaspoon Curry Powder (page 232)
¼ cup cold water
1 teaspoon mustard powder
2 slices ginger root, or ¹⁄₁₆ teaspoon ginger powder

⅓ pound bean sprouts
2 cups broccoli flowerettes
1 cup Chinese or American white cabbage, shredded
1 square bean curd, sliced
2 tablespoons Soy Sauce Substitute (page 227)
1 tablespoon low-sodium chicken bouillon
1 tablespoon sesame seed oil

1. In bowl, combine first 2 ingredients. Let stand ½ hour. Drain, reserving liquid. Slice mushrooms. Set aside.
2. In wok, combine chicken stock, onion, sherry, vinegar, and curry powder. Turn heat to medium and bring to a slow boil. Reduce heat to low and simmer 15 minutes.
3. While soup is cooking, in second bowl, combine cold water and mustard powder, stirring until mustard is dissolved. Stir into soup.
4. Add mushrooms and reserved mushroom liquid plus ginger root. Raise heat to medium and bring to a second boil. Continue boiling 5 minutes.
5. Reduce heat to low. Add bean sprouts, broccoli, cabbage, and bean curd. Simmer 5 minutes.
6. Stir in soy sauce, bouillon, and oil. Simmer 5 minutes more. Discard ginger root.

Per serving: 153 calories; 45.9 mg. sodium; 13.6 gm. carbohydrates; 6.0 gm. fat.

* If not available, substitute 8 large fresh mushrooms and omit boiling water.

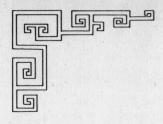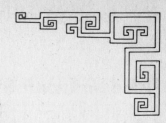

Salads

Salads as we know them—colorful combinations of crispy, crunchy, raw vegetables—do not exist in China. The reason is twofold.

First, the Chinese method of fertilization leaves a poisonous residue on produce that can only be neutralized by high heat. Therefore, unless a vegetable has a thick, protective skin, it is always cooked before being eaten. Second, vegetables are rarely offered as a separate course. The Chinese meal, which includes individual vegetable dishes, is served all at once rather than in stages as is the custom here.

Nevertheless, Chinese vegetables—in solo or combination—make delectable salads. Because they are generally stir-fried, they retain their tender, crisp texture and full flavor, whether served piping hot or chilled, plain or with a light dressing of your choice.

But Americans love salads, and there is nothing to prevent us from taking those delectable Chinese vegetables and turning them into one of our favorite courses, which is exactly what we have done. In fact, vegetables prepared the Chinese way make exotically lovely salads that are both crispy and crunchy. So here in America, Chinese salads—or, at least, salads with a Chinese flair—do exist after all.

What is more, you can turn these already special salads into extraordinary specialties just by doing some combining such as adding chopped lettuce and sliced tomato to Green Bean and Fruit Salad (page 105), for example. Top off this mixture with tidbits of meat, fish, or poultry, and you will have created an original, unusual, and easy main dish.

Try the offerings developed for this chapter. Then create others of your own. You will see how salads with an Oriental touch can spruce up your entire meal.

Fish Salad with Bean Curd   SERVES 4

Hoisin Rice in Four (page 211) is a wonderful accompaniment for this Cantonese-type dish.

½ pound flounder fillet or squid cut in 1-inch chunks
1 egg white
1 tablespoon lemon juice
1 tablespoon peanut oil
2 slices ginger root, minced, or ⅟₁₆ teaspoon ginger powder
1 large square bean curd, sliced
4 cups Chinese or American white cabbage, shredded
Dash of Five-Spice Powder (page 228)

Black pepper to taste
½ teaspoon sugar
¼ cup unsalted peanuts, crushed
⅓ cup Fish Stock (page 67)
1 teaspoon low-sodium chicken bouillon
2 scallions, chopped, including greens

1. In bowl, combine first 3 ingredients; cover and refrigerate 15 minutes.
2. In wok, heat oil over low heat. Add ginger and bean curd. Stir-fry 30 seconds.
3. Add cabbage. Stir-fry 2 minutes.
4. Stir in five-spice powder, pepper, and sugar, blending thoroughly. Push mixture to sides of wok.
5. Add peanuts and fish mixture. Stir-fry 2 minutes more.
6. Add fish stock and bouillon. Raise heat to high and bring mixture to a boil.
7. Reduce heat to medium. Add scallions and cook until liquid is absorbed.
8. Serve hot or cold over noodles or rice.

Per serving with flounder: 289.5 calories; 81.6 mg. sodium; 12.2 gm. carbohydrates; 12.2 gm. fat.
Per serving with squid: 242.4 calories; 37.0 mg. sodium; 13.0 gm. carbohydrates; 12.3 gm. fat.

Assorted Seafood Salad

SERVES 8

Reminiscent of the eastern school, this dish is a lovely main course, accompanied by Many-Flavored Fried Rice (page 213).

½ pound sole fillets, cut into
  1-inch chunks
½ pound haddock fillets, cut into
  1-inch chunks
½ pound red snapper fillets or
  swordfish steak, cut into 1-inch
  chunks
4 tablespoons cider vinegar, divided

⅓ cup lemon juice, divided
1 tablespoon honey
½ cup boiling water
4 teaspoons sesame seed paste
4 radishes, sliced thin
½ pound bean sprouts
1 head iceberg lettuce, chopped

1. In bowl, combine first 3 ingredients plus 2 tablespoons vinegar and 4 tablespoons lemon juice. Cover and refrigerate at least 2 hours, stirring occasionally.
2. While fish is marinating, in second bowl, combine remaining vinegar and lemon juice plus honey, stirring to blend thoroughly. Set aside.
3. In third bowl, combine water and sesame seed paste, stirring to blend thoroughly. Stir into vinegar-lemon mixture. Set aside.
4. In fourth bowl, combine radishes, bean sprouts, and lettuce, tossing to blend. Set aside.
5. In wok, poach fish in marinade 3 minutes. Add to lettuce mixture.
6. Pour sesame paste mixture over fish mixture. Toss to blend.

Per serving with snapper: 147.5 calories 72.1 mg. sodium; 9.8 gm. carbohydrates; 3.5 gm. fat.
Per serving with swordfish: 154.6 calories; 53.0 mg. sodium; 9.8 gm. carbohydrates; 4.4 gm. fat.

Lobster Salad Cantonese   SERVES 4

2 radishes, sliced thin
1 cucumber, halved, seeded, and
  cut in strips
½ can (4 ounces) water chestnuts,
  chopped
1 cup broccoli flowerettes,
  blanched
½ head iceberg lettuce, shredded
¼ cup lemon juice

1 tablespoon cider vinegar
1 tablespoon dry sherry
2 tablespoons peanut oil
¼ cup unsalted almonds, crushed
1 tablespoon dried cilantro (or
  parsley)
½ teaspoon paprika
Black pepper to taste
8 ounces lobster meat, chopped

1. In bowl, combine first 5 ingredients. Toss to blend. Set aside.
2. In second bowl, combine all remaining ingredients except lobster meat.
3. Pour dressing over vegetables. Add lobster. Toss to blend.

Per serving: 295 calories; 159.4 mg. sodium; 17.8 gm. carbohydrates; 16.7 gm. fat.

Spiced Scallops
and Cashews in Tomatoes   SERVES 4

This Cantonese dish is just as delicious with shrimp. Serve with Sweet and
Pungent Chicken (page 138) and boiled white rice for one terrific meal.

4 tomatoes, cored, pulp removed
  and reserved
⅛ teaspoon ginger powder
1/16 teaspoon ground coriander
2 tablespoons dried cilantro (or
  parsley)
1 teaspoon vegetable oil
½ pound bay scallops

Black pepper to taste
2 scallions, minced, including
  greens
2 tablespoons unsalted cashews,
  crushed
¼ cup cold water
1 teaspoon mustard powder

1. Preheat oven to 375°.
2. In 9-inch square casserole, place tomatoes. Sprinkle ginger powder,
   coriander, and cilantro in hollows. Add just enough water to cover
   bottom of casserole. Bake 10 minutes. Remove from oven.
3. In wok, heat oil over low heat. Add scallops, pepper, and scallions.
   Stir-fry 1 minute. Transfer to platter. Stir in cashews.

4. In small bowl, combine water and mustard powder, blending thoroughly. Stir into scallop mixture.
5. Stuff scallop mixture into tomatoes. Either heat 5 minutes more, or cover and chill ½ hour.

VARIATION: *Spiced Shrimp and Cashews in Tomatoes*—Substitute ½ pound shelled deveined shrimp for the scallops and proceed as above.

Per serving with scallops: 133.9 calories; 160.3 mg. sodium; 11.9 gm. carbohydrates; 5.0 gm. fat.
Per serving with shrimp: 139.8 calories; 88.9 mg. sodium; 10.8 gm. carbohydrates; 5.3 gm. fat.

Ginger Squid Salad in Soy Sauce   SERVES 4

This delightful Cantonese salad is an excellent companion to Asparagus in Oyster Sauce (page 189).

1 pound squid, cleaned, halved, and cut in strips
2 slices ginger root, minced, or ⅟₁₆ teaspoon ginger powder
¼ cup lemon juice
1 teaspoon peanut oil
1 red pepper, julienned
1 green pepper, julienned
1 teaspoon dry sherry

½ cup Meat Stock (page 69)
2 ounces vermicelli, boiled al dente*
2 tablespoons Soy Sauce Substitute (page 227)
1 scallion, minced, including greens

1. In bowl, combine first 3 ingredients. Let stand ½ hour.
2. In wok, heat oil over low heat. Add red and green peppers. Stir-fry 2 minutes.
3. Add sherry. Stir-fry to blend.
4. Add meat stock and squid mixture. Simmer 5 minutes, stirring often.
5. In large bowl, combine vermicelli and squid mixture. Toss to blend.
6. Stir in soy sauce. Garnish with scallion. Serve warm or chilled.

Per serving: 192.3 calories; 24.6 mg. sodium; 21.5 gm. carbohydrates; 3.2 gm. fat.

* Do not add salt to boiling water.

Steamed Chicken
with Vegetable Hot Sauce Salad   SERVES 8

This is Hunan at its hottest and best.

1 3-pound chicken, halved or
  quartered
5 cups boiling water, divided
2 teaspoons low-sodium chicken
  bouillon
2 tablespoons dry sherry
2 tablespoons Soy Sauce Substitute
  (page 227)
2 tablespoons honey
1 teaspoon Chili Oil (page 230)
1 onion, minced

4 fresh mushrooms, chopped
1 slice ginger root, minced, or
  pinch of ginger powder
1 can (8 ounces) bamboo shoots,
  sliced
1 teaspoon Chili Paste (page 230)
1 red pepper, seeded and chopped
1 cucumber, scraped, seeded, and
  minced

1. On heatproof plate, place chicken. Then place plate on rack over 4 cups boiling water. Cover and steam ½ hour, or until chicken is fork tender. Transfer chicken to platter. Let cool. Remove skin and chop chicken into bite-size pieces. Set aside.
2. In bowl, combine remaining boiling water, bouillon, sherry, soy sauce, and honey, blending thoroughly. Set aside.
3. In wok, heat oil over low heat. Add onion, mushrooms, and ginger. Stir-fry 30 seconds.
4. Add bamboo shoots and chili paste. Stir-fry 30 seconds more.
5. Add red pepper. Stir-fry 30 seconds more.
6. Spoon vegetable mixture over chicken. Garnish with cucumber.
7. Serve sauce on the side.

Per serving: 203.7 calories; 81.2 mg. sodium; 28.4 gm. carbohydrates; 6.5 gm. fat.

Chicken Salad Canton with Peanut Sauce

SERVES 8

This sauce is so versatile that it works with equal success on fish or meat.

1 3-pound chicken
8 cups water
1½ cups lemon juice
½ cup dry sherry
⅓ cup unsalted peanuts, crushed
⅓ cup red wine vinegar
¼ cup peanut oil
¼ cup hot water
2 tablespoons Soy Sauce Substitute (page 227)
2 tablespoons low-sodium ketchup

4 scallions, chopped, including greens
1/16 teaspoon ground Szechwan peppercorns
1½ pounds bean sprouts
2 tomatoes, sliced thin
2 tablespoons dried cilantro (or parsley)
1 tablespoon low-sodium chicken bouillon
1 tablespoon cornstarch

1. In wok or Dutch oven, place first 4 ingredients. Turn heat to medium and bring to a slow boil. Continue boiling ½ hour, or until chicken is fork tender but not overdone, turning occasionally. Remove to platter. Let stand ½ hour. Reserve stock.
2. While chicken is cooking, in bowl, combine peanuts, vinegar, oil, and hot water. Stir to blend.
3. Add soy sauce, ketchup, scallions, and Szechwan pepper. Stir thoroughly. Cover and refrigerate at least ½ hour.
4. Skin chicken and cut the meat from the bone in bite-size pieces.
5. On platter, place bean sprouts. Arrange chicken on top. Place tomato slices over all, and garnish with cilantro. Cover and refrigerate.
6. Over medium heat, bring reserved chicken stock to a boil. Continue boiling until liquid is reduced by half. Then stir in bouillon and cook 5 minutes more.
7. Stir in cornstarch and continue stirring until cornstarch is dissolved and mixture starts to thicken.
8. In large bowl, combine vinegar and hot stock mixtures. Let stand 15 minutes. Pour half the sauce over the chicken. Serve remaining sauce on the side as a dip.

Per serving: 418.5 calories; 72.4 mg. sodium; 23.6 gm. carbohydrates; 22.1 gm. fat.

Chicken with Vegetable Marinade   SERVES 4

Fukien in derivation with mustard powder for bite.

1 cup cauliflowerettes
2 carrots, scraped and cut into
  1-inch rounds
1 green pepper, seeded and sliced
4 radishes, sliced thin
⅓ cup lemon juice
1 teaspoon mustard powder
2 tablespoons cider vinegar

2 tablespoons honey
⅓ cup boiling water
1 tablespoon low-sodium chicken
  bouillon
2 cups cooked chicken, cubed
1 cup bean sprouts
2 tablespoons dried cilantro (or
  parsley)

1. In bowl, combine first 4 ingredients. Toss to blend.
2. In second bowl, combine lemon juice and mustard powder, stirring until mustard is completely dissolved.
3. Stir in vinegar, honey, boiling water, and bouillon, blending thoroughly.
4. Pour dressing over cauliflower mixture. Cover and refrigerate 1 hour.
5. Add chicken and bean sprouts. Toss to blend.
6. Garnish with cilantro.

Per serving: 210.4 calories; 96.4 mg. sodium; 28.2 gm. carbohydrates; 4.0 gm. fat.

Chicken Salad of Many Flavors   SERVES 8

Serve this Hunan-style dish with Chicken Livers and Oysters (page 163) for a perfectly delightful meal.

1 3-pound chicken
12 cups water
⅓ cup orange juice
2 tablespoons dry sherry
2 tablespoons red wine vinegar
½ tablespoon lemon juice
1 tablespoon Chili Oil (page 230)
2 teaspoons sesame seed oil

2 slices ginger root, minced, or ⅟₁₆
  teaspoon ginger powder
⅟₁₆ teaspoon ground Szechwan
  peppercorns
4 scallions, chopped, including
  greens
1 cucumber, scraped and sliced
1 head iceberg lettuce, shredded

1. In wok or Dutch oven, place chicken and water. Turn heat to high and bring to a boil. Continue boiling 20 minutes, or until chicken is fork tender. Transfer chicken to warm platter. Let stand until cool. Then remove skin and chop chicken into bite-size pieces.

2. In bowl, combine all remaining ingredients except cucumber and lettuce.
3. In second bowl, combine cucumber, lettuce, and chicken. Toss to blend.
4. Pour dressing over chicken mixture. Toss to blend.

Per serving: 200.2 calories; 75.5 mg. sodium; 6.0 gm. carbohydrates; 8.6 gm. fat.

Chicken and Snow Pea Pod Salad   SERVES 4

The exotic influence of Szechwan makes its presence felt here.

1 cup cooked rice
2 tablespoons Soy Sauce Substitute
   (page 227)
2 tablespoons lemon juice
2 tablespoons sesame seed oil,
   divided
1 onion, minced
2 slices ginger root, minced, or ⅟₁₆
   teaspoon ginger powder
1 fresh chili pepper, minced, or
   dash of hot pepper flakes

1 teaspoon paprika
16 snow pea pods, cut diagonally
   in thirds
1 teaspoon dry sherry
1 cup cooked chicken, cubed
2 scallions, minced, including
   greens

1. In bowl, combine first 3 ingredients plus 1 tablespoon sesame seed oil. Stir to blend thoroughly.
2. In wok, heat remaining oil over low heat. Add onion, ginger, and chili pepper. Stir-fry 2 minutes, or until onion is golden.
3. Stir in paprika. Then push onion mixture to sides of wok. Add snow pea pods and sherry. Stir-fry 1 minute.
4. Spoon snow pea pod mixture over rice. Stir to blend well.
5. Add chicken and stir through.
6. Garnish with scallions.

Per serving: 202.9 calories; 21.4 mg. sodium; 22.5 gm. carbohydrates; 1.0 gm. fat.

Duck Salad with Pears

SERVES 8

Very unusual and very good, compliments of Imperial Peking.

½ duck (about 2 pounds), skinned
8 cups water
2 slices ginger root, or ¹⁄₁₆ teaspoon
  ginger powder
½ cup Six-Fruit Sauce (page 242)
2 tablespoons peanut (or sesame
  seed) oil
Dash of hot pepper flakes
¹⁄₁₆ teaspoon garlic powder
3 tablespoons dry sherry
¾ cup orange juice

4 pears, cored and halved
1 stick cinnamon, or ⅛ teaspoon
  ground cinnamon
2 teaspoons low-sodium chicken
  bouillon
4 scallions, chopped, including
  greens
1 head Boston lettuce, cut into
  bite-size pieces

1. In wok or Dutch oven, combine first 3 ingredients. Turn heat to high and bring to a boil. Continue boiling 5 minutes. Then reduce heat to low and simmer 1 hour, or until duck is tender. Transfer duck to warm platter, reserving stock. Slice meat off bone. Set aside.
2. In bowl, combine fruit sauce, oil, hot pepper flakes, and garlic powder, blending thoroughly. Set aside.
3. Preheat oven to 350°.
4. In 8-inch square casserole, combine sherry and orange juice.
5. Add pears, cut side down. Add cinnamon stick. Cover and bake ½ hour.
6. Reduce heat to 300°. Add more juice, if necessary, to prevent sticking. Turn pears, cut side up. Cover and bake 15 minutes more, or until pears are fork tender. Transfer pears to warm platter. Let stand 20 minutes.
7. While pears are baking, over high heat, bring reserved duck stock to a boil. Continue boiling ½ hour, or until stock is reduced to approximately 1 cup.
8. Stir in bouillon and scallions.
9. Pour stock mixture into Six-Fruit Sauce mixture. Stir to blend.
10. Divide lettuce equally among 8 plates.
11. Slice each pear half in quarters and ring them around the lettuce.
12. Place equal portions of sliced duck on each bed of lettuce.
13. Spoon some of the sauce over the duck. Serve remainder on the side.
    Note: This dish can be prepared in stages—the duck one day, the pears the next.

Per serving: 232.3 calories; 54.2 mg. sodium; 24.2 gm. carbohydrates; 9.4 gm. fat.

Sugar Beef Salad

SERVES 8

This dish is typical of the Fukien blending of soy sauce and sugar.

½ pound bottom round
2 cloves garlic, minced
1 large onion, chopped
2 slices ginger root, or ⅟₁₆ teaspoon
 ginger powder
Water to cover
¼ cup orange juice
¼ cup dry sherry
¼ cup Soy Sauce Substitute (page
 227)

⅛ teaspoon Five-Spice Powder
 (page 228)
3 tablespoons sugar
½ head lettuce, chopped
3 cups watercress, chopped
2 cups cauliflowerettes, steamed
2 tangerines, peeled and sectioned

1. In wok, over high heat, sear meat on all sides. Transfer to platter.
2. To wok, add garlic, onion, and ginger. Stir-fry 30 seconds.
3. Reduce heat to low. Return meat to wok. Add water to cover. Cover and simmer ½ hour.
4. Add orange juice, sherry, soy sauce, and five-spice powder. Cover and simmer 1 hour, turning meat occasionally.
5. Stir in sugar. Cover and simmer ½ hour more.
6. Transfer beef to casserole. Let cool ½ hour. Slice meat very thin. Cover with sauce. Cover and refrigerate overnight.
7. Distribute lettuce and watercress evenly among 4 plates. Spoon meat and sauce on top. Garnish with cauliflower and tangerines.

Per serving: 162.1 calories; 44.8 mg. sodium; 17.1 gm. carbohydrates; 6.4 gm. fat.

Beef Strips Bamboo   SERVES 4

A delicate and different salad with a northern influence.

½ pound flank steak, cut in thin
  strips
½ cup Fish Stock (page 67)
2 tablespoons white vinegar
1 star anise
2 tablespoons dry red wine
2 teaspoons vegetable oil
2 cloves garlic, minced
2 slices ginger root, minced, or ⅟₁₆
  teaspoon ginger powder
2 teaspoons orange (or lemon) peel,
  minced, or ½ teaspoon orange
  (or lemon) peel powder
½ can (4 ounces) bamboo shoots,
  sliced

1 cup cooked rice
1 tablespoon low-sodium beef
  bouillon
2 scallions, minced, including
  greens
1½ cups Chinese or American
  white cabbage, shredded
½ teaspoon sugar
1 cucumber, scraped and sliced
  thin

1. In bowl, combine first 5 ingredients. Cover and refrigerate at least 1 hour. Drain, reserving marinade. Discard star anise.
2. In wok, heat oil over low heat. Add garlic and ginger. Stir-fry 1 minute.
3. Add orange peel and bamboo shoots. Stir-fry 30 seconds.
4. Add rice, bouillon, and scallions plus 1 tablespoon reserved marinade. Stir-fry 2 minutes. Remove mixture to large bowl.
5. Add beef and 1 more tablespoon marinade. Stir-fry 1 minute, or until beef loses all pink color. Remove to rice mixture.
6. Add cabbage and sugar. Stir-fry 1 minute. Raise heat to medium. Add remaining marinade and cook until liquid has evaporated, stirring often. Remove to rice mixture.
7. Toss mixture to blend well. Garnish with cucumber. Serve warm or chilled.

Per serving: 315.3 calories; 96.1 mg. sodium; 28.0 gm. carbohydrates; 8.2 gm. fat.

Beef Strips and Cauliflower in Mustard Sauce

SERVES 4

This delicious dish with a refreshing northern zip makes a lovely light main-course salad.

½ pound flank steak, cut in very thin strips
2 tablespoons red wine vinegar
2 scallions, chopped, including greens
1½ tablespoons sesame seed oil, divided

¼ pound cauliflowerettes
½ cup boiling water
2 teaspoons low-sodium beef bouillon
2 teaspoons mustard powder
½ teaspoon sugar
1 head lettuce, shredded

1. In bowl, combine first 3 ingredients. Cover and refrigerate at least 6 hours.
2. In wok, heat ½ tablespoon oil over medium heat. Add cauliflower. Reduce heat to low and cook 2 minutes, stirring occasionally.
3. While cauliflower is cooking, in second bowl, combine water, bouillon, mustard, sugar, and remaining oil. Stir to completely dissolve bouillon and sugar. Set aside.
4. Drain meat and add to wok, reserving marinade. Raise heat to medium and stir-fry until meat loses all pink color. Transfer meat and cauliflower to a salad bowl.
5. Add meat marinade to bouillon mixture. Stir to blend. Pour over meat mixture.
6. Add lettuce. Toss to blend thoroughly and serve. Or chill meat mixture 1 hour; then toss with lettuce and serve.

Per serving: 203.2 calories; 59.6 mg. sodium; 8.8 gm. carbohydrates; 10.3 gm. fat.

Pork and Zucchini Salad
SERVES 4

The sweetness typical of eastern Chinese cuisine is evident in this dish.

½ cup red wine vinegar
2 teaspoons sesame seed oil
¼ cup pineapple juice
1 teaspoon vegetable oil
1 zucchini, quartered and cut in
  thin strips
½ can (4 ounces) water chestnuts,
  sliced
Black pepper to taste

2 teaspoons low-sodium chicken
  bouillon
¼ teaspoon ground coriander
1 cup leftover cooked pork, cubed
¼ cup dry sherry
1 tablespoon Soy Sauce Substitute
  (page 227)
1 head lettuce, shredded

1. In bowl, combine first 3 ingredients. Let stand 20 minutes.
2. In wok, heat vegetable oil over low heat. Add zucchini, water chestnuts, and pepper. Stir-fry 2 minutes.
3. Add all remaining ingredients except lettuce. Stir to blend. Raise heat to medium and cook 2 minutes, stirring often.
4. Transfer pork mixture to large bowl. Add lettuce. Toss to blend.
5. Pour vinegar mixture over all. Toss to blend thoroughly.

Per serving: 208 calories; 53.7 mg. sodium; 17.7 gm. carbohydrates; 11.0 gm. fat.

Pork and Bean Sprout Salad
SERVES 4

The chili powder adds a western flair to what would otherwise be a Cantonese dish. Broccoli and Minced Shrimp (page 192) is a good accompaniment.

½ pound ground pork
1 tablespoon Soy Sauce Substitute
  (page 227)
1 tablespoon cider vinegar
1 egg white
¼ teaspoon Chili Powder (page
  231)
1 tablespoon vegetable oil

1 onion, minced
½ can (4 ounces) water chestnuts,
  minced
¾ pound bean sprouts
1 teaspoon sugar
½ cup Meat Stock (page 69)
2 endives

1. In bowl, combine first 5 ingredients, stirring to blend thoroughly. Set aside.
2. In wok, heat oil over low heat. Add onion and water chestnuts. Stir-fry 1 minute, or until onion is wilted.

3. Add pork mixture and stir-fry 3 minutes, or until pork loses all pink color.
4. Push pork mixture to sides of wok. Add bean sprouts and sugar. Stir to blend.
5. Add meat stock. Raise heat to medium and cook until liquid is absorbed, stirring occasionally.
6. Mound pork mixture in center of platter. Arrange endive leaves around pork and use as spoons. Serve warm or chilled.

Per serving: 271.1 calories; 66.9 mg. sodium; 20.3 gm. carbohydrates; 13.6 gm. fat.

Ginger Lamb with Radish and Leek   SERVES 4

Although lamb is primarily enjoyed in the North, the western style in this dish lends a scrumptious balance to this distinctly flavored meat. This should be served with boiled white rice.

8 ounces lamb (any cut), shredded
⅛ teaspoon ground Szechwan peppercorns
2 cloves garlic, minced
4 scallions, cut into 1-inch pieces, including greens
2 bunches watercress, chopped
2 teaspoons sugar
4 radishes, sliced
2 tablespoons dry sherry

2 tablespoons Soy Sauce Substitute (page 227)
1 teaspoon vegetable oil
1 leek, chopped, including greens
1 teaspoon low-sodium beef bouillon
1 cucumber, sliced in ¼-inch rounds

1. In bowl, combine first 4 ingredients. Let stand 15 minutes.
2. In second bowl, combine watercress and sugar. Let stand 15 minutes.
3. To lamb mixture, add radishes, sherry, and soy sauce. Stir to blend. Let stand 15 minutes more. Drain, reserving marinade.
4. In wok, heat oil over low heat. Add leek and watercress mixture. Stir-fry 30 seconds. Push mixture to sides of wok.
5. Add lamb and radish mixture. Turn heat to high and stir-fry 30 seconds.
6. Add bouillon and stir to blend. Continue stir-frying until lamb loses all pink color. Stir in reserved marinade.
7. Remove mixture to platter and mound in the middle. Surround with cucumber slices.

Per serving: 225.1 calories; 89.8 mg. sodium; 14.1 gm. carbohydrates; 6.5 gm. fat.

Mongolian Lamb Salad   SERVES 4

This tangy northern dish works just as well with leftover pork or cold flounder. Serve with Mushroom and Corn Soup (page 82), and you will have a no-fuss meal.

3 tablespoons low-sodium chili
  ketchup
2 tablespoons Soy Sauce Substitute
  (page 227)
1 tablespoon cider vinegar
1 tablespoon dry sherry
2 teaspoons sesame seed oil
2 cloves garlic, minced
1/16 teaspoon ginger powder
4 scallions, chopped, including
  greens
4 tablespoons cold water

1 1/2 teaspoons mustard powder
2 teaspoons sugar
1 cup, tightly packed, diced leftover
  lamb
1 cucumber, diced
1 red pepper, minced
1 tablespoon dried cilantro (or
  parsley)
1 head lettuce (any kind),
  shredded

1. In bowl, combine first 4 ingredients. Stir to blend. Cover and refrigerate 1 hour.
2. In wok, heat oil over low heat. Add garlic, ginger, and scallions. Stir-fry 1 minute. Set aside.
3. In second bowl, combine water, mustard powder, and sugar, stirring to dissolve.
4. Stir scallion mixture into ketchup mixture.
5. In large bowl, combine lamb, cucumber, red pepper, cilantro, and lettuce. Toss to blend.
6. Pour scallion-ketchup mixture over all. Toss to blend.
7. Pour mustard mixture over all. Toss to blend.

Per serving with lamb: 248.1 calories; 94.0 mg. sodium: 17.8 gm. carbohydrates; 7.8 gm. fat.
Per serving with pork: 242.8 calories; 81.4 mg. sodium; 17.8 gm. carbohydrates; 9.5 gm. fat.
Per serving with flounder: 183.5 calories; 96.0 mg. sodium; 17.8 gm. carbohydrates; 3.8 gm. fat.

Sweet and Hot Carrots and Radishes

SERVES 4

Do not let the "hot" fool you. This dish is very Cantonese.

2 large carrots, cut into ½-inch
  rounds and steamed
4 radishes, sliced
2 tablespoons vegetable oil
¼ cup hot water
1 tablespoon sugar

¼ cup white vinegar
Dash of hot pepper flakes
2 tablespoons Soy Sauce Substitute
  (page 227)
1 tablespoon dry sherry

In large bowl, combine all ingredients. Cover and chill at least 2 hours.

Per serving: 133.2 calories; 50.5 mg. sodium; 15.7 gm. carbohydrates; 7.9 gm. fat.

Fried Noodle Salad

SERVES 4

This is adapted from a popular Szechwan dish which usually fries the noodles pancake-style and often adds meat or fish, as well as vegetables. We prefer a rapid stir-fry, which requires less oil.

4 ounces vermicelli, cooked al
  dente*
2 tablespoons lemon juice
1 tablespoon sesame seed oil
1 green pepper, sliced
1 red pepper, sliced

4 fresh mushrooms, sliced
⅛ teaspoon Szechwan Pepper Spice
  (page 229)
2 tablespoons low-sodium chili
  ketchup

1. In bowl, combine first 2 ingredients. Toss to blend. Set aside.
2. In wok, heat oil over low heat. Add green and red peppers. Stir-fry 1 minute.
3. Add mushrooms. Stir-fry 1 minute more.
4. Add Szechwan pepper spice. Stir to blend.
5. Add noodle mixture. Raise heat to medium and stir-fry 1 minute.
6. Stir in ketchup and stir-fry 1 minute more.
7. May be served hot or cold.

Per serving: 275 calories; 22.8 mg. sodium; 50.2 gm. carbohydrates: 4.7 gm. fat.

* Do not add salt to boiling water.

Watercress and Noodle Salad   SERVES 4

The oyster sauce is the secret ingredient in this dish from Canton.

4 ounces vermicelli, cooked al
   dente*
¼ cup Oyster Sauce (page 234)
2 tablespoons Soy Sauce Substitute
   (page 227)

1 tablespoon vegetable oil
2 cloves garlic, minced
1 large carrot, julienned
3 cups watercress, chopped
½ teaspoon sugar

1. In bowl, combine first 3 ingredients. Toss to blend. Set aside.
2. In wok, heat oil over low heat. Add garlic and carrot. Stir-fry 2 minutes.
3. Add watercress. Raise heat to medium and stir-fry 1 minute more.
4. Stir in sugar, blending well.
5. Spoon watercress mixture over noodle mixture. Toss to blend.

Per serving: 250.1 calories; 70.0 mg. sodium; 42.4 gm. carbohydrates; 5.2 gm. fat.

* Do not add salt to boiling water.

Szechwan Vegetable Salad   SERVES 8

Although this salad—a wonderful combination of textures and flavors—takes a little longer than most salads to assemble and make, it's so fantastic it's worth it.

8 dried black mushrooms*
1 cup boiling water
4 tablespoons dry red wine
2 teaspoons low-sodium beef
   bouillon
2 teaspoons sesame seed oil
½ pound asparagus, trimmed and
   cut into 1½-inch pieces
½ teaspoon sugar
1 tablespoon Chili Oil (page 230)
1 small eggplant, pared and cubed

2 scallions, minced, including
   greens
1⁄16 teaspoon ground coriander
2 red peppers, halved
1 cup Chicken Stock (page 68)
2 tablespoons cold water
1 tablespoon cornstarch
1 teaspoon dry sherry
1 tablespoon lemon juice
2 tangerines, peeled and sectioned
1 cucumber, diced

1. In bowl, combine first 2 ingredients. Let stand ½ hour.
2. Pour mushrooms plus liquid and wine into a saucepan. Turn heat to medium and bring to a slow boil. Reduce heat to low. Add bouillon, cover and simmer 15 minutes, or until liquid is almost absorbed.
3. While mushrooms are cooking, in wok, heat sesame seed oil over low heat. Add asparagus and stir-fry 2 minutes. Stir in sugar and stir-fry 1 minute more. Remove to platter.

4. In wok, heat chili oil over low heat. Add eggplant and stir-fry 2 minutes.
5. Add scallions and coriander. Stir to blend. Cover and simmer 10 minutes, stirring occasionally.
6. Preheat oven to broil.
7. On broiler pan, place red peppers, cut side down. Broil 6 inches from heat 3 minutes, or until skin starts to blacken and blister. Turn and broil 1 minute more. Transfer to dish and cut each half into 6 strips.
8. In second saucepan, over medium heat, bring chicken stock to a boil. Reduce heat to low and simmer 5 minutes.
9. In bowl, combine water and cornstarch, stirring to dissolve. Stir into stock.
10. Stir sherry and lemon juice into stock. Simmer until sauce starts to thicken, stirring occasionally.
11. On flat salad platter, mound eggplant mixture in center.
12. Arrange asparagus, pepper slices, and tangerine sections around the eggplant.
13. Scatter cucumber over all.
14. Dice mushrooms and scatter over all.
15. Serve sauce on the side.

Per serving: 97.5 calories; 23.7 mg. sodium; 12.0 gm. carbohydrates; 4.1 gm. fat.

* If not available, substitute 8 large fresh mushrooms, sliced, and use ½ cup boiling water.

Marinated Broccoli Stems and Cauliflower

SERVES 4

This dish is popular throughout China. We have substituted cider vinegar for soy sauce and added the spark of orange peel.

8 broccoli stems, cut in ½-inch
  rounds
2 cups cauliflowerettes
⅓ cup cider vinegar
2 teaspoons orange peel, minced,
  or ¼ teaspoon orange peel
  powder

1 tablespoon sugar
2 tablespoons vegetable oil
1 tablespoon sesame seed oil
¼ cup hot water

In large jar, combine all ingredients. Shake to blend well. Refrigerate overnight.

Per serving: 163.1 calories; 24.9 mg. sodium; 14.5 gm. carbohydrates; 11.6 gm. fat.

Cucumber and Onion Salad   SERVES 4

You will love this northern dish.

2 cucumbers, scraped, seeded, and
  chopped
1 teaspoon unsalted cashews or
  peanuts, crushed
2 tablespoons Hoisin Sauce
  Substitute (page 228)

2 tablespoons cider vinegar
1 tablespoon sugar
3 tablespoons orange juice
2 scallions, chopped, including
  greens

1. In bowl, combine first 2 ingredients. Toss to blend. Cover and refrigerate 15 minutes.
2. In second bowl, combine remaining ingredients. Let stand 15 minutes.
3. Pour scallion dressing over cucumber mixture. Toss to blend thoroughly.

Per serving with cashews: 117.4 calories; 38.5 mg. sodium; 11.8 gm. carbohydrates;
  1.0 gm. fat.
Per serving with peanuts: 117.8 calories; 38.4 mg. sodium; 11.1 gm. carbohydrates;
  1.1 gm. fat.

Bean Sprout and Green Bean Salad   SERVES 4

Graced with the flavors of western China.

½ pound green beans, steamed
¼ cup lemon juice
2 tablespoons cider vinegar
¼ cup boiling water
1 teaspoon low-sodium chicken
  bouillon
1 teaspoon sugar

Black pepper to taste
1½ tablespoons sesame seed oil,
  divided
½ pound bean sprouts
2 cloves garlic, minced
2 radishes, minced

1. In bowl, combine first 3 ingredients. Toss to blend.
2. In second bowl, combine water, bouillon, sugar, and pepper, stirring until bouillon is dissolved. Let stand 5 minutes. Then pour over green bean mixture. Stir to blend.
3. In wok, heat 1 tablespoon oil over low heat. Add bean sprouts and garlic. Stir-fry 2 minutes, or until bean sprouts are lightly browned.
4. Stir bean sprout mixture into green bean mixture. Stir in remaining ½ tablespoon oil, blending thoroughly.
5. Garnish with minced radish. Serve warm or chilled.

Per serving: 157.6 calories; 12.0 mg. sodium; 15.6 gm. carbohydrates; 8.8 gm. fat.

Green Bean and Fruit Salad SERVES 8

This reflects the influence of Shantung, with its wealth of fruits.

1½ pounds green beans, halved
  diagonally and steamed
6 tablespoons cider vinegar,
  divided
1 apple, cored and sliced
1 pear, cored and sliced
1 orange, peeled and sectioned
1 can (8 ounces) dietetic pineapple
  chunks, drained (reserve half
  the juice)

⅓ cup boiling water
2 tablespoons honey
¼ cup unsalted almond slivers
  (optional)
1 small cucumber, scraped and
  diced

1. In bowl, combine green beans and 3 tablespoons vinegar. Toss to blend. Cover and refrigerate 15 minutes.
2. In wok, combine remaining vinegar and all fruit. Turn heat to low. Simmer 3 minutes, stirring occasionally.
3. While fruit is cooking, combine water and honey, stirring until honey is well blended. Pour into wok and stir-fry 30 seconds, or until fruit is thoroughly coated.
4. Spoon fruit mixture over green beans. Toss to blend.
5. Garnish with almond slivers, if desired, and cucumber.

Per serving without almonds: 106.9 calories; 14.1 mg. sodium; 50.5 gm. carbohydrates; 0.5 gm. fat.
Per serving with almonds: 149.6 calories; 14.4 mg. sodium; 51.9 gm. carbohydrates; 4.4 gm. fat.

Eggplant Curry Salad

SERVES 4

Turn this tasty Yunnan dish into a main course by adding either ½ pound of chopped, cooked white fish or the chopped meat of a 1-pound lobster to the finished salad; or add ½ pound small shrimp, shelled, deveined, and chopped, to Step 6 and stir-fry until shrimp turn pink.

8 small dried black mushrooms*
1 cup hot water
1 tablespoon vegetable oil
1 onion, minced
2 cloves garlic, minced
1 leek, chopped, including greens
1 small eggplant, peeled and diced
¼ teaspoon Szechwan Pepper Spice (page 229)
1 tablespoon dry sherry

2 teaspoons low-sodium chicken bouillon
2 teaspoons Curry Powder (page 232)
1 cucumber, scraped and sliced in ¼-inch rounds
1 large carrot, julienned

1. In bowl, combine first 2 ingredients. Let stand ½ hour. Drain, reserving liquid.
2. In wok, heat oil over low heat. Add onion, garlic, and leek. Stir-fry 1 minute, or until onion is wilted.
3. Add eggplant and Szechwan pepper spice. Stir to blend. Cover and cook 15 minutes, stirring occasionally.
4. Stir in sherry and mushrooms.
5. Stir bouillon into reserved mushroom liquid. Add curry powder, blending well. Stir into wok.
6. Raise heat to medium and stir-fry 2 minutes more. Transfer mixture to platter. Garnish with cucumber and carrots.

Per serving plain: 176.7 calories; 36.8 mg. sodium; 26.6 gm. carbohydrates; 5.0 gm. fat.
Per serving with fish: 222 calories; 78.9 mg. sodium; 26.6 gm. carbohydrates; 5.5 gm. fat.
Per serving with lobster: 202.7 calories; 96.8 mg. sodium; 26.7 gm. carbohydrates; 5.6 gm. fat.
Per serving with shrimp: 228.7 calories; 116.8 mg. sodium; 27.5 gm. carbohydrates; 5.3 gm. fat.

* If not available, substitute 8 small fresh mushrooms.

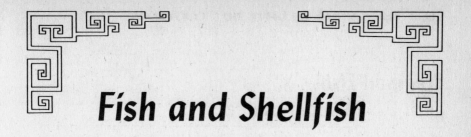

Fish and Shellfish

Thanks to its four major rivers, which cut swaths through the land, its brimming lakes, and generous coastline, China is bountifully supplied with a dazzling selection of fresh fish and shellfish all year long. It is not surprising, then, that seafood is a mainstay of the Chinese diet, relished far more there than it is in the United States.

Shellfish are served any number of ways—whole (in the shell for maximum juicy flavor), cut up, steamed, fried, the featured ingredient or one of many. Unfortunately, shellfish are relatively high in sodium and therefore are often forbidden to those of us on low-salt diets.

But not to worry. Chicken breast, London broil, and any firm fish such as haddock, red snapper, or swordfish are excellent substitutes for any shellfish. There is little difference in calories, carbohydrates, and fat, but there is up to an 80 percent decrease in sodium when compared to shellfish like scallops, which have the highest sodium content in this book (76 milligrams per ounce).

The shellfish recipes in this section were carefully planned to taste just as delicious with a substitute of your choice as with the original, so either way, you can enjoy them.

Fish are another matter. They are perfect food for just about everyone because they are rich in protein, low in carbohydrates and sodium, and have a moderate fat content.

The Chinese generally prepare fish whole—either steamed or fried, so the fish can bathe in their own sweet juices. In deference to American taste, however, fish fillets are used most often in this book. Either way, the end results will give exquisite taste sensations you might not have expected of fish.

Just wait until you taste Braised Fish and Peanuts (page 109), Mixed Seafood in Hoisin Sauce (page 126), and Salmon with Green Beans Mandarin (page 117). This chapter will make fish lovers of you all.

Hot – good

Steamed Fish
with Chili Ginger-Sauce

SERVES 4

There are not many dishes hotter or better than this one in the Hunan tradition.

1 1½-pound flounder or striped bass, scored on both sides
2 slices ginger root, minced, or ¹⁄₁₆ teaspoon ginger powder
½ tablespoon ground Szechwan peppercorns
1 tablespoon sugar
1 teaspoon vegetable oil
1 onion, minced

1 can (8 ounces) bamboo shoots, sliced
1½ cups water
2 tablespoons low-sodium beef bouillon
4 tablespoons Chili Paste (page 230)

1. In 9 x 13-inch casserole, place fish. Rub all over with ginger, Szechwan pepper, and sugar. Let stand 15 minutes.
2. In wok, heat oil over low heat. Add onion and bamboo shoots. Stir-fry 30 seconds.
3. Add fish and remaining ingredients. Cover and simmer 5 minutes.
4. With tongs, turn fish. Raise heat to medium. Cover and cook 10 minutes more, or until fish flakes easily, adding more water if necessary to prevent sticking.

Per serving with flounder: 220.2 calories; 109.1 mg. sodium; 28.0 gm. carbohydrates; 3.6 gm. fat.
Per serving with bass: 253.6 calories; 8.8 mg. sodium; 23.0 gm. carbohydrates; 6.2 gm. fat.

Fair

Braised Fish and Peanuts

SERVES 8

The Cantonese willingness to experiment is evident here. Serve with Honeyed Carrots and Watercress (page 195).

½ pound flounder or cod fillets, cut in 1-inch chunks
½ pound swordfish or red snapper fillets, cut in 1-inch chunks
1 pint shucked oysters, liquid reserved
3 tablespoons lemon juice
Dash of hot pepper flakes
2 teaspoons peanut oil
2 cloves garlic, minced
2 slices ginger root, minced, or ⅟₁₆ teaspoon ginger powder
¼ pound shrimp, shelled, deveined, and minced

1½ tablespoons unsalted peanuts
1 cup boiling water, divided
1 tablespoon low-sodium chicken bouillon
1 tablespoon dry sherry
1 teaspoon mustard powder
1 teaspoon cornstarch
1 cup snow pea pods, halved diagonally
3 scallions, chopped, including greens

1. In bowl, combine first 5 ingredients. Cover and refrigerate 1 hour.
2. In wok, heat oil over low heat. Add garlic, ginger, shrimp, and peanuts. Stir-fry 2 minutes, or until shrimp loses all pink color.
3. Add fish and oyster mixture plus oyster liquid. Cover and simmer 5 minutes.
4. While wok mixture is simmering, in bowl, combine boiling water and bouillon. Set aside.
5. In second bowl, combine sherry, mustard, and cornstarch. Set aside.
6. Turn heat under wok to high. Add bouillon mixture and snow pea pods. Bring mixture to a boil.
7. Add cornstarch mixture and scallions. Stir until mixture thickens.

Per serving:
Flounder with swordfish: 143 calories; 76.5 mg. sodium; 5.7 gm. carbohydrates; 5.2 gm. fat.
Flounder with red snapper: 136 calories; 95.7 mg. sodium; 5.7 gm. carbohydrates; 4.3 gm. fat.
Cod with swordfish: 143 calories; 74.2 mg. sodium; 5.7 gm. carbohydrates; 5.1 gm. fat.
Cod with red snapper: 136 calories; 93.4 mg. sodium; 5.7 gm. carbohydrates; 4.2 gm. fat.

Braised Fish in
Mustard and Tomato Sauce

SERVES 4

The taste is Cantonese, but the pleasure belongs to all. Try this one with Sweet and Hot Chicken Mushroom Soup (page 72).

1 pound halibut, red snapper, or salmon fillets
1 tablespoon low-sodium chicken bouillon
2 teaspoons sesame seed oil, divided
1 cup Chinese or American white cabbage, shredded
1 teaspoon sugar
3 tablespoons dry sherry
2 teaspoons mustard powder
2 tomatoes, diced
Black pepper to taste
2 scallions, chopped, including greens

1. On heatproof dish, place fish. Rub with bouillon. Let stand 15 minutes.
2. Place dish on rack over boiling water. Cover and steam 15 minutes, or until fish flakes easily. Transfer fish to warm platter.
3. While fish is cooking, in small skillet, heat oil over low heat. Add cabbage and stir-fry 2 minutes.
4. Stir in sugar. Cover and simmer 2 minutes more.
5. While cabbage is cooking, in bowl, combine sherry and mustard. Stir into cabbage along with tomatoes, pepper, and scallions. Stir-fry 2 minutes.
6. Spoon cabbage mixture over fish.

Per serving with halibut: 194.1 calories; 75.1 mg. sodium; 10.0 gm. carbohydrates; 4.9 gm. fat.
Per serving with red snapper: 111.1 calories; 89.9 mg. sodium; 10.0 gm. carbohydrates; 4.5 gm. fat.
Per serving with salmon: 328.1 calories; 86.5 mg. sodium; 10.0 gm. carbohydrates; 18.8 gm. fat

Good

Crispy Sweet and Sour Fish

SERVES 4

Every region has a sweet and sour fish recipe. The balance of sweetish sherry and "salty" soy sauce in this version reflects the eastern influence.

1½-pound sea bass, scaled and gutted, head and tail intact
¼ cup boiling water
1 teaspoon low-sodium beef bouillon
¼ cup dry sherry
¼ cup Soy Sauce Substitute (page 227)
⅔ cup cold water
¼ cup cornstarch
2 cups vegetable oil
2 cloves garlic, minced
2 slices ginger root, minced, or ¹⁄₁₆ teaspoon ginger powder

½ can (4 ounces) bamboo shoots, sliced
2 carrots, scraped and cut into ⅛-inch rounds
4 fresh mushrooms, sliced
4 scallions, chopped, including greens
1 tablespoon sugar
¼ cup low-sodium ketchup
3 tablespoons red wine vinegar
½ cup Chicken Stock (page 68)

1. In 9 x 13-inch casserole, place fish. Make small diagonal cuts on both sides.
2. In bowl, combine boiling water and bouillon, stirring until bouillon is dissolved.
3. Stir in sherry and soy sauce.
4. Pour bouillon mixture over fish. Let stand 10 minutes, turning once. Remove fish from marinade and wipe dry. Reserve marinade.
5. In second bowl, combine cold water and cornstarch, blending thoroughly.
6. Coat fish with ⅔ cup of cornstarch mixture.
7. In wok, heat oil over high heat until crackling. Carefully lower fish into oil head first. Deep-fry 5 to 7 minutes, or until golden brown, turning with tongs if necessary. Remove to warm platter.
8. Drain off all but 1 tablespoon oil. Add garlic, ginger, bamboo shoots, and carrots. Stir-fry 1 minute.
9. Add mushrooms and scallions. Stir-fry 30 seconds.
10. Add remaining fish marinade and last 4 ingredients. Stir to blend.
11. Add remaining cornstarch mixture. Stir until mixture thickens.
12. Pour sauce over fish. Serve immediately.

Per serving: 460.8 calories; 127.7 mg. sodium; 28.5 gm. carbohydrates; 21.4 gm. fat.

Poached Bass with Hot Sauce and Vegetables

SERVES 8

Decidedly eastern, and, believe it or not, the spices do not overwhelm the sweet flavor of the bass. Serve with Soy Sauce Substitute (page 227) and Chinese Mustard (page 10) as dips.

8⅓ cups water
1 4-pound sea bass, scaled and gutted, head and tail intact
4 slices ginger root, or ⅛ teaspoon ginger powder
2 carrots, scraped and cut into strips
1 cup cauliflowerettes
½ pound green beans
1½ cups boiling water
3 tablespoons Soy Sauce Substitute (page 227)

4 teaspoons low-sodium chicken bouillon
1 teaspoon Curry Powder (page 232)
1 teaspoon dried cilantro (or parsley)
2 teaspoons sesame seed oil
4 scallions, chopped, including greens

1. In wok, bring 8⅓ cups water to a boil over high heat. Lower fish into water head first. Reduce heat to simmer.
2. Add ginger and carrots. Cover and simmer 10 minutes.
3. Add cauliflower and green beans. Cover and simmer 20 minutes more, or until fish flakes easily.
4. While fish is cooking, in bowl, combine all remaining ingredients. Stir to blend. Set aside.
5. When fish is done, transfer to warm platter. Pour soy sauce mixture over all.
6. Drain vegetables and arrange around fish. Discard ginger.

Per serving: 209 calories; 135.8 mg. sodium; 25.5 gm. carbohydrates; 4.1 gm. fat.

Braised Cod in Pork Sauce

SERVES 4

The mouthwatering flavor of this dish is Cantonese, although steaming is generally preferred in this southern region.

¾ pound cod fillets
3 tablespoons Soy Sauce Substitute (page 227)
2 teaspoons vegetable oil
2 cloves garlic, minced
2 slices ginger root, minced, or ¹⁄₁₆ teaspoon ginger powder

¼ pound ground pork
4 fresh mushrooms, sliced
2 cups Chicken Stock (page 68)
2 cups broccoli flowerettes
¼ cup cold water
2 teaspoons cornstarch

1. In bowl, combine first 2 ingredients. Cover and refrigerate 15 minutes.
2. In wok, heat oil over low heat. Add garlic, ginger, and pork. Stir-fry 3 minutes, or until pork loses all pink color.
3. Add mushrooms. Stir-fry 30 seconds. Remove mixture to platter.
4. Raise heat to high. Add chicken stock and bring to a boil.
5. Reduce heat to low. Add fish mixture. Cover and simmer 5 minutes.
6. Add broccoli. Cover and simmer 3 minutes more.
7. While fish mixture is simmering, in bowl, combine water and cornstarch. Set aside.
8. To wok, add pork mixture. Stir to blend.
9. Raise heat to medium. Add cornstarch mixture. Cook until mixture thickens, stirring frequently.

Per serving: 243 calories; 111.6 mg. sodium; 8.7 gm. carbohydrates; 0.9 gm. fat.

Lemon Cod and Vegetables

SERVES 8

Boiled white rice is all you need for this eastern-style temptation.

1½ pounds cod fillets, cut in 1-inch chunks
2 tablespoons lemon juice
2 cups Chicken Stock (page 68), divided
1 can (8 ounces) bamboo shoots
½ can (4 ounces) water chestnuts, sliced
1 onion, chopped
2 slices ginger root, or ¹⁄₁₆ teaspoon ginger powder

1 tablespoon low-sodium beef bouillon
2 tablespoons dry sherry
1 teaspoon sugar
1 teaspoon cornstarch
¼ cup cold water
1 teaspoon sesame seed oil

1. In saucepan, combine cod, lemon juice, and ¾ cup chicken stock. Turn heat to low. Cover and simmer 5 minutes.
2. Add remaining chicken stock, vegetables, and ginger. Raise heat to medium and bring to a slow boil. Reduce heat to low and simmer 5 minutes more.
3. Stir in beef bouillon. Then stir in sherry and sugar. Simmer 5 minutes more.
4. While fish is cooking, in bowl, combine cornstarch and water. Stir into fish mixture. Raise heat to high and stir until mixture starts to bubble.
5. Stir in sesame seed oil.

Per serving: 136 calories; 79.0 mg. sodium; 9.9 gm. carbohydrates; 2.3 gm. fat.

Flounder in Silk

SERVES 4

In this adaptation of an eastern specialty, we have simplified the preparation by marinating the fish, thus speeding the cooking. And, of course, we have omitted the ham generally used.

1 pound flounder fillets, cut in
  1-inch chunks
1 egg white, lightly beaten
2 tablespoons cornstarch, divided
Black pepper to taste
1 teaspoon lemon peel powder
1 cup Meat Stock (page 69),
  divided
4 teaspoons vegetable oil, divided

1 clove garlic, sliced
2 slices ginger root, minced, or $\frac{1}{16}$
  teaspoon ginger powder
3 tablespoons dried cilantro (or
  parsley)
2 teaspoons dry sherry
1 teaspoon low-sodium chicken
  bouillon

1. In bowl, combine flounder, egg white, 1 tablespoon cornstarch, pepper, and lemon peel. Mix thoroughly. Cover and refrigerate at least 1 hour.
2. In second bowl, combine remaining cornstarch and 2 tablespoons meat stock. Mix to dissolve cornstarch. Set aside.
3. In wok, heat 2 teaspoons oil over high heat. Add flounder, reduce heat to medium, and stir-fry, separating chunks, for 1 minute. Remove fish and drain on paper towels.
4. To wok, add remaining oil, garlic, and ginger. Stir-fry 1 minute.
5. Add cilantro and stir-fry briefly. Add sherry, remaining meat stock, and cornstarch mixture. Stir until sauce thickens slightly.
6. Add fish and bouillon. Cook briefly, stirring to blend. Discard garlic.

Per serving: 189 calories; 102.7 mg. sodium; 10.7 gm. carbohydrates; 6.8 gm. fat.

Flounder in
Szechwan Pepper Sauce   SERVES 4

The taste has punch, but a subtle one. It is delicious with Beef Strips and Cauliflower in Mustard Sauce (page 97).

1 pound flounder fillets
2 scallions, chopped, including
    greens
Dash of Five-Spice Powder (page
    228)
¼ cup dry sherry
1 star anise (optional)
2 teaspoons low-sodium beef
    bouillon

1 tablespoon peanut oil
1 red or green pepper, sliced thin
¹⁄₁₆ teaspoon ground Szechwan
    peppercorns
1 cup Chicken Stock (page 68)
1 teaspoon sugar
1 tablespoon cornstarch

1. In 9 x 13-inch casserole, combine first 6 ingredients. Cover and refrigerate 2 hours, turning occasionally. Remove fish from marinade, reserving the latter.
2. In wok, heat oil over low heat. Add red pepper. Stir-fry 1 minute.
3. Add Szechwan pepper and fillets. Simmer 1 minute.
4. Add chicken stock and sugar. Raise heat to medium. Cover and cook 5 minutes.
5. While fish is cooking, in bowl, combine fish marinade with cornstarch. Stir into wok mixture and continue cooking, stirring until sauce thickens.

Per serving: 194.1 calories; 110.3 mg. sodium; 9.3 gm. carbohydrates; 6.1 gm. fat.

Salmon with Green Beans Mandarin

SERVES 8

Salmon is not common to China, but we prefer its distinctive taste, which balances the sweet and pungent flavors here, to the milder bass or carp more likely to be used in this northern-style dish.

¾ cup boiling water, divided
2 teaspoons low-sodium beef
  bouillon
1 tablespoon low-sodium chicken
  bouillon
1 tablespoon cornstarch
2 tablespoons cold water
1¼ pounds salmon fillets, cut in
  1-inch chunks
1 onion, minced
1 tablespoon lemon juice
1 tablespoon peanut oil

2 slices ginger root, minced, or ⅟₁₆
  teaspoon ginger powder
1 pound green beans, halved
  diagonally
1 teaspoon sugar
2 cloves garlic, minced
1 can (15 ounces) mandarin
  oranges, plus juice
¼ cup unsalted cashews, chopped
1 tablespoon dry sherry

1. In bowl, combine ¼ cup boiling water and beef bouillon. Set aside.
2. In second bowl, combine ½ cup boiling water and chicken bouillon. Set aside.
3. In third bowl, combine cornstarch and cold water. Set aside.
4. In large bowl, place salmon. Cover with onion, beef bouillon mixture, and lemon juice. Let stand.
5. In wok, heat oil over low heat. Add ginger, green beans, sugar, and garlic. Stir-fry 3 minutes.
6. Stir in mandarin oranges and juice plus cashews and sherry. Cook 3 minutes, stirring often.
7. Stir in fish and marinade plus chicken bouillon mixture. Cook 5 minutes, or until fish is fork tender.
8. Stir in cornstarch mixture. Raise heat to medium and cook until mixture thickens, stirring frequently.

Per serving: 283 calories; 58.1 mg. sodium; 55.5 gm. carbohydrates; 14.9 gm. fat.

Salmon with Zucchini in Soy Sauce   SERVES 8

The eastern region is famous for its fish and their preparation. This dish is a prime example. Serve with Cucumber and Onion Salad (page 104) for a real treat.

1½ tablespoons fresh coriander (or parsley), chopped
1 cup Chicken Stock (page 68)
8 dried black mushrooms*
2 cloves garlic, blanched and mashed
2 slices ginger root, or ¹⁄₁₆ teaspoon ginger powder
1½ pounds salmon fillets, cut in 1-inch chunks
¼ cup Soy Sauce Substitute (page 227)

1 tablespoon cornstarch
1 tablespoon sesame seed oil
1 large zucchini, cut into matchstick strips
Black pepper to taste
2 teaspoons low-sodium beef bouillon
1 teaspoon mustard powder
1 teaspoon sugar
2 scallions, chopped, including greens

1. In wok, combine first 5 ingredients. Bring to a slow boil over medium heat.
2. Add salmon. Reduce heat to low. Cover and simmer 15 minutes, or until fish flakes easily. Remove fish to warm platter. Reserve sauce.
3. While fish is cooking, in bowl, combine soy sauce and cornstarch. Set aside.
4. In skillet, heat oil over medium-low heat. Add zucchini, pepper, and bouillon. Stir-fry 1 minute.
5. Stir in mustard and sugar plus reserved sauce. Raise heat to medium and bring to a slow boil.
6. Stir in scallions and soy sauce mixture. Continue cooking until mixture starts to thicken. Pour over salmon.

Per serving: 247 calories; 68.1 mg. sodium; 6.8 gm. carbohydrates; 14.4 gm. fat.

* If not available, substitute 8 large fresh mushrooms, sliced.

Delicious

Red Snapper with Asparagus

SERVES 4

This is a delicacy every region will claim.

2 tablespoons vegetable oil, divided
1 pound asparagus, trimmed and
   cut in 2-inch pieces
1½ teaspoons sugar
1 pound red snapper fillets, cut in
   1-inch chunks
⅛ teaspoon ginger powder
2 cloves garlic, minced
½ cup boiling water

1 teaspoon low-sodium chicken
   bouillon
Dash of hot pepper flakes
¼ cup cold water
1 tablespoon cornstarch
½ cup Brown Sauce (page 233)
4 scallions, chopped, including
   greens

1. In wok, heat 1 tablespoon oil over medium-low heat. Add asparagus and stir-fry 2 minutes. Stir in sugar, blending thoroughly.
2. Push asparagus to sides of wok. To well created in center, add remaining oil, fish, ginger, and garlic. Stir-fry 2 minutes.
3. In bowl, combine boiling water, bouillon, and hot pepper flakes. Stir into fish mixture.
4. Raise heat to high and bring to a boil. Reduce heat to low and simmer 2 minutes.
5. While fish is cooking, in second bowl, combine cold water and cornstarch. Stir into fish mixture.
6. Add brown sauce, stirring to blend thoroughly.
7. Add scallions. Raise heat to medium and cook, stirring constantly, until mixture thickens.

Per serving: 264.6 calories; 90.9 mg. sodium; 17.8 gm. carbohydrates; 10.2 gm. fat.

Steamed Snapper with Pork Sauce   SERVES 8

The aromatic flavor of the Szechwan pepper spice is more pungent than biting in this dish of Fukien origin. An excellent counterpoint is Mandarin Rice with Peppers (page 214).

1 4-pound red snapper, scored on both sides
2½ tablespoons Szechwan Pepper Spice (page 229)
2 scallions, minced, including greens
2 slices ginger root, minced, or ¹⁄₁₆ teaspoon ginger powder
2 teaspoons sesame seed oil

1 leek, chopped, including greens
1 teaspoon dry sherry
¼ pound ground pork
½ cup boiling water
2 teaspoons low-sodium chicken bouillon
Black pepper to taste

1. In 9 x 13-inch casserole, place fish. Rub all over with Szechwan pepper spice, scallions, and ginger. Cover and refrigerate ½ hour.
2. In wok, heat oil over medium-low heat. Add leek and stir-fry 1 minute.
3. Add sherry and pork. Stir-fry 1 minute more, or until pork loses all pink color.
4. Add water, bouillon, and pepper, blending thoroughly. Remove from heat.
5. Place fish on heatproof dish on rack over boiling water. Spoon pork mixture over fish. Cover and steam ½ hour, or until fish flakes easily. Serve immediately.

Per serving: 221.8 calories; 23.8 mg. sodium; 2.8 gm. carbohydrates; 5.2 gm. fat.

Swordfish with Hot Sauce

SERVES 8

It is fitting that the Peking tradition inspired this royally elegant meal.

3 swordfish steaks (½ pound each)
¼ cup lemon juice
¼ cup orange juice
1 tablespoon red wine vinegar
Black pepper to taste
3 tablespoons low-sodium ketchup
2 tablespoons dry sherry
1 teaspoon low-sodium
   Worcestershire sauce (optional)
½ cup boiling water
2 teaspoons low-sodium chicken
   bouillon

1 tablespoon Chili Oil (page 230)
2 slices ginger root, minced, or
   ⅟₁₆ teaspoon ginger powder
2 scallions, chopped, including
   greens
2 cloves garlic, minced
¼ cup unsalted walnuts, crushed
2 tablespoons cold water
2 teaspoons cornstarch

1. In 9 x 13-inch casserole, combine first 8 ingredients. Cover and refrigerate at least 2 hours, turning fish occasionally.
2. In bowl, combine boiling water and bouillon. Set aside.
3. In wok, heat oil over low heat. Add ginger, scallions, garlic, and walnuts. Stir-fry 1 minute. Spoon around fish, along with half the marinade.
4. Preheat oven to broil.
5. Broil fish 6 inches from heat 5 minutes. Turn and broil 5 minutes more, or until fish flakes easily. Transfer fish to platter.
6. While fish is cooking, in bowl, combine cold water and cornstarch. Set aside.
7. When fish is done, in saucepan, combine remaining fish marinade and bouillon mixture. Bring to a slow boil over medium heat.
8. Reduce heat to low. Stir in cornstarch mixture. Cook, stirring constantly until mixture thickens. Pour sauce over fish.

Per serving: 184 calories; 3.3 mg. sodium; 6.1 gm. carbohydrates; 9.9 gm. fat.

Fragrant Fried Trout

SERVES 4

The Fukien tradition is well represented in this sumptuous meal. Good accompaniments might include Stir-Fried Snow Pea Pods (page 200) and boiled white rice.

2 trout (brook or rainbow), ¾ pound each, scored on each side
1 clove garlic, minced
2 egg whites
1 tablespoon low-sodium chicken bouillon
1½ tablespoons cornstarch
4 scallions, chopped, including greens
1 star anise
Pinch of Five-Spice Powder (page 228)

2 tablespoons Soy Sauce Substitute (page 227)
2 teaspoons red wine vinegar
1 slice ginger root, minced, or pinch of ginger powder
1½ tablespoons lemon peel, minced, or ¾ teaspoon lemon peel powder
2 tablespoons vegetable oil
¼ cup hot water
2 tablespoons sugar

1. In 9 x 13-inch casserole, combine first 5 ingredients. Let stand 10 minutes, turning once.
2. In bowl, combine scallions, star anise, five-spice powder, soy sauce, vinegar, ginger, and lemon peel. Set aside.
3. In wok, heat oil over low heat. Add fish and fry 7 minutes. Turn and fry 7 minutes more, adding 1 to 2 tablespoons soy sauce mixture, if necessary, to prevent sticking.
4. Transfer fish to warm platter.
5. To wok, add hot water, sugar, and remaining soy sauce mixture. Stir until sugar is dissolved. Spoon sauce over fish. Discard star anise.

Per serving: 362.5 calories; 64.2 mg. sodium; 15.8 gm. carbohydrates; 21.5 gm. fat.

Twice-Cooked Seafood

SERVES 8

Very Chinese, very good, but typical of no one region.

½ pound small shrimp, shelled, deveined, and chopped
3 tablespoons dry sherry
1 teaspoon cider vinegar
Black pepper to taste
½ pound cleaned squid, cut in 2-inch chunks
¼ cup lemon juice
2 teaspoons low-sodium chicken bouillon
8 dried black mushrooms*
1½ cups hot Chicken Stock (page 68)

⅓ cup cold water
1 teaspoon mustard powder
2 teaspoons cornstarch
1 tablespoon sesame seed oil
2 cloves garlic, minced
2 cups Chinese or American white cabbage, shredded
½ teaspoon sugar
2 cans (16 ounces) low-sodium corn niblets, drained
4 scallions, chopped, including greens

1. In bowl, combine first 4 ingredients. Cover and refrigerate ½ hour.
2. In second bowl, combine squid, lemon juice, and bouillon. Cover and refrigerate ½ hour.
3. In third bowl, combine mushrooms and chicken stock. Let stand ½ hour.
4. In fourth bowl, combine water, mustard powder, and cornstarch. Set aside.
5. In wok, heat oil over low heat. Add garlic and cabbage. Stir-fry 2 minutes.
6. Add sugar and stir to blend. Cover and simmer 2 minutes more.
7. Push cabbage to sides of wok. To well created in center, add shrimp mixture and corn. Stir-fry 1 minute. Push to sides of wok.
8. Add squid mixture and mushrooms and chicken stock. Stir-fry 2 minutes.
9. Stir in scallions and cornstarch mixture. Raise heat to high and cook until mixture thickens.

Per serving: 182 calories; 59.4 mg. sodium; 14.1 gm. carbohydrates; 3.8 gm. fat.

* If not available, substitute 8 large fresh mushrooms, sliced.

Seafood Casserole Cantonese   SERVES 8

Delicious served with Carrots and Ginger Apple (page 195) and boiled white rice.

1 1-pound lobster, cut into 2-inch
  pieces
¾ pound perch fillets, cut into 1-inch
  chunks
1 pint shucked oysters, liquid
  reserved
4 tablespoons dry sherry
1 tablespoon low-sodium beef
  bouillon
1 tablespoon peanut (or vegetable)
  oil
1 cup fresh mushrooms, sliced
3 cloves garlic, minced
2 slices ginger root, minced, or ¹⁄₁₆
  teaspoon ginger powder

2 tablespoons Black Bean Sauce
  (page 232)
¼ pound ground pork
2 cups Chicken Stock (page 68)
¼ cup cold water
1 tablespoon cornstarch
¼ head Chinese or American white
  cabbage, chopped
3 scallions, chopped, including
  greens
1 egg, lightly beaten

1. In bowl, combine first 5 ingredients. Cover and refrigerate 20 minutes.
2. In wok, heat oil over low heat. Add mushrooms, garlic, and ginger. Stir-fry 30 seconds.
3. Add black bean sauce and pork and stir-fry 1 minute more, or until pork loses all pink color.
4. Add seafood mixture to wok along with chicken stock. Raise heat to medium and bring to a slow boil. Reduce heat to low and simmer 3 minutes.
5. While wok mixture is cooking, in bowl, combine water and cornstarch. Set aside.
6. To wok, add cabbage and scallions. Raise heat to medium and slowly allow egg to stream into wok, stirring constantly.
7. Add reserved oyster liquid and cornstarch mixture, stirring until sauce thickens.

Per serving: 196 calories; 250.7 mg. sodium; 8.2 gm. carbohydrates; 7.2 gm. fat.

Seafood Sticks

SERVES 4

Traditionally a Peking dish known as Dragon and Phoenix Legs: Dragon being shrimp, and Phoenix, the chicken. In our version, as you see, we have used seafood only. It is just as good this way.

¼ pound shrimp, shelled,
   deveined, and minced
½ pound carp or flounder fillets,
   chopped
1 small onion, minced
½ cup bean sprouts, minced
⅟₁₆ teaspoon celery seed
¾ cup water

6 tablespoons cornstarch
1 tablespoon dry sherry
Black pepper to taste
1 teaspoon sesame seed oil
1 large sheet aluminum foil or
   waxed paper
1 cup vegetable oil

1. In blender or food processor, combine first 5 ingredients. Grind briefly.
2. In bowl, combine water and cornstarch. Set aside.
3. In second bowl, combine seafood mixture, sherry, pepper, and sesame seed oil, blending thoroughly. Divide into 8 equal portions.
4. Cut cellophane into 8 2 x 4-inch rectangles. Place one portion of seafood down the center of each rectangle.
5. Rub a little cornstarch mixture around edges of each rectangle. Fold long side toward center, slightly overlapping. Then fold up short ends.
6. Place sticks, folded side down, on heatproof plate. Place on rack over boiling water. Cover and steam 10 minutes. Transfer sticks to platter. Let cool 20 minutes.
7. In wok, heat vegetable oil over high heat until crackling.
8. Dip each seafood stick into remaining cornstarch mixture. Then lower into oil, using a strainer.
9. Deep-fry sticks until golden brown. Remove with strainer and drain. Cut away wrapper.

Per serving with carp: 302 calories; 70.9 mg. sodium; 23.7 gm. carbohydrates; 15.7 gm. fat.
Per serving with flounder: 281 calories; 86.9 mg. sodium; 23.7 gm. carbohydrates; 13.8 gm. fat.

Mixed Seafood in Hoisin Sauce · SERVES 8

This Cantonese dish is so delicious your guests will ask for more.

¾ pound shrimp, shelled,
deveined, and halved lengthwise
¾ pound scallops, halved
1 teaspoon low-sodium chicken
bouillon
2 egg whites, beaten
2½ tablespoons cornstarch
4 cups water
2 tablespoons vegetable oil, divided
2 slices ginger root, minced, or
1/16 teaspoon ginger powder

1 onion, minced
1½ tablespoons low-sodium beef
bouillon
2 tablespoons dry sherry
2 cups broccoli or cauliflower
flowerettes
1 teaspoon cider vinegar
Black pepper to taste
5 tablespoons Hoisin Sauce
Substiute (page 228)
¼ cup unsalted slivered almonds

1. In bowl, combine first 5 ingredients, blending thoroughly. Cover and refrigerate ½ hour.
2. In wok, bring water to a boil over high heat. Scatter seafood mixture into water and continue boiling until coating turns white. Drain into colander.
3. In wok, heat oil over low heat. Add ginger and onion. Stir-fry 1 minute.
4. Add remaining ingredients except seafood mixture. Stir-fry 30 seconds.
5. Spoon seafood mixture on top. Cover. Raise heat to medium and cook 1 minute.

Per serving with broccoli: 198 calories; 184.0 mg. sodium; 13.6 gm. carbohydrates; 7.5 gm. fat.
Per serving with cauliflower: 197 calories; 183.4 mg. sodium; 13.4 gm. carbohydrates; 7.4 gm. fat.

Drunken Lobster Plus Pork SERVES 4

Peking could not have done better in the days of the Imperial Family.

1 3-pound lobster, steamed and
   chopped into 2-inch pieces
¼ cup dry sherry
¼ cup white wine
Black pepper to taste
¼ pound pork, shredded
1 egg white
½ teaspoon celery seed
1 teaspoon cornstarch
1 cup boiling water

8 dried black mushrooms*
1 tablespoon peanut oil
1 can (8 ounces) water chestnuts,
   sliced
1 cup broccoli flowerettes
3 tablespoons Soy Sauce Substitute
   (page 227)
3 scallions, chopped, including
   greens

1. In bowl, combine first 4 ingredients. Cover and refrigerate ½ hour.
2. In second bowl, combine pork, egg white, celery seed, and cornstarch. Set aside.
3. In third bowl, combine boiling water and mushrooms. Let stand ½ hour.
4. In wok, heat oil over low heat. Add water chestnuts and broccoli. Stir-fry 1 minute.
5. Add pork mixture. Stir-fry 2 minutes more, or until pork loses all pink color.
6. Add lobster, including marinade.
7. Drain mushrooms and add to wok mixture.
8. Add soy sauce and scallions. Stir to blend. Raise heat to high and cook until mixture begins to boil, stirring often.

Per serving: 288 calories; 228.8 mg. sodium; 19.4 gm. carbohydrates; 10.4 gm. fat.

* If not available, substitute 8 large fresh mushrooms, sliced, and omit boiling water.

Lobster Casserole in Four Colors   SERVES 4

The northern influence is evident in this dish, which is fit for a king.

1 egg
½ teaspoon low-sodium chicken
  bouillon
2 teaspoons dry sherry
¹⁄₁₆ teaspoon ginger powder
¹⁄₁₆ teaspoon garlic powder
Black pepper to taste
1 tablespoon peanut (or vegetable)
  oil

1 clove garlic, minced
1 leek, chopped, including greens
1 can (8 ounces) bamboo shoots,
  chopped
1½ cups Chicken Stock (page 68),
  divided
¼ cup cold water
2 teaspoons cornstarch
1 pound lobster meat, chopped

1. Preheat oven to 325°.
2. In bowl, beat together first 6 ingredients. Set aside.
3. In wok, heat oil over low heat. Add garlic, leek, and bamboo shoots. Stir-fry 1 minute.
4. Add ½ cup chicken stock and cook 5 minutes. Transfer to 6-inch square casserole.
5. In second bowl, combine water and cornstarch. Stir into casserole.
6. Add remaining chicken stock, lobster, and egg mixture. Bake ½ hour, or until lightly browned on top.

Per serving: 234 calories; 269.5 mg. sodium; 17.2 gm. carbohydrates; 8.6 gm. fat.

Lemon Lobster   SERVES 4

Of no specific region, but sure to be loved by all, the flavors of this dish go especially well with Chinese Chicken and Rice (page 215).

1 pound lobster meat, chopped
3 tablespoons Soy Sauce Substitute
  (page 227)
2 teaspoons dry sherry
2 teaspoons peanut (or vegetable)
  oil
2 slices ginger root, or ¹⁄₁₆ teaspoon
  ginger powder
1 clove garlic, minced
1 onion, sliced

4 scallions, chopped, including
  greens
1 cup snow pea pods, halved
  diagonally
⅓ cup lemon juice
1 teaspoon low-sodium chicken
  bouillon
1 teaspoon low-sodium beef
  bouillon

1. In bowl, combine first 3 ingredients. Cover and refrigerate 15 minutes.

2. In wok, heat oil over low heat. Add ginger, garlic, and onion. Stir-fry 1 minute, or until onion is wilted.
3. Add scallions and snow pea pods. Stir-fry 30 seconds.
4. Raise heat to high. Add lobster mixture, lemon juice, and both bouillons. Cook 5 minutes, or until mixture bubbles around the edges.

Per serving: 179 calories; 255.7 mg. sodium; 13.7 gm. carbohydrates; 5.7 gm. fat.

Scallops in Soy Sauce
SERVES 8

When you serve this lovely eastern-style delight, Peanutty Noodles with Chicken (page 211) is a good companion.

1½ pounds scallops
¾ cup Soy Sauce Substitute (page 227), divided
3 scallions, chopped, including greens
1/16 teaspoon ginger powder

2 cups boiling water
16 dried black mushrooms*
2 teaspoons cornstarch
1 tablespoon sesame seed oil
1 teaspoon lemon juice

1. In bowl, combine scallops, ½ cup soy sauce, scallions, and ginger. Cover and refrigerate ½ hour. Drain, reserving marinade.
2. In second bowl, combine boiling water and mushrooms. Let stand ½ hour. Drain.
3. In third bowl, combine remaining soy sauce and cornstarch. Set aside.
4. In wok, heat oil over medium heat. Add scallops. Stir-fry 30 seconds.
5. Add reserved scallop marinade and mushrooms. Raise heat to high. Cook 3 minutes, stirring occasionally.
6. Add cornstarch mixture and lemon juice. Cook until mixture thickens, stirring frequently.

Per serving: 113.6 calories; 235.8 mg. sodium; 7.3 gm. carbohydrates; 2.8 gm. fat.

* If not available, substitute 16 large fresh mushrooms, sliced, and omit boiling water.

Scallops in Orange Sauce

SERVES 4

This northern dish needs no explanation—just tasting.

¾ pound scallops
Black pepper to taste
1 egg white
2 tablespoons cornstarch, divided
1 teaspoon sesame seed oil
2 scallions, chopped, including
   greens
4 fresh mushrooms, sliced
2 teaspoons low-sodium chicken
   bouillon

1 tablespoon dry sherry
1 tablespoon orange peel, minced,
   or dash of orange peel powder
¼ cup water
2 tablespoons Soy Sauce Substitute
   (page 227)
1 red pepper, cut in strips
1 teaspoon low-sodium ketchup
   (optional)

1. In bowl, combine first 4 ingredients. Cover and refrigerate ½ hour.
2. In wok, heat oil over low heat. Add scallions and mushrooms. Stir-fry
   30 seconds.
3. Add bouillon, sherry, orange peel, and water. Stir to blend.
4. Add scallop mixture and remaining ingredients. Cover and simmer 5
   minutes.
5. Raise heat to medium and bring mixture to a slow boil. Continue boiling 3 minutes.

Per serving: 136 calories; 235.5 mg. sodium; 12.7 gm. carbohydrates; 2.4 gm. fat.

Excellent — too much cornstarch

Scallops and Almonds

SERVES 4

So easy. So Cantonese. Great with a side dish of Hot Ribs (page 35) and
boiled white rice.

¾ pound scallops
2 tablespoons dry sherry
1½ tablespoons low-sodium
   chicken bouillon
1 tablespoon sesame seed oil,
   divided
½ pound green beans, halved
   diagonally

½ can (4 ounces) water chestnuts,
   sliced
1 clove garlic, minced
1 slice ginger root, minced, or pinch
   of ginger powder
¼ cup unsalted slivered almonds
Black pepper to taste

1. In bowl, combine first 3 ingredients. Let stand 10 minutes.

2. In wok, heat oil over low heat. Add green beans, water chestnuts, garlic, and ginger. Stir-fry 2 minutes.
3. Add almonds and pepper. Stir to blend.
4. Add scallop mixture. Cover and simmer 5 minutes.

Per serving: 243 calories; 241.2 mg. sodium; 53.3 gm. carbohydrates; 12.2 gm. fat.

Braised Shrimp Bamboo   SERVES 4

A thoroughly enjoyable and light eastern-style treat. Combine with Szechwan Fried Rice (page 208) for a sumptuous meal.

½ pound shrimp, shelled, deveined, and halved lengthwise
2 tablespoons Soy Sauce Substitute (page 227)
1 tablespoon sesame seed oil
1 onion, minced
1 clove garlic, minced
3 tablespoons dry sherry
1 teaspoon cornstarch
½ teaspoon mustard powder
½ tablespoon sugar

1 tablespoon low-sodium tomato paste
1 can (8 ounces) bamboo shoots, sliced
½ cup boiling water
2 teaspoons low-sodium chicken bouillon
2 scallions, chopped, including greens

1. In bowl, combine first 2 ingredients. Let stand 15 minutes, stirring occasionally.
2. In wok, heat oil over low heat. Add onion and garlic and stir-fry 1 minute.
3. In bowl, combine sherry, cornstarch, and mustard powder. Set aside.
4. To wok, add shrimp mixture. Stir-fry 30 seconds.
5. Add sherry mixture, sugar, tomato paste, and bamboo shoots. Stir to blend thoroughly. Cover and simmer 5 minutes.
6. While shrimp mixture is cooking, in bowl, combine boiling water and bouillon. Stir into wok mixture along with scallions. Raise heat to medium and cook 1 minute more, or until mixture starts to bubble, stirring often.

Per serving: 148.1 calories; 89.0 mg. sodium; 14.4 gm. carbohydrates; 5.3 gm. fat.

Steamed Shrimp with Pork Sauce   SERVES 4

When something tastes as good as this Cantonese dish, it deserves equally delicious accompaniments. Try Yunnan Curried Mushrooms (page 29) and Hot and Sour Soup I (page 70) plus boiled white rice.

½ pound small shrimp, shelled, deveined, and halved lengthwise
1 tablespoon lemon juice
1 clove garlic, minced
2 slices ginger root, minced, or ¹⁄₁₆ teaspoon ginger powder
2 tablespoons Soy Sauce Substitute (page 227)

⅛ pound ground pork
½ can (4 ounces) bamboo shoots, minced
1 teaspoon dry sherry
Black pepper to taste
Dash of orange peel powder

1. In bowl, combine first 2 ingredients. Cover and refrigerate ½ hour.
2. In second bowl, combine remaining ingredients, blending thoroughly.
3. On heatproof platter, place shrimp mixture. Shred pork mixture over all.
4. Set platter on rack over boiling water. Cover and steam 10 minutes.
5. Serve immediately.

Per serving: 133 calories; 92.5 mg. sodium; 9.1 gm. carbohydrates; 3.1 gm. fat.

Red and Green Shrimp   SERVES 8

Hoisin Rice in Four (page 211) is a wonderful side dish for this Cantonese treat.

1½ pounds small shrimp
1 egg white
1 tablespoon lemon juice
1 teaspoon low-sodium chicken bouillon
Dash of hot pepper flakes
2½ tablespoons cornstarch, divided
½ cup water
1 cup vegetable oil

1 clove garlic, minced
½ pound snow pea pods
2 tomatoes, chopped fine
2 tablespoons dry sherry
3 scallions, chopped, including greens
1 teaspoon low-sodium beef bouillon

1. In bowl, combine first 5 ingredients plus 1 tablespoon cornstarch. Cover and refrigerate ½ hour.
2. In second bowl, combine remaining cornstarch and water. Set aside.

3. In wok, heat oil over high heat until crackling. Add shrimp mixture. Reduce heat to medium and fry 1 minute, or until coating is golden all over.
4. With strainer, remove shrimp to platter.
5. Pour off all but 1 tablespoon oil. Reduce heat to low. Add garlic, snow pea pods, and tomatoes. Stir-fry 1 minute.
6. Add sherry, scallions, bouillon, and shrimp. Stir to blend.
7. Add cornstarch mixture and stir until mixture thickens.

Per serving: 181 calories; 124.6 mg. sodium; 12.5 gm. carbohydrates; 6.7 gm. fat.

Braised Shrimp with Leek

SERVES 4

This Szechwan-style dish is easy to make and simply delicious. Wonderful with Beef (or Chicken) Lo Mein (page 218).

⅓ cup water
1½ teaspoons mustard powder
1 tablespoon vegetable oil
1 leek cut in 1-inch rounds, greens chopped
1 clove garlic, minced
1 fresh chili pepper, minced
1 tablespoon orange peel, minced, or ½ teaspoon orange peel powder

¾ pound medium shrimp, shelled, deveined, and halved lengthwise
1 tablespoon dry sherry
1 teaspoon low-sodium beef bouillon

1. In bowl, combine first 2 ingredients. Set aside.
2. In wok, heat oil over low heat. Add leek, garlic, and chili pepper. Stir-fry 30 seconds.
3. Add orange peel and stir-fry 30 seconds more.
4. Add shrimp. Stir to blend.
5. Add sherry, bouillon, and mustard mixture. Cover and simmer 5 minutes, or until shrimp turn pink all over.

Per serving: 140 calories; 124.5 mg. sodium; 7.1 gm. carbohydrates; 4.7 gm. fat.

Shrimp in Pepper Sauce   SERVES 4

Don't be put off by the long list of ingredients in this Szechwan-style meal.
There are very few steps, and the result—well, judge for yourself.

¾ pound small shrimp
2 tablespoons Soy Sauce Substitute
   (page 227)
1 tablespoon white vinegar
2 tablespoons water
½ tablespoon cornstarch
1 egg white
2 teaspoons vegetable oil
2 fresh chili peppers, seeded and
   minced
1/16 teaspoon Szechwan peppercorns
1 green pepper, sliced thin

1 cup unsalted slivered almonds
1 clove garlic, minced
1 slice ginger root, minced, or dash
   of ginger powder
1 small leek, sliced, including
   greens
1 teaspoon sesame seed oil
2 tablespoons dry sherry or dry
   white vermouth
¼ cup boiling water

1. In bowl, combine first 6 ingredients, blending thoroughly. Cover and
   refrigerate ½ hour.
2. In wok, heat vegetable oil over low heat. Add chili peppers, Szechwan
   peppercorns, green pepper, almonds, garlic, ginger, and leek. Stir-fry
   2 minutes.
3. Push vegetable mixture to sides of wok. To well created in center, add
   sesame seed oil.
4. Add shrimp mixture. Raise heat to medium and stir-fry until shrimp
   turn pink all over.
5. Raise heat to high. Add remaining ingredients and stir-fry until mixture
   thickens.

Per serving: 230.5 calories; 132.8 mg. sodium; 12.8 gm. carbohydrates; 11.3 gm. fat.

Squid and Mushrooms

SERVES 4

The mildly sweet flavor of the squid is beautifully complemented by the alternating sweet, "salty," and pungent accents that punctuate this eastern dish.

1 pound cleaned squid, cut in 1-inch chunks
1½ cups boiling water, divided
1 tablespoon cider vinegar
8 dried black mushrooms*
1 tablespoon low-sodium chicken bouillon
¼ cup cold water
1 tablespoon cornstarch
1 tablespoon vegetable oil
1 onion, minced

2 slices ginger root, or ¹⁄₁₆ teaspoon ginger powder
2 tablespoons Soy Sauce Substitute (page 227)
1 cup snow pea pods
1 teaspoon sugar
2 teaspoons dry sherry
4 scallions, chopped, including greens

1. In bowl, combine squid, ½ cup boiling water, and vinegar. Let stand ½ hour, then drain.
2. In second bowl, combine remaining boiling water and mushrooms. Let stand ½ hour. Then drain, reserving ⅔ cup mushroom liquid.
3. In third bowl, combine reserved mushroom liquid with bouillon, stirring until bouillon is dissolved. Set aside.
4. In fourth bowl, combine cold water and cornstarch. Set aside.
5. In wok, heat oil over low heat. Add onion and ginger. Stir-fry 1 minute, or until onion is wilted.
6. Add squid and soy sauce. Stir to blend.
7. Add snow pea pods. Raise heat to medium and stir-fry 1 minute.
8. Stir in sugar, sherry, scallions, and mushrooms.
9. Raise heat to high. Add bouillon mixture and cornstarch mixture, blending thoroughly. Cook until mixture bubbles around the edges, stirring frequently. Discard ginger.

Per serving: 240 calories; 14.5 mg. sodium; 18.8 gm. carbohydrates; 5.9 gm. fat.

* If not available, substitute 8 large fresh mushrooms, sliced, and omit 1 cup boiling water.

Squid and Cabbage with Duck Sauce

SERVES 4

Eloquent in its simplicity, this dish with a northern flair is excellent served with Chicken with Vegetable Marinade (page 92).

1 pound cleaned squid, cut in
  1-inch chunks
3 tablespoons lemon juice
1½ tablespoons sesame seed oil,
  divided
2 cups Chinese or American white
  cabbage, shredded

1 teaspoon sugar
¼ cup cold water
1 teaspoon mustard powder
Black pepper to taste
2 tablespoons Duck Sauce (page
  234)

1. In bowl, combine first 2 ingredients. Let stand 20 minutes.
2. In wok, heat 1 tablespoon oil over low heat. Add cabbage. Stir-fry 2 minutes.
3. Stir in sugar. Cover and cook 2 minutes more.
4. While cabbage is cooking, in bowl, combine water and mustard powder. Set aside.
5. Push cabbage mixture to sides of wok. To well formed in center, add remaining oil.
6. Raise heat to medium. Add squid mixture and stir-fry 30 seconds.
7. Add pepper and mustard mixture, blending thoroughly.
8. Stir in duck sauce, blending thoroughly, and cook 1 minute more.

Per serving: 144.1 calories; 30.1 mg. sodium; 8.2 gm. carbohydrates; 3.1 gm. fat.

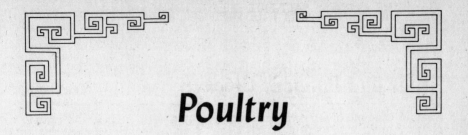

Poultry

In China, poultry almost always means chicken. Smaller birds, such as squab and pheasant, are too expensive for everyday fare and are reserved as delicacies of the banquet table. As for duck, though we Americans regard Peking duck or pressed duck as Chinese specialties, in truth, these dishes are not nearly as popular in China as they are here.

Chicken is another matter. Although as plentiful as pork, chicken is held in much greater esteem, in part because it is companion to the cock, which symbolizes sun, vigor, male potency, benevolence, and universal life.

Chicken blends with and enhances the various tastes and textures of every regional cooking style. For family dining, it is usually cut up and prepared in any of the more than 100 ways the Chinese have devised. For banquets, it is roasted whole and served with a luxurious sauce.

So whether you like your chicken hot or sweet, spicy or mellow, in succulent shreds, silky velveted tidbits, or tempting nuggets, there is a Chinese chicken dish to charm your senses, and tantalize your palate.

Spicy Fried Chicken   SERVES 8

Green Beans with Pork Bits (page 198) go well with this Szechwan dish.

¼ teaspoon ground cinnamon
¹⁄₁₆ teaspoon hot pepper flakes
3 cloves garlic, minced
1 teaspoon sugar
2 tablespoons dried cilantro (or parsley)

2 tablespoons low-sodium beef bouillon
4 whole chicken breasts, skinned, boned, and cut in 1-inch chunks
¼ cup cornstarch
½ cup vegetable oil, divided

1. In large dish, combine first 6 ingredients, blending thoroughly.
2. Roll chicken pieces in spice mixture. Let stand 20 minutes.
3. Add cornstarch. Toss to blend.
4. In wok, heat half the oil over medium heat. Add half the chicken and stir-fry until crust turns golden brown. Transfer to platter.
5. Repeat Step 4 with remaining oil and chicken.

Per serving: 283.6 calories; 59.6 mg. sodium; 9.5 gm. carbohydrates; 17.5 gm. fat.

Sweet and Pungent Chicken SERVES 4

Another example of the creative Cantonese style.

2 slices ginger root, chopped, or
⅟₁₆ teaspoon ginger powder
4 scallions, chopped, including
greens
2 teaspoons low-sodium chicken
bouillon
1 tablespoon low-sodium
Worcestershire sauce
2 tablespoons dry sherry
¼ cup water
4 tablespoons Soy Sauce Substitute
(page 227), divided
2 whole chicken breasts, skinned,
boned, and cubed
Dash of Five-Spice Powder (page
228)

2 tablespoons white vinegar
⅟₁₆ teaspoon ground Szechwan
peppercorns
2 teaspoons orange peel, minced,
or ½ teaspoon orange peel
powder
1½ tablespoons vegetable (or
peanut) oil
1 pound green beans, halved
diagonally
½ teaspoon sugar
1 teaspoon sesame seed oil

1. In blender or food processor, combine first 6 ingredients plus 2 tablespoons soy sauce. Puree.
2. In bowl, combine chicken and scallion mixture. Toss to blend. Let stand 15 minutes. Drain, reserving marinade.
3. In second bowl, combine remaining soy sauce, five-spice powder, vinegar, Szechwan pepper, and orange peel. Set aside.
4. In wok, heat vegetable oil over medium heat. Add chicken and stir-fry 1 minute, or until chicken turns white all over.
5. Push chicken to sides of wok. Add green beans and 2 tablespoons soy sauce mixture. Stir-fry 30 seconds.
6. Stir in sugar and remaining soy sauce mixture, blending thoroughly.
7. Stir in chicken marinade and sesame seed oil. Stir-fry 30 seconds.

Per serving: 237.1 calories; 65.9 mg. sodium; 12.6 gm. carbohydrates; 42.2 gm. fat.

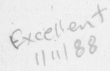
Excellent
11/11/88

Excellent

Stuffed Chicken of Many Flavors   SERVES 8

This dish with northern overtones requires a little work in preparation, but it isn't hard and the result is memorably worth the effort.

1 3-pound chicken, cleaned, washed, and dried
2 cloves garlic, blanched and mashed
1 teaspoon Szechwan peppercorns, crushed
½ teaspoon ground cinnamon
¼ teaspoon ground nutmeg
1 onion, minced
1 tablespoon vegetable oil
2 cloves garlic, minced
2 slices ginger root, minced, or ¹⁄₁₆ teaspoon ginger powder
½ can (4 ounces) water chestnuts, chopped
½ can (4 ounces) bamboo shoots, sliced

6 scallions, chopped, including greens
3 tablespoons dry sherry
½ cup dried cilantro (or parsley)
6 tablespoons Soy Sauce Substitute (page 227), divided
¼ cup unsalted walnuts, crushed
2½ cups boiled white rice
½ cup lemon juice, divided
4 teaspoons low-sodium chicken bouillon
2 tablespoons sesame seed oil

1. With knife, cut the membrane between the skin of the chicken and the meat.
2. With fingers, hold back the skin and rub the meat with the mashed garlic, Szechwan peppercorns, cinnamon, nutmeg, and onion. Then lower the skin to cover the meat.
3. In wok, heat vegetable oil over low heat. Add minced garlic, ginger, and water chestnuts. Stir-fry 1 minute.
4. Add bamboo shoots and scallions. Stir-fry 30 seconds.
5. Add sherry, cilantro, 3 tablespoons soy sauce, and walnuts. Stir-fry 1 minute.
6. Add rice and 2 tablespoons lemon juice plus bouillon. Stir-fry 2 minutes.
7. Stir in sesame seed oil and remaining soy sauce, blending thoroughly.
8. Preheat oven to 375°.
9. Stuff chicken with rice mixture. Place chicken, breast side up, on rack in roasting pan. Roast 15 minutes.
10. Reduce heat to 325° and roast 1 hour more, or until chicken is fork tender and juices run clear, basting occasionally with remaining lemon juice.

Per serving: 360.8 calories; 81.2 mg. sodium; 30.7 gm. carbohydrates; 16.4 gm. fat.

Peanutty Chicken and Scallions   SERVES 8

You will love this savory, succulent, and sticky Szechwan dish. For balance, try it with Rice and Mixed Vegetables (page 212).

1 cup boiling water
4 teaspoons low-sodium chicken
  bouillon
3 tablespoons low-sodium peanut
  butter
2 tablespoons peanut oil
4 whole chicken breasts, skinned,
  boned and cut in 1-inch chunks
½ green pepper, chopped

¹⁄₁₆ teaspoon hot pepper flakes
4 cloves garlic, minced
2 tablespoons dry sherry
1 tablespoon red wine vinegar
2 teaspoons sugar
2 tablespoons raisins*
6 scallions, chopped, including
  greens

1. In small saucepan, combine boiling water and bouillon. Turn heat to low and cook 5 minutes.
2. Add peanut butter and simmer 5 minutes, stirring often.
3. While bouillon mixture is heating, in wok, heat oil over low heat. Add chicken, green pepper, hot pepper flakes, and garlic. Stir-fry 2 minutes, or until chicken turns white.
4. Stir in sherry, vinegar, sugar, and 2 tablespoons bouillon mixture. Heat 1 minute.
5. Stir in raisins. Cook 2 minutes more.
6. Add remaining bouillon mixture and scallions. Cook 2 minutes more, stirring frequently.

Per serving: 169.1 calories; 33.0 mg. sodium; 12.0 gm. carbohydrates; 8.5 gm. fat.

* Preserved in nonsodium ingredient.

Lemon Chicken
SERVES 4

Every region has its own special way of preparing this dish, for Lemon Chicken is one of the most popular dishes in and from China. It is also one of the easiest to prepare. Below is our variation of this delectable offering. Accent simply with Snow Pea Pods and Bamboo Shoots (page 200) and boiled white rice.

2 half chicken breasts, boned, skinned, and cut into 4 equal strips
⅓ cup lemon juice, divided
½ cup all-purpose flour
⅔ cup water
1 tablespoon low-sodium chicken bouillon
¹⁄₁₆ teaspoon ginger powder
Black pepper to taste

Juice plus grated rind from 1 large lemon
4 tablespoons sugar
4 tablespoons white vinegar
¾ cup Chicken Stock (page 68), divided
1 teaspoon cornstarch
1½ cups vegetable oil

1. In bowl, combine chicken and 2 tablespoons lemon juice. Let stand 15 minutes, turning once.
2. In second bowl, combine remaining lemon juice, flour, and water, stirring to form a batter. Then stir in bouillon, ginger, and pepper, blending thoroughly. (Batter should be a little runny.)
3. In saucepan, combine fresh lemon juice and rind, sugar, vinegar, chicken stock, and cornstarch. Stir to blend. Set aside.
4. In wok, heat oil over high heat until sizzling.
5. Dip chicken in batter and deep-fry until golden brown. Drain.
6. While chicken is frying, heat lemon sauce over medium-low heat until it bubbles around the edges.
7. Cut chicken into bite-size pieces. Pour sauce over all.

Per serving: 331.8 calories; 38.3 mg. sodium; 42.8 gm. carbohydrates; 11.4 gm. fat.

Glazed Chicken and Vegetables   SERVES 4

The light, glazed sauce and chopped vegetable combination signal another meal from a Cantonese kitchen.

2 half chicken breasts, skinned, boned, and shredded
1 tablespoon low-sodium chicken bouillon
1 tablespoon dry sherry
1 egg white
2 tablespoons cornstarch, divided
2 cups Chicken Stock (page 68)
2 tablespoons Soy Sauce Substitute (page 227)
1 teaspoon cider (or red wine) vinegar
Black pepper to taste

2 tablespoons sesame seed oil
1 carrot, scraped and cut in ¼-inch rounds
2 slices ginger root, minced, or ¹⁄₁₆ teaspoon ginger powder
1 cup broccoli flowerettes, chopped
8 fresh mushrooms, sliced
¼ cup cold water
1½ teaspoons mustard powder
4 scallions, chopped, including greens

1. In bowl, combine first 4 ingredients plus 1 tablespoon cornstarch, blending thoroughly. Cover and refrigerate ½ hour.
2. In second bowl, combine chicken stock, soy sauce, vinegar, and pepper. Set aside.
3. In wok, heat oil over medium heat. Add carrot, ginger, broccoli, and mushrooms. Stir-fry 1 minute.
4. Add chicken stock mixture. Reduce heat to low and simmer 1 minute.
5. While mixture is cooking, in third bowl, combine remaining cornstarch, water, and mustard powder. Set aside.
6. Raise heat under wok mixture to medium. When sauce starts to bubble around the edges, add chicken mixture and scallions, stirring to blend. Cook 1 minute, or until chicken turns white all over.
7. Stir in cornstarch mixture and continue stirring until sauce thickens.

Per serving: 241.9 calories; 68.2 mg. sodium; 15.9 gm. carbohydrates; 11.5 gm. fat.

Excelent

Chow Mein

SERVES 4

One of the best-known and most popular Chinese dishes, chow mein is usually a combination of meats and vegetables, or vegetables alone. The combinations vary from region to region depending on the fresh local produce.

2 tablespoons vegetable oil, divided
1 onion, sliced
1 cup Chinese or American white
  cabbage, shredded
¼ pound pork, shredded
1 half chicken breast, skinned,
  boned, and cubed
2 tablespoons Soy Sauce Substitute
  (page 227), divided

2 teaspoons dry sherry
1½ teaspoons cornstarch
½ can (4 ounces) bamboo shoots,
  sliced
⅓ pound bean sprouts

1. In wok, heat 1 tablespoon oil over low heat. Add onion and cabbage. Stir-fry 2 minutes. Set aside.
2. In bowl, combine pork, chicken, ½ tablespoon soy sauce, sherry, and cornstarch. Toss to blend.
3. Reheat wok mixture over low heat. Add pork and chicken mixture. Turn heat to medium and continue stir-frying 2 minutes, or until chicken is white all over. Transfer mixture to bowl.
4. To wok, add remaining tablespoon oil. Add bamboo shoots and bean sprouts. Stir-fry 2 minutes.
5. Add meat and cabbage mixture plus remaining soy sauce. Stir-fry 2 minutes more.

Per serving: 370.6 calories; 45.7 mg. sodium; 49.6 gm. carbohydrates; 14.8 gm. fat.

Curried Chicken with Pineapple   SERVES 4

Although curry came to China via Yunnan and Kweichou, the Cantonese like it as much as their western neighbors. This dish is one delectable example. Serve it with Fried Rice and Oysters (page 207) or Noodles with Sesame Paste Sauce (page 222).

1 tablespoon vegetable oil
2 whole chicken breasts, skinned, boned, and cut into 1-inch chunks
2 cloves garlic, minced
1 leek, chopped, including greens
Black pepper to taste
1 tablespoon Curry Powder (page 232)

2 tomatoes, chopped
1 can (8 ounces) dietetic crushed pineapple, drained, juice reserved
1 teaspoon cornstarch
1 tablespoon cold water
2 scallions, chopped, including greens

1. In wok, heat oil over low heat. Add chicken, garlic, leek, and pepper. Stir-fry 1 minute, or until chicken turns white all over.
2. Stir in curry powder and tomatoes. Stir-fry 2 minutes more.
3. Stir in pineapple. Simmer 2 minutes, stirring occasionally.
4. While mixture is cooking, in bowl, combine reserved pineapple juice, cornstarch, and water. Stir into wok along with scallions and stir-fry 1 minute more, or until mixture thickens.

Per serving: 216.2 calories; 56.4 mg. sodium; 17.3 gm. carbohydrates; 6.5 gm. fat.

Steamed Chicken in Oyster Sauce   SERVES 4

Adapted from a Cantonese specialty, but we prefer steaming to simmering. The oyster sauce is not fishy at all, but rather a delicate accent for the chicken. Beef Lo Mein (page 218) completes the meal.

8 dried black mushrooms*
1 cup boiling water
2 whole chicken breasts, skinned, boned, and cubed
4 scallions, chopped, including greens

2 slices ginger root, shredded, or ¹⁄₁₆ teaspoon ginger powder
1 tablespoon dry sherry
2 teaspoons low-sodium beef bouillon
⅓ cup Oyster Sauce (page 234)

1. In bowl, combine first 2 ingredients. Let stand ½ hour. Drain, reserving half the liquid. Cut each mushroom in half. Set aside.

2. On double-duty aluminum foil, place chicken. Top with mushrooms, scallions, and ginger.
3. Add sherry, bouillon, oyster sauce, and remaining mushroom liquid. Wrap tightly.
4. On heatproof platter, place aluminum foil package. Place platter on rack in steamer over boiling water. Cover and steam 1 hour.

Per serving: 145.1 calories; 68.5 mg. sodium; 4.3 gm. carbohydrates; 3.6 gm. fat.

* If not available, substitute 8 small fresh mushrooms, halved, and use only ½ cup boiling water.

Garlic Chicken with Snow Pea Pods   SERVES 4

It seems like a lot of garlic, but all it is is a lot of good Szechwan taste.

6 cloves garlic, blanched and mashed
2 whole chicken breasts, boned, skinned, and sliced into thin strips
¼ cup water, divided
1 teaspoon mustard powder
1½ teaspoons cornstarch
2 fresh chili peppers, seeded and minced, or ⅟₁₆ teaspoon hot pepper flakes

3 tablespoons dry sherry
2 teaspoons vegetable oil
⅔ cup Chicken Stock (page 68)
1 tablespoon low-sodium beef bouillon
1 teaspoon cider vinegar
4 scallions, chopped, including greens
1 cup snow pea pods, halved diagonally

1. In bowl, combine first 2 ingredients. Stir to blend. Set aside.
2. In second bowl, combine half the water and mustard powder. Set aside.
3. In third bowl, combine remaining water and cornstarch. Set aside.
4. In fourth bowl, combine chili peppers and sherry. Set aside.
5. In wok, heat oil over low heat. Add chicken mixture and stir-fry 3 minutes, or until chicken turns white all over.
6. Add chicken stock, bouillon, and vinegar. Stir to blend.
7. Add scallions and snow pea pods. Simmer 5 minutes.
8. Add mustard powder and cornstarch mixtures plus sherry mixture. Raise heat to medium and cook until mixture thickens, stirring occasionally.

Per serving: 209.3 calories; 69.0 mg. sodium; 12.0 gm. carbohydrates; 6.3 gm. fat.

Pungent Creamed
Corn Chicken   SERVES 4

Each ingredient works in counterpoint with every other in this marvelous dish of eastern influence. Steaming brings it all into savory harmony. Serve with Braised Leeks in Soy Sauce (page 198).

2 whole chicken breasts, skinned
  and halved
1½ tablespoons low-sodium
  chicken bouillon
2 tablespoons Soy Sauce Substitute
  (page 227)
1 can (8 ounces) low-sodium
  creamed corn
1 tablespoon dry sherry

Dash of Five-Spice Powder (page
  228)
1/16 teaspoon ground nutmeg
1 green pepper, minced
1/16 teaspoon ginger powder
Black pepper to taste
1 teaspoon sesame seed oil
2 scallions, chopped, including
  greens

1. On heatproof platter, place chicken. Rub with bouillon. Set aside.
2. In bowl, combine soy sauce, corn, and sherry, blending thoroughly.
3. Stir in remaining ingredients. Spoon over chicken.
4. Cover platter with aluminum foil. Place on rack in steamer over boiling water. Cover and steam 45 minutes, or until chicken is fork tender.

Per serving: 209 calories; 65.9 mg. sodium; 16.5 gm. carbohydrates; 5.8 gm. fat.

Stir-Fried Chicken Legs
with Soy Sauce Peaches   SERVES 4

This has the understated subtlety of Canton, although the results will be loudly proclaimed. Cucumber and Onion Salad (page 104) is a refreshing accompaniment.

8 chicken drumsticks, skinned,
  boned, and cut in 1-inch chunks
1 can (8 ounces) dietetic peaches,
  sliced, including juice
Black pepper to taste
2 tablespoons Soy Sauce Substitute
  (page 227)

1 tablespoon sesame seed oil
2 tablespoons cold water
1 teaspoon cornstarch
6 scallions, chopped, including
  greens

1. In bowl, combine first 4 ingredients. Stir to blend. Let stand 20 minutes. Drain, reserving marinade.

2. In wok, heat oil over low heat. Add chicken and peaches and simmer 2 minutes, stirring occasionally.
3. While chicken mixture is simmering, in bowl, combine cold water and cornstarch. Set aside.
4. To wok, add scallions and reserved marinade. Stir to blend.
5. Add cornstarch mixture and continue stirring until mixture thickens.

Per serving: 296 calories; 138.3 mg. sodium; 8.0 gm. carbohydrates; 11.8 gm. fat.

Sweet Chicken and Mushrooms SERVES 4

One of the milder dishes in the Szechwan repertoire and simply marvelous with Many-Flavored Fried Rice (page 213).

4 chicken thighs
1¾ cups hot water
2 teaspoons low-sodium beef bouillon
2 tablespoons red wine vinegar
1 stick cinnamon
1 star anise
Dash of Five-Spice Powder (page 228)
1 teaspoon sesame seed oil
8 dried black mushrooms, or 4 fresh mushrooms, halved

1 tablespoon vegetable oil
1 onion, minced
1 slice ginger root, minced, or pinch of ginger powder
1 teaspoon Szechwan peppercorns
3 tablespoons dry sherry
1 teaspoon cornstarch
½ teaspoon mustard powder

1. In 8-inch square casserole, combine first 9 ingredients. Cover and refrigerate at least 2 hours, turning chicken occasionally.
2. Preheat oven to 350°.
3. Bake chicken, covered, 40 minutes, turning once. Transfer to warm platter. Reserve marinade.
4. In wok, heat oil over low heat. Add onion, ginger, and Szechwan peppercorns. Stir-fry 1 minute.
5. Stir in chicken marinade. Simmer 2 minutes, stirring occasionally.
6. While sauce is simmering, in bowl, combine sherry, cornstarch, and mustard powder, blending thoroughly. Stir into wok mixture and continue stirring until mixture thickens. Discard cinnamon stick, star anise, and Szechwan peppercorns.
7. Pour sauce over chicken.

Per serving: 157.5 calories; 51.4 mg. sodium; 9.2 gm. carbohydrates; 8.8 gm. fat.

Chicken Sub Gum

SERVES 4

We have taken a few liberties with this traditional Cantonese dish because sub gum means a variety of foods, diced and stir-fried. The dish originated as a tasty way to prepare leftovers.

2 tablespoons peanut oil
1 onion, sliced
½ green pepper, chopped
2 half chicken breasts, skinned, boned, and diced
1 tablespoon dry sherry
½ can (4 ounces) bamboo shoots, sliced
½ can (4 ounces) water chestnuts, chopped

1 cup Chinese or American white cabbage, shredded
½ teaspoon sugar
¼ cup unsalted almonds, chopped
½ cup Chicken Stock (page 68)
2 teaspoons low-sodium chicken bouillon
¼ cup Black Bean Sauce (page 232)

1. In wok, heat oil over medium-low heat. Add onion, pepper, and chicken. Stir-fry until chicken turns white all over.
2. Add sherry, bamboo shoots, and water chestnuts. Stir-fry 1 minute.
3. Push chicken mixture to sides of wok. To well created in center, add cabbage. Stir-fry 1 minute.
4. Stir in sugar. Then add almonds, chicken stock, and bouillon. Reduce heat to low and simmer 5 minutes, stirring often.
5. Stir in black bean sauce and simmer 5 minutes more, stirring often.

Per serving: 291.8 calories; 53.8 mg. sodium; 21.9 gm. carbohydrates; 18.1 gm. fat.

Chicken Plus Four

SERVES 4

A combination of regional influences: peppercorns from Szechwan, the eastern blending of soy sauce and sugar, the light sauce, representative of Canton. The result is a Chinese meal sure to please.

2 whole chicken breasts, skinned, boned, and cut in 1-inch chunks
¼ teaspoon garlic powder
⅟₁₆ teaspoon ginger powder
⅟₁₆ teaspoon ground Szechwan peppercorns
2 egg whites
2 tablespoons cornstarch, divided
¼ cup cold water
2 tablespoons Soy Sauce Substitute (page 227)

2 tablespoons white vinegar
½ tablespoon sugar
1½ tablespoons peanut (or vegetable) oil
1 can (8 ounces) bamboo shoots, sliced
4 fresh mushrooms, sliced
¼ cup unsalted almonds, crushed
2 tablespoons dried cilantro (or parsley)

1. In bowl, combine first 5 ingredients plus 1 tablespoon cornstarch. Stir to blend. Cover and refrigerate 1 hour.
2. In second bowl, combine remaining cornstarch and water. Set aside.
3. In third bowl, combine soy sauce, vinegar, and sugar. Set aside.
4. In wok, heat oil over medium heat. Add chicken mixture and stir-fry 1 minute, or until chicken turns white all over. With slotted spoon, transfer to platter.
5. To wok, add bamboo shoots and mushrooms. Stir-fry briefly.
6. Add almonds and stir to blend.
7. Add chicken and cornstarch and soy sauce mixtures. Reduce heat to low and stir until mixture thickens.
8. Stir in cilantro.

Per serving: 275.1 calories; 36.6 mg. sodium; 20.7 gm. carbohydrates; 15.4 gm. fat.

Chicken in Hot Cashew Sauce
SERVES 4

This dish smolders teasingly with western sizzle.

2 half chicken breasts, skinned,
  boned, and cubed
Black pepper to taste
1 egg white
2 tablespoons dry red wine
1½ tablespoons cornstarch, divided
¼ cup water
1½ tablespoons peanut oil, divided
1 onion, chopped
1 clove garlic, minced
2 fresh chili peppers, seeded and
  minced, or ⅟₁₆ teaspoon hot
  pepper flakes

2 cups Chinese or American white
  cabbage, shredded
4 fresh mushrooms, chopped
¼ cup unsalted cashews, crushed
1 cup Chicken Stock (page 68),
  divided
2 tablespoons Black Bean Sauce
  (page 232)
2 tablespoons dry sherry

1. In bowl, combine first 4 ingredients plus ½ tablespoon cornstarch. Stir to blend thoroughly. Cover and refrigerate ½ hour.
2. In second bowl, combine remaining cornstarch and water. Set aside.
3. In wok, heat 1 tablespoon oil over low heat. Add onion, garlic, and chili peppers. Stir-fry 30 seconds.
4. Add cabbage. Stir to blend. Cover and simmer 2 minutes.
5. Push cabbage mixture to sides of wok. Add mushrooms. Stir-fry 30 seconds.
6. Add remaining oil and chicken mixture. Raise heat to medium and stir-fry until chicken turns white all over.
7. Stir in cashews and 3 tablespoons chicken stock. Stir-fry 1 minute.
8. Add remaining chicken stock, black bean sauce, and sherry. Bring to a boil.
9. Add cornstarch mixture and continue stirring until mixture thickens.

Per serving: 307.1 calories; 71.1 mg. sodium; 22.2 gm. carbohydrates; 15.9 gm. fat.

Chicken in Hot Yellow Bean Sauce   SERVES 4

Bean Curd, Tomatoes, and Mushrooms (page 191) is especially good with this dish of Cantonese origin.

2 whole chicken breasts, skinned, boned, and diced
1 egg white
1 teaspoon low-sodium beef bouillon
1½ tablespoons cornstarch, divided
½ cup Meat Stock (page 69)
1 tablespoon peanut (or vegetable) oil
1 onion, sliced

⅟₁₆ teaspoon hot pepper flakes
½ can (4 ounces) bamboo shoots, chopped
1 tablespoon dry sherry
1 red pepper, chopped
3 tablespoons Yellow Bean Sauce (page 236)
2 scallions, chopped, including greens

1. In bowl, combine first 3 ingredients plus ½ tablespoon cornstarch, blending thoroughly. Cover and refrigerate ½ hour.
2. In second bowl, combine remaining cornstarch and meat stock. Set aside.
3. In wok, heat oil over low heat. Add onion, pepper flakes, and bamboo shoots. Stir-fry 1 minute.
4. Add chicken and stir-fry until chicken turns white all over.
5. Push chicken mixture to sides of wok. To well created in center, add sherry and red pepper. Stir-fry 30 seconds.
6. Add sweet bean sauce and scallions. Stir-fry 30 seconds.
7. Add meat stock mixture. Raise heat to medium and continue stirring until mixture thickens.

Per serving: 204 calories; 50.1 mg. sodium; 24.4 gm. carbohydrates; 6.7 gm. fat.

Chicken and Shrimp

SERVES 8

This Cantonese version of surf and turf is a sure winner.

2 tablespoons sesame seed oil, divided
1 leek, chopped, including greens
2 slices ginger root, minced, or ⅟₁₆ teaspoon ginger powder
2 cloves garlic, minced
3 whole chicken breasts, skinned, boned, and cut in 1-inch chunks
Black pepper to taste
¼ pound small shrimp, shelled, deveined, and chopped

1 tablespoon dry sherry
1 tablespoon low-sodium chili ketchup
3 scallions, chopped, including greens
¼ cup unsalted walnuts, crushed
1 cup Chicken Stock (page 68)
1 tablespoon cornstarch

1. In wok, heat half the oil over low heat. Add leek, ginger, and garlic. Stir-fry 1 minute.
2. Add chicken and pepper. Stir-fry until chicken turns white all over.
3. Push chicken mixture to sides of wok. To well created in the center, add remaining oil.
4. Raise heat to medium. Add shrimp and stir until shrimp turn pink all over.
5. Stir in sherry, chili ketchup, scallions, and walnuts, blending thoroughly. Simmer 1 minute.
6. While wok mixture is simmering, in bowl, combine chicken stock and cornstarch. Stir into wok mixture.
7. Raise heat to high and continue stirring until mixture bubbles around the edges and thickens.

Per serving: 165 calories; 43.3 mg. sodium; 6.1 gm. carbohydrates; 9.7 gm. fat.

Chicken and Oysters

SERVES 4

Savory yet subtle, this is a true representative of Cantonese cuisine.

1 whole chicken breast, skinned, boned, and cubed
1 pint shucked oysters, liquid reserved
1 egg white
2½ teaspoons cornstarch, divided
2 tablespoons cold water
⅔ cup boiling water
1 teaspoon low-sodium beef bouillon
2 teaspoons low-sodium chicken bouillon

2 tablespoons dry sherry
1 teaspoon mustard powder
1 tablespoon vegetable oil
1 leek, chopped, including greens
2 cloves garlic, minced
2 slices ginger root, minced, or $\frac{1}{16}$ teaspoon ginger powder
1 pound asparagus, trimmed and cut diagonally in 2-inch pieces
2 scallions, chopped, including greens

1. In bowl, combine chicken, oysters, egg white, and 1 teaspoon cornstarch. Stir to blend. Cover and refrigerate 1 hour.
2. In second bowl, combine remaining cornstarch and water. Set aside.
3. In third bowl, combine boiling water and beef and chicken bouillons. Set aside.
4. In fourth bowl, combine sherry and mustard powder. Set aside.
5. In wok, heat oil over low heat. Add leek, garlic, and ginger. Stir-fry 1 minute.
6. Add asparagus plus 2 tablespoons bouillon mixture. Stir-fry 1 minute more.
7. Push asparagus mixture to sides of wok. Add chicken and oyster mixture. Stir-fry 2 minutes, or until chicken turns white all over.
8. Add remaining bouillon mixture plus reserved oyster liquid. Stir to blend.
9. Raise heat to medium. Add scallions and cook 1 minute, stirring constantly. Stir in sherry and mustard mixture.
10. Stir in cornstarch mixture and continue stirring until mixture thickens.

Per serving: 205.4 calories; 85.2 mg. sodium; 18.9 gm. carbohydrates; 6.9 gm. fat.

Five-Spice Chicken   SERVES 8

Duck is the traditional main ingredient for this Cantonese dish. In using duck, however, choose a 4-pound bird since duck has more fat and waste than chicken. Saucy Noodles with Vegetables (page 220) is an excellent accompaniment.

1 teaspoon Five-Spice Powder (page 228)
¾ cup boiling water
2 tablespoons lemon juice
2 teaspoons low-sodium beef bouillon
2 teaspoons low-sodium chicken bouillon

2 tablespoons Soy Sauce Substitute (page 227)
2 teaspoons sugar
⅛ teaspoon cayenne pepper
1 tablespoon sesame seed oil
1 tablespoon cognac
1 3-pound chicken

1. In large bowl, combine all ingredients except chicken, stirring to blend well.
2. Add chicken and turn to coat thoroughly with marinade. Cover and let stand 1 hour, turning chicken occasionally.
3. Preheat oven to 450°.
4. Line a shallow roasting pan with aluminum foil. Place chicken on rack in roasting pan. Reserve marinade.
5. Reduce heat to 350°. Roast chicken 1 hour, or until juices run clear and skin is browned. Baste often with marinade.
6. Remove skin and cut chicken in bite-size pieces.
7. Skim fat off pan juices and serve remaining gravy on the side.

Per serving with chicken: 166.5 calories; 66.1 mg. sodium; 3.2 gm. carbohydrates; 7.9 gm. fat.
Per serving with duck: 224.9 calories; 90.6 mg. sodium; 3.2 gm. carbohydrates; 12.0 gm. fat.

Mandarin Chicken

SERVES 8

From the North, this dish will definitely be on your repeat list. Add Spiced Shrimp and Cashews in Tomatoes (page 89) and boiled white rice to please the eye as well as the palate.

2 cups water
1 3-pound chicken
½ cup lemon juice, divided
2 tablespoons garlic powder, divided
1 tablespoon mustard powder, divided
2 cans (22 ounces) mandarin oranges, plus juice

3 tablespoons sugar
2 tablespoons cider vinegar
¼ cup dry red wine
4 scallions, chopped, including greens
2 tablespoons cognac

1. Preheat oven to 450°.
2. Line a roasting pan with aluminum foil. Pour in water. Truss chicken and place, breast side down, on rack in roasting pan.
3. Pour half the lemon juice over chicken. Sprinkle with half the garlic and mustard powders.
4. Roast 20 minutes, or until skin is golden brown.
5. Turn chicken breast side up. Pour on remaining lemon juice. Sprinkle with remaining garlic and mustard powders.
6. Roast 20 minutes more, or until skin is golden brown. Transfer to platter. Let cool 15 minutes. Cut into bite-size pieces. Remove skin and discard.
7. While chicken is cooling, in saucepan, combine remaining ingredients except cognac. Cook over low heat 10 minutes, stirring occasionally.
8. Pour sauce over chicken. Then pour on cognac and flame.

Per serving: 202 calories; 62.6 mg. sodium; 16.8 gm. carbohydrates; 5.5 gm. fat.

Sugar-Sesame Cornish Hens
in Lemon Sherry
SERVES 8

The elegant flavors of the North are very apparent in this dish that will do every hostess proud. Good served with Braised Zucchini in Six-Fruit Sauce (page 202) or Broccoli in Garlic Sauce (page 193).

4 Cornish hens (about 1 pound
   each)
½ cup lemon juice
¼ cup dry sherry
1/16 teaspoon ground coriander
1/16 teaspoon ginger powder
Black pepper to taste
1¾ cups boiling water, divided

2 tablespoons low-sodium chicken
   bouillon
1 tablespoon lemon peel, minced,
   or 1 teaspoon lemon peel powder
2 tablespoons sesame seed oil
3 tablespoons sugar
1 tablespoon sesame seeds

1. In 9 x 13-inch casserole, place hens. Pour lemon juice over all.
2. In bowl, combine sherry, coriander, ginger, and pepper. Pour over hens.
3. In second bowl, combine 1 cup boiling water, bouillon, lemon peel, and oil. Pour over hens. Cover and refrigerate at least 2 hours, turning hens occasionally.
4. Preheat oven to 325°.
5. In third bowl, combine remaining water, sugar, and sesame seeds. Set aside.
6. Roast hens, breast side up, 1 hour, or until fork tender, basting occasionally with sugar mixture.
7. Cut each hen in half. Spoon pan juices over all.

Per serving: 173.5 calories; 44.5 mg. sodium; 8.8 gm. carbohydrates; 7.3 gm. fat.

Crispy Spiced Duck

SERVES 8

Below is our version of a classic Szechwan specialty. We have opted for anise rather than Szechwan pepper and our own blend of spices rather than the premixed five-spice powder. Serve this aromatic dish with Rice and Mixed Vegetables (page 212).

1 tablespoon Anise Pepper Spice
  (page 229)
½ teaspoon garlic powder
⅛ teaspoon ginger powder
⅛ teaspoon ground cinnamon
1/16 teaspoon ground coriander
1/16 teaspoon clove powder
Black pepper to taste
4 scallions, chopped, including
  greens

1 teaspoon sugar
2 tablespoons dry sherry
1 3- to 4-pound duck, excess fat
  removed
⅓ cup lemon juice, divided
1 cup water

1. In bowl, combine first 10 ingredients, stirring to blend. Rub mixture on duck—inside and out.
2. On heatproof plate, place duck. Place on rack in steamer over boiling water. Cover and steam 1 hour.
3. While duck is steaming, preheat oven to 450°.
4. Transfer duck, breast side up, to rack in roasting pan. Pour half the lemon juice over all.
5. Add water to pan. Roast duck 20 minutes.
6. Pour on remaining lemon juice. Reduce heat to 350° and roast 20 minutes more, or until skin is crispy and juices run clear.
7. Let stand 20 minutes before carving very thin.

Per serving: 198.7 calories; 85.2 mg. sodium; 2.1 gm. carbohydrates; 9.4 gm. fat.

Roast Duck with Eggplant

SERVES 8

The influence here is eastern. It is, indeed, a lovely mix of flavors and textures.

1 4-pound duck
2 cloves garlic, blanched and mashed
¾ cup boiling water
¼ cup dark molasses
2 tablespoons low-sodium beef bouillon
Black pepper to taste
1 teaspoon vegetable oil

1 leek, chopped, including greens
1 eggplant, skinned and cubed
2 tablespoons low-sodium chili ketchup
1½ cups boiled white rice
Dash of clove powder
Dash of ground cinnamon
2 tablespoons dry sherry

1. On rack in roasting pan, place duck, breast side up. Rub all over with garlic.
2. In bowl, combine water, molasses, bouillon, and pepper. Stir to blend. Set aside.
3. Preheat oven to 450°.
4. In wok, heat oil over low heat. Add leek and eggplant. Stir-fry to blend. Cover and steep 20 minutes, stirring occasionally.
5. Stir in chili ketchup, rice, clove powder, cinnamon, sherry, and 2 tablespoons molasses mixture. Stir to blend. Cover and steep 10 minutes more.
6. Stuff duck with eggplant mixture. Roast 15 minutes.
7. Reduce heat to 350°. Baste with molasses mixture. Roast 2 hours more, or until juices run clear, basting occasionally with molasses mixture.
8. Let stand 20 minutes. Remove stuffing to bowl. Carve duck.

Per serving: 303.5 calories; 96.6 mg. sodium; 22.1 gm. carbohydrates; 11.1 gm. fat.

Odd-Spiced Duck

SERVES 8

Not really odd, just unusual. Complement this Shanghai-style dish with Scallop and Corn Soup (page 105) and Green Bean and Fruit Salad (page 79).

1 4-pound duck, chopped into bite-size pieces, excess fat removed
1 stick cinnamon
2 slices ginger root, or 1/16 teaspoon ginger powder
2 carrots, scraped and cut in 1/4-inch rounds
1 1/2 cups water

1/4 cup Soy Sauce Substitute (page 227)
1 can (16 ounces) dietetic pears, sliced, including juice
2 scallions, minced, including greens

1. In wok, place first 5 ingredients. Turn heat to medium and bring to a slow boil. Reduce heat. Cover and simmer 1 hour, stirring occasionally.
2. Add remaining ingredients. Raise heat to medium and bring to a boil. Reduce heat. Cover and simmer 1/2 hour more, or until duck is fork tender. With slotted spoon, transfer duck to warm platter. Remove skin.
3. Skim fat off gravy. Then raise heat to medium and bring to a boil. Continue boiling 5 minutes. Discard cinnamon stick and ginger root.
4. Pour gravy over duck.

Per serving: 233.3 calories; 98.1 mg. sodium; 8.0 gm. carbohydrates; 9.8 gm. fat.

Duck and Pungent Fruit Sauce SERVES 8

Not as tart as Duck in Citrus Sauce (page 161), but the bite of ginger to balance the fruit is magic in this equally flavorful northern treat. Broccoli in Garlic Sauce (page 193) is a perfect side dish.

2 tablespoons Chili Oil (page 230)
1 4-pound duck, skinned, boned, and cut into 2-inch pieces
2 cloves garlic, minced
2 slices ginger root, minced, or 1/16 teaspoon ginger powder
8 fresh mushrooms, sliced
1 can (8 ounces) dietetic peaches, drained, juice reserved
1 can (8 ounces) dietetic pears, drained, juice reserved

1/4 cup cider vinegar
2 tablespoons dry sherry
1 cup water
3 tablespoons sugar
2 tablespoons low-sodium chicken bouillon
4 scallions, cut in 1-inch pieces, including greens

1. In wok, heat oil over medium heat. Add duck, garlic, and ginger and stir-fry 2 minutes, or until duck is white all over.
2. Stir in mushrooms, peaches, and pears and simmer 2 minutes, stirring occasionally.
3. Add reserved peach and pear juices, vinegar, sherry, water, and sugar. Raise heat to high and bring to a boil, stirring constantly.
4. Reduce heat to low. Cover and simmer 1/2 hour.
5. Stir in bouillon and scallions. Cover and simmer 10 minutes more, stirring occasionally.

Per serving: 285.4 calories; 94.8 mg. sodium; 13.8 gm. carbohydrates; 13.9 gm. fat.

Duck in Citrus Sauce

SERVES 8

The Shantung version of duck à l'orange, this dish is sure to impress. Serve Watercress and Noodle Salad (page 102) alongside to make a perfect meal.

1 4-pound duck
1 tablespoon garlic powder
2 onions, chopped
½ cup water
½ cup orange juice
1 orange, seeded, cut into chunks, skin intact
1 lemon, seeded, cut into chunks, skin intact

½ cup dry sherry
2 tablespoons red wine vinegar
2 tablespoons low-sodium beef bouillon
1 teaspoon paprika
1 tablespoon cornstarch
2 leeks, chopped, including greens

1. In 9 x 13-inch casserole, place duck. Sprinkle with garlic powder.
2. Scatter onions around duck.
3. Pour water and orange juice over all.
4. Scatter orange and lemon over duck.
5. Pour sherry over all. Cover and refrigerate overnight, turning occasionally. Drain, reserving marinade, including orange and lemon.
6. Preheat oven to 450°.
7. On rack in roasting pan, place duck, breast side up. Roast ½ hour, or until skin turns brown, basting occasionally with marinade liquid.
8. Reduce heat to 350° and roast 1½ hours more, or until duck is fork tender and juices run clear.
9. While duck is roasting, in saucepan, cook marinade over very low heat 20 minutes.
10. While marinade is cooking, in bowl, combine vinegar, bouillon, paprika, and cornstarch. Stir into marinade along with leeks. Cook 10 minutes more, or until mixture thickens, stirring often.
11. Let duck stand at room temperature 20 minutes before carving. Spoon sauce over all.

Per serving: 273.6 calories; 98.8 mg. sodium; 18.7 gm. carbohydrates; 10.4 gm. fat.

Braised Duck in Sherry-Soy Sauce   SERVES 8

A true Shanghai delicacy that is complemented by Piquant Tomatoes and Cucumber (page 201).

1 4-pound duck, chopped into
  bite-size pieces, excess fat
  removed
1 cup Meat Stock (page 69)
2 slices ginger root, or ¹⁄₁₆ teaspoon
  ginger powder
1 cup boiling water
8 dried black mushrooms*

⅓ cup dry sherry
½ cup Soy Sauce Substitute (page
  227)
4 scallions, chopped, including
  greens

1. In wok, combine first 3 ingredients. Let stand ½ hour, stirring occasionally.
2. In bowl, combine boiling water and mushrooms. Let stand ½ hour. Drain, reserving liquid. Cut each mushroom in half.
3. To wok, add reserved mushroom liquid and sherry. Turn heat to medium and bring to a slow boil. Reduce heat to low. Cover and simmer 1 hour.
4. Add mushroms, soy sauce, and scallions. Cover and simmer 45 minutes more, or until duck is fork tender.
5. With slotted spoon, remove duck to warm platter. Remove skin before eating.
6. Skim fat off gravy. Discard ginger. Serve gravy on side.

Per serving: 231.4 calories; 99.8 mg. sodium; 5.3 gm. carbohydrates; 10.8 gm. fat.

* If not available, substitute 8 large fresh mushrooms, sliced.

Chicken Livers Sesame

SERVES 4

Good with Glazed Green Beans (page 197) and Mandarin Rice with Peppers (page 214).

2 teaspoons sesame seed oil
1 pound chicken livers
1 leek, chopped, including greens
1/16 teaspoon ginger powder
Black pepper to taste

1 can (8 ounces) water chestnuts, chopped
1 tablespoon sesame seeds
1 teaspoon sugar

1. In wok, heat oil over low heat. Add livers, leek, ginger powder, pepper, and water chestnuts. Stir-fry 3 minutes, or until livers lose all pink color.
2. Stir in sesame seeds and sugar. Stir-fry 2 minutes more.

Per serving: 247.1 calories; 93.2 mg. sodium; 8.7 gm. carbohydrates; 55.2 gm. fat.

Chicken Livers and Oysters

SERVES 8

Boiled white rice and Cauliflower with Pork Soup (page 75) complete the menu for a lovely, light meal, starring this Cantonese-style dish.

1 pound chicken livers
1 egg white
2 tablespoons Soy Sauce Substitute (page 227)
1 teaspoon low-sodium chicken bouillon
1 tablespoon peanut (or vegetable) oil
1 leek, chopped, including greens

2 cloves garlic, minced
1/16 teaspoon ginger powder
1 can (8 ounces) bamboo shoots, sliced
1/4 pound snow pea pods, halved diagonally
1 teaspoon dry sherry
1 pint oysters, including liquid

1. In bowl, combine first 4 ingredients, blending thoroughly. Cover and refrigerate 15 minutes.
2. In wok, heat oil over low heat. Add leek, garlic, and ginger powder. Stir-fry 1 minute.
3. Add bamboo shoots. Stir-fry 30 seconds.
4. Add liver mixture. Raise heat to medium and stir-fry 1 minute, or until livers lose all pink color.
5. Push liver mixture to sides of wok. To well created in center, add snow pea pods and sherry. Stir-fry 30 seconds.
6. Add oysters plus liquid. Cook 1 minute, stirring constantly.

Per serving: 154.7 calories; 78.4 mg. sodium; 9.9 gm. carbohydrates; 5.3 gm. fat.

Chicken Livers Fukien

SERVES 4

This dish makes a perfect meal with Hoisin Rice in Four (page 211).

1 pound chicken livers
⅓ cup dry red wine
1 tablespoon low-sodium beef
  bouillon
8 dried black mushrooms*
1 cup boiling water
½ tablespoon low-sodium chicken
  bouillon
1 tablespoon peanut oil
2 carrots, scraped, cut in ¼-inch
  rounds and blanched

2 scallions, minced, including
  greens
½ teaspoon sugar
Dash of clove powder
Black pepper to taste
½ cup Chicken Stock (page 68)
1½ tablespoons cornstarch
1 tablespoon dried cilantro (or
  parsley)

1. In bowl, combine first 3 ingredients. Set aside.
2. In second bowl, combine mushrooms, water, and chicken bouillon. Let stand ½ hour. Drain, reserving marinade. Cut each mushroom in half.
3. In wok, heat oil over medium-low heat. Add carrots and scallions. Stir-fry 1 minute.
4. Add sugar, clove powder, and pepper, stirring to blend.
5. Add liver mixture and mushroms. Reduce heat to low. Cover and simmer 15 minutes.
6. Add mushroom marinade. Cover and simmer 10 minutes more.
7. While wok mixture is cooking, in bowl, combine chicken stock and cornstarch. Stir into wok mixture along with cilantro. Raise heat to high and cook, stirring constantly until mixture thickens.

Per serving: 264.1 calories; 99.0 mg. sodium; 61.1 gm. carbohydrates; 9.2 gm. fat.

* If not available, substitute 8 large fresh mushrooms, sliced.

Meats

In China, meat is synonymous with pork, which is enjoyed at least once every day. Otherwise, the Chinese are not overly fond of red meat. They have never acquired a taste for beef, because there is virtually no land for grazing. However, just how mouth-watering beef can be when touched by the art of the Orient is evident in dishes like Beef and Bean Sprouts (page 176).

Because of its strong odor and heavy, distinctive flavor, lamb is especially distasteful to the delicate Chinese nose and palate. For this reason, lamb is used primarily in hotly spiced Szechwan dishes. Only the Muslims of the North, whose religion bans pork, prefer and regularly eat lamb, which they raise.

So, in the end, the Chinese always come back to pork, which is prepared in an infinite number of ways: red-roasted whole, cubed, shredded, ground. Ironically, this greatly savored food is considered too humble and commonplace for banquets. As far as I am concerned, however, pork dishes like. Hot and Spicy Pork with Oysters (page 171) would do any table and any occasion proud.

Although Westerners appreciate the delicious versatility of pork, the American preference has always been beef. That is why there are more beef recipes than pork in this chapter, but not just any beef—only London broil, flank steak, or bottom round, because these are lower in calories, fat, and sodium than other cuts.

But whatever your meat preference, it is sure to be most flavorful when prepared in the Oriental manner.

Red Pork Roast

SERVES 8

A northern variation of a most traditional meal originating in Shanghai. The combination of different wines and spices will make you want to go on eating. Try it with Bamboo Shoots in Mushroom Sauce (page 190).

2-pound pork roast, bone in
2 quarts cold water
10 cloves
4 slices ginger root, or ⅛ teaspoon
   ginger powder
¼ cup dry vermouth or dry sherry
½ cup dry red wine
2 sticks cinnamon (2 inches each),
   or ⅛ teaspoon ground cinnamon

1 tablespoon garlic powder
2 tablespoons sugar
2 tablespoons lemon juice
2 teaspoons low-sodium beef
   bouillon
2 teaspoons low-sodium chicken
   bouillon

1. In wok or Dutch oven, combine pork and water. Turn heat to high and bring to a boil. Continue boiling 5 minutes. Remove from heat. Let cool. Then stud pork with cloves.
2. Return to heat and bring to a second boil. Reduce heat to low.
3. Add ginger, vermouth, wine, cinnamon sticks, and garlic powder. Cover and simmer 1½ hours, turning meat often.
4. Uncover and continue to cook ½ hour more, or until meat is tender, adding water if necessary to prevent meat from sticking.
5. Remove pork to platter. Discard cloves.
6. Stir remaining ingredients into remaining wok liquid. Raise heat to medium and cook 5 minutes, or until mixture thickens, stirring frequently. Discard cinnamon sticks.
7. Slice pork and pour gravy over all.

Per serving: 320.3 calories; 84.9 mg. sodium; 5.8 gm. carbohydrates; 16.8 gm. fat.

Spiced Pork with Cabbage

SERVES 4

Serve this Cantonese-style dish with Noodles of Land and Sea (page 225).

1½ tablespoons vegetable oil
1 onion, chopped
½ pound pork, cubed
Black pepper to taste
Dash of ginger powder
⅟₁₆ teaspoon ground cinnamon
1 teaspoon paprika
1 star anise
2 cups Chinese or American white
   cabbage, shredded

1 tablespoon sugar
¾ cup Chicken Stock (page 68)
1 tablespoon dry sherry
2 tablespoons Soy Sauce Substitute
   (page 227)
2 tablespoons cold water
1 tablespoon cornstarch

1. In wok, heat oil over low heat. Add onion and pork and stir-fry 2 minutes, or until pork loses all pink color.
2. Stir in pepper, ginger powder, cinnamon, paprika, and star anise. Stir to blend.
3. Push pork mixture to sides of wok. To well created in center, add cabbage and sugar. Stir-fry 2 minutes.
4. Add chicken stock, sherry, and soy sauce. Cover and simmer 5 minutes.
5. While pork mixture is simmering, in bowl, combine water and cornstarch. Stir into wok mixture.
6. Raise heat to medium. Cook, stirring constantly until mixture thickens. Discard star anise.

Per serving: 271.3 calories; 81.2 mg. sodium; 15.9 gm. carbohydrates; 20.4 gm. fat.

Pork and Kumquats

SERVES 8

Of no particular region, but the special taste of this dish is absolutely marvelous.

1½ tablespoons vegetable oil, divided
1¼ pounds pork, cut into 1-inch chunks
1 teaspoon mustard powder
1 onion, sliced thin
¼ pound snow pea pods, halved diagonally
2 stalks broccoli, flowerettes and stems, chopped
8 fresh mushrooms, sliced
2 tomatoes, cut in wedges

Black pepper to taste
2 cloves garlic, minced
1 can (16 ounces) kumquats, drained, liquid reserved
1 tablespoon cornstarch
1 cup boiling water
4 teaspoons low-sodium beef bouillon
1 teaspoon sesame seed oil

1. In wok, heat 1 tablespoon vegetable oil over medium heat. Add pork and mustard powder. Stir-fry 2 minutes, or until pork is browned all over. Transfer to platter.
2. In wok, heat remaining vegetable oil over low heat. Add all vegetables, pepper, and garlic. Stir-fry 2 minutes.
3. Stir in kumquats and simmer 2 minutes, stirring occasionally.
4. While wok mixture is cooking, in bowl, combine kumquat liquid and cornstarch. Set aside.
5. In second bowl, combine boiling water and bouillon. Set aside.
6. Return pork to wok. Raise heat to high. Add cornstarch and bouillon mixtures. Cook, stirring constantly, until mixture thickens.
7. Stir in sesame seed oil.

Per serving: 319 calories; 73.6 mg. sodium; 24.9 gm. carbohydrates; 15.4 gm. fat.

Pork and Bean Curd

SERVES 4

Another treat in the Cantonese style. Delightful with Assorted Seafood Salad (page 87).

2 tablespoons sesame seed oil,
  divided
½ pound pork, cubed
2 cloves garlic, minced
1 onion, chopped
1 large square bean curd, chopped
4 scallions, chopped, including
  greens

4 fresh mushrooms, sliced
½ cup Shrimp Sauce (page 240)
½ cup boiling water
2 teaspoons low-sodium chicken
  bouillon
2 tablespoons cold water
1 tablespoon cornstarch

1. In wok, heat 1 tablespoon oil over low heat. Add pork, garlic, and onion. Stir-fry 2 minutes, or until pork loses all pink color.
2. Push pork mixture to sides of wok. To well created in center, add remaining oil. Add bean curd, scallions, and mushrooms. Stir-fry 1 minute more.
3. Add shrimp sauce. Cover and simmer 2 minutes.
4. While mixture is simmering, in bowl, combine boiling water and bouillon. Stir into wok mixture.
5. In second bowl, combine cold water and cornstarch. Stir into wok mixture. Raise heat to medium and stir constantly until mixture thickens.

Per serving: 318.7 calories; 71.5 mg. sodium; 15.2 gm. carbohydrates; 18.2 gm. fat.

Pork and Almonds

SERVES 4

This Cantonese-flavored dish goes well with just about anything.

1 tablespoon vegetable oil
1 onion, minced
½ pound pork, shredded
1 can (8 ounces) bamboo shoots,
    sliced
1 tablespoon dry sherry
2 tablespoons Soy Sauce Substitute
    (page 227)
¼ cup unsalted slivered almonds

½ cup Meat Stock (page 69),
    divided
1 red pepper, julienned
1 teaspoon sugar
2 tablespoons Black Bean Sauce
    (page 232)
1 teaspoon cornstarch

1. In wok, heat oil over low heat. Add onion and stir-fry 1 minute.
2. Add pork and stir-fry 1 minute more.
3. Add bamboo shoots and sherry. Stir-fry 30 seconds.
4. Add soy sauce and almonds. Raise heat to medium and stir-fry 1 minute.
5. Add 1 tablespoon meat stock and red pepper. Stir-fry 30 seconds.
6. Stir in sugar.
7. Stir in black bean sauce. Reduce heat to low and simmer 1 minute.
8. In bowl, combine remaining meat stock and cornstarch, stirring until cornstarch is dissolved.
9. Stir cornstarch mixture into wok. Continue stirring until mixture thickens.

Per serving: 324.1 calories; 50.6 mg. sodium; 17.7 gm. carbohydrates; 20.9 gm. fat.

Hot and Spicy Pork with Oysters   SERVES 8

The wonderfully succulent and varied flavors of this dish could only be found in the western region. Try it with Asparagus in Mustard Sauce (page 189).

1¼ pounds pork, sliced thin
¼ cup Soy Sauce Substitute (page 227)
¼ cup dry sherry
2 slices ginger root, or ⅟₁₆ teaspoon ginger powder
4 scallions, chopped, including greens
⅟₁₆ teaspoon Five-Spice Powder (page 228)

1 tablespoon Chili Oil (page 230)
2 pints oysters, drained, liquid reserved
¾ cup boiling water
1½ tablespoons low-sodium chicken bouillon
¼ cup cold water
2 tablespoons cornstarch

1. In large bowl, combine first 6 ingredients. Stir to blend. Cover and refrigerate 1 hour. Drain. Reserve marinade.
2. In wok, heat chili oil over medium heat. Add pork and stir-fry 1 minute, or until pork loses all pink color. Transfer to platter.
3. Add oysters and stir-fry 10 seconds. Transfer to platter.
4. Add pork marinade and bring to a boil.
5. While marinade is cooking, in bowl, combine oyster liquid, boiling water, and bouillon. Stir into wok mixture. Reduce heat to low and simmer 2 minutes, stirring occasionally.
6. While sauce is cooking, in second bowl, combine cold water and cornstarch. Stir into wok mixture.
7. Return pork to wok and cook until mixture thickens, stirring frequently.
8. Stir in oysters and cook 30 seconds more.

Per serving: 287 calories; 119.0 mg. sodium; 9.8 gm. carbohydrates; 12.7 gm. fat.

Braised Pork with Orange Rings
SERVES 8

Simmered to perfection in the Fukien manner, this dish is a wonderful treat with any accompaniment. Two good choices are Asparagus in Mustard Sauce (page 189) or Bean Curd, Tomatoes, and Mushrooms (page 19).

1½ pounds pork loin, cubed
10 cups boiling water
4 slices ginger root, or ⅛ teaspoon ginger powder
1 tablespoon vegetable oil
2 cloves garlic, minced
4 scallions, chopped, including greens

Black pepper to taste
2 tablespoons dry sherry
½ cup water
1 tablespoon sugar
⅓ cup Soy Sauce Substitute (page 227)
1 orange, sliced in ⅛-inch rings

1. In wok or Dutch oven, combine first 3 ingredients. Turn heat to medium and bring to a boil. Reduce heat to low. Cover and simmer 20 minutes. Drain pork. Discard ginger. Set aside.
2. In wok, heat oil over medium heat. Add pork, garlic, scallions, and pepper. Stir-fry 30 seconds.
3. Add sherry. Stir-fry 30 seconds more.
4. Add all remaining ingredients. Reduce heat to low and simmer 20 minutes more, or until pork is fork tender.

Per serving: 266.1 calories; 63.8 mg. sodium; 6.9 gm. carbohydrates; 14.4 gm. fat.

Szechwan Pork with Vegetables

SERVES 8

Every mouthful sparks a different taste sensation.

1½ pounds pork, cubed
2 tablespoons Soy Sauce Substitute
  (page 227), divided
1 teaspoon cider vinegar
1 teaspoon lemon juice
1½ tablespoons cornstarch, divided
⅓ cup cold water, divided
4 teaspoons Chili Oil (page 230),
  divided
2 slices ginger root, minced, or ¹⁄₁₆
  teaspoon ginger powder
2 cloves garlic, minced
1 small eggplant, peeled and cubed

1½ cups cauliflowerettes
1 green pepper, chopped
1 tablespoon dry sherry
1 tablespoon sugar
½ teaspoon mustard powder
½ teaspoon Anise Pepper Spice
  (page 229)
2 scallions, chopped, including
  greens

1. In bowl, combine pork, 1 tablespoon soy sauce, vinegar, lemon juice, and ½ tablespoon cornstarch. Stir to blend. Cover and refrigerate ½ hour. Drain, reserving marinade.
2. While pork is marinating, in second bowl, combine remaining cornstarch and ¼ cup cold water.
3. In wok, heat 2 teaspoons chili oil over low heat. Add ginger, garlic, eggplant, and cauliflower. Cover and simmer ½ hour, stirring occasionally.
4. Push vegetable mixture to sides of wok. Add remaining chili oil and green pepper. Stir-fry briefly.
5. Add pork and stir-fry 5 minutes more, or until pork loses all pink color.
6. Stir in sherry and sugar, blending thoroughly.
7. Stir in remaining soy sauce and pork marinade.
8. Add remaining water and mustard powder, blending thoroughly.
9. Stir in remaining ingredients. Cover and simmer 2 minutes.

Per serving: 263.1 calories; 66.4 mg. sodium; 10.8 gm. carbohydrates; 12.8 gm. fat.

Szechwan Beef   SERVES 8

This dish delivers a real zing.

1½ tablespoons peanut (or sesame) oil, divided
3 cloves garlic, minced
1 pound sirloin steak, sliced in ½-inch strips
⅛ teaspoon hot pepper flakes
¹⁄₁₆ teaspoon ginger powder
2 tablespoons white vinegar
Dash of Five-Spice Powder (page 228)

1 green pepper, chopped
1 can (8 ounces) bamboo shoots
2 tablespoons low-sodium ketchup
3 tablespoons dry sherry
1 tablespoon low-sodium beef bouillon
¼ cup boiling water
4 scallions, chopped, including greens

1. In wok, heat 1 tablespoon oil over low heat. Add garlic, beef, hot pepper flakes, and ginger. Stir-fry 2 minutes, or until beef loses all pink color.
2. Stir in vinegar and five-spice powder.
3. Push beef to sides of wok. To well created in center, add remaining oil. Add green pepper and bamboo shoots. Stir-fry 2 minutes.
4. Stir in ketchup, sherry, and bouillon, blending thoroughly.
5. Raise heat to medium. Stir in boiling water, blending thoroughly.
6. Stir in scallions and cook 1 minute, stirring constantly.

Per serving: 258 calories; 46.2 mg. sodium; 5.3 gm. carbohydrates; 19.1 gm. fat.

Chinese Barbecued Beef

SERVES 4

Pork loin or 4 half chicken breasts can be substituted for the beef in this northern specialty.

1 cup boiling water
3 tablespoons low-sodium chili ketchup
2 tablespoons red wine vinegar
2 tablespoons Hoisin Sauce Substitute (page 228)
½ can (8 ounces) dietetic pineapple, crushed, including juice
2 tablespoons dry sherry
1½ teaspoons mustard powder

⅛ teaspoon garlic powder
⅛ teaspoon ginger powder
Black pepper to taste
¾ pound flank steak, cut in thick strips (2 x 1 x 6 inches)
6 tablespoons Soy Sauce Substitute (page 227)

1. In 9 x 13-inch casserole, combine all but last 2 ingredients. Stir to blend thoroughly.
2. Add beef strips. Cover and refrigerate at least 2 hours, turning beef occasionally.
3. Preheat oven to 375°.
4. Transfer beef to shallow roasting pan. Add enough cold water to cover the bottom of the pan. Roast beef 10 minutes. Reduce heat to 325°.
5. Spoon 4 to 6 tablespoons of marinade over the beef. Roast 10 minutes more.
6. Turn beef and repeat Step 5. Continue roasting, turning and basting beef every 10 minutes until all marinade is gone.
7. Remove beef to platter. Slice thin. Spoon on soy sauce. Serve warm or cold.

Per serving with beef: 219 calories; 68.1 mg. sodium; 8.9 gm. carbohydrates; 7.2 gm. fat.
Per serving with pork: 273 calories; 72.4 mg. sodium; 8.9 gm. carbohydrates; 13.7 gm. fat.
Per serving with chicken: 166 calories; 62.4 mg. sodium; 8.9 gm. carbohydrates; 5.1 gm. fat.

Beef and Bean Sprouts   SERVES 4

In the imaginative spirit of the Cantonese tradition, serve this with Sweet and Hot Chicken Mushroom Soup (page 72).

8 dried black mushrooms*
1 cup boiling water
⅓ cup cold water, divided
1 tablespoon cornstarch
2 teaspoons mustard powder
1 small apple, pared, cored, and
  chopped fine
¼ cup dry sherry
¼ cup Hoisin Sauce Substitute
  (page 228)
½ pound flank steak, sliced into
  thin strips
1 tablespoon vegetable oil

1 clove garlic, minced
½ pound bean sprouts
½ cup Chicken Stock (page 68)
2 teaspoons low-sodium chicken
  bouillon
4 scallions, chopped, including
  greens

1. In bowl, combine first 2 ingredients. Let stand ½ hour. Drain, reserving half the liquid. Set aside.
2. In second bowl, combine 4 tablespoons cold water and cornstarch. Set aside.
3. In third bowl, combine remaining cold water and mustard powder. Set aside.
4. In fourth bowl, combine apple, sherry, hoisin sauce, and steak. Let stand 20 minutes, stirring occasionally. Drain, reserving marinade.
5. In wok, heat oil over low heat. Add garlic and bean sprouts. Stir-fry 1 minute.
6. Push bean sprout mixture to sides of wok. Add steak. Raise heat to high and stir-fry 1 minute.
7. Add remaining mushroom liquid and chicken stock. Stir to blend.
8. Stir in bouillon, scallions, and reserved steak marinade. Stir to blend.
9. Stir in cornstarch mixture. Then stir in mustard mixture. Stir-fry continuously until mixture thickens.

Per serving: 310 calories; 51.9 mg. sodium; 21.8 gm. carbohydrates; 11.8 gm. fat.

* If not available, substitute 8 large fresh mushrooms, sliced, and omit boiling water.

Beef in Hot Peanut Sauce

SERVES 8

Cool down this Szechwan delight with Minced Oysters (page 53) served on a bed of lettuce and tomatoes.

¼ cup dry sherry
¼ cup apple juice
2 tablespoons low-sodium peanut butter
2 tablespoons sesame seed oil, divided
1 pound sirloin steak, cut in ½-inch strips
¼ teaspoon hot pepper flakes
1 tablespoon low-sodium beef bouillon
1 tablespoon low-sodium chicken bouillon

¹⁄₁₆ teaspoon anise powder
2 slices ginger root, minced, or ¹⁄₁₆ teaspoon ginger powder
1 can (8 ounces) bamboo shoots
2 stalks broccoli flowerettes and stems, chopped
½ pound vermicelli, cooked al dente*
4 scallions, chopped, including greens

1. In small saucepan, combine first 3 ingredients. Cook over very low heat, stirring frequently to blend peanut butter.
2. While sauce is heating, in wok, heat 1 tablespoon oil over medium heat. Add steak, hot pepper flakes, beef and chicken bouillons, anise powder, and ginger. Stir-fry until beef loses all pink color. Transfer to platter.
3. In wok, heat remaining oil over low heat. Add bamboo shoots and broccoli. Stir-fry 2 minutes.
4. Add vermicelli, meat mixture, and peanut sauce. Stir-fry, blending thoroughly, 2 minutes.
5. Stir in scallions. Heat, stirring constantly, 1 minute.

Per serving: 394.8 calories; 50.7 mg. sodium; 29.1 gm. carbohydrates; 21.7 gm. fat.

* Do not add salt to boiling water.

Braised Steak in Oyster Sauce SERVES 8

This Cantonese dish is literally as easy as one, two, three. Eggplant Curry Salad (page 106) is an excellent accompaniment.

1½ pounds chuck steak, cut in
   1-inch cubes
1 large onion, minced
1 cup champagne, or ¾ cup dry
   white wine plus ¼ cup salt-free
   seltzer
⅓ cup Soy Sauce Substitute (page
   227)

4 large carrots, scraped and cut into
   ½-inch rounds
½ cup Oyster Sauce (page 234)
3 tablespoons cold water
1½ tablespoons cornstarch

1. In wok, combine first 5 ingredients. Turn heat to medium and bring to a slow boil. Reduce heat to low and simmer 1 hour.
2. Add oyster sauce and simmer ½ hour more, or until meat is tender.
3. While meat is cooking, in bowl, combine water and cornstarch. Stir into wok mixture. Raise heat to medium and stir constantly until mixture thickens.

Per serving: 339 calories; 57.8 mg. sodium; 13.6 gm. carbohydrates; 18.4 gm. fat.

Chinese Pepper Steak

SERVES 8

A nationally popular dish, made special with the northern touch of red wine. A sparkling side dish selection is Ginger-Sherry Shrimp (page 55).

1½ pounds London broil, ½ inch thick, cut into ½-inch strips
⅓ cup dry red wine
2 teaspoons sugar
2 tablespoons peanut oil, divided
4 cloves garlic, minced
1 onion, sliced
1 green pepper, sliced thin
1 red pepper, sliced thin
8 fresh mushrooms, sliced
1/16 teaspoon ginger powder

½ cup boiling water
2 teaspoons low-sodium beef bouillon
2 tablespoons cold water
1 tablespoon cornstarch
2 tablespoons Yellow Bean Sauce (page 236)

1. In large bowl, combine first 3 ingredients. Cover and refrigerate overnight, turning beef occasionally. Drain, reserving marinade. Pat beef dry.
2. In wok, heat 1 tablespoon oil over medium heat. Add beef and garlic and stir-fry 2 minutes, or until beef loses all pink color. Transfer to platter.
3. In wok, heat remaining oil over low heat. Add onion, green and red peppers, mushrooms, and ginger powder. Stir-fry 2 minutes.
4. Add marinade and cook 2 minutes more, stirring occasionally.
5. While vegetables are cooking, in bowl, combine boiling water and bouillon. Set aside.
6. In second bowl, combine cold water and cornstarch. Set aside.
7. Raise heat under wok mixture to high. Add beef and bouillon mixtures. Cook, stirring occasionally, until mixture starts to bubble around the edges.
8. Stir in cornstarch mixture. Cook, stirring constantly, until mixture thickens.
9. Reduce heat to low. Stir in sweet bean sauce, blending thoroughly.
10. Slice steak very thin. Spoon sauce over all.

Per serving: 249.2 calories; 72.6 mg. sodium; 12.3 gm. carbohydrates; 10.1 gm. fat.

Fruit Steak

SERVES 4

A sweetly simple dish from Canton. Excellent served with Braised Leeks in Soy Sauce (page 198) or Carrot and Eggplant Chili (page 194).

¾ pound flank steak, pricked all
   over with fork
2 teaspoons garlic powder
¼ teaspoon ginger powder
Black pepper to taste
1½ tablespoons peanut oil
1 orange, chopped, including rind
1½ cups boiling water
4 teaspoons low-sodium beef
   bouillon

4 scallions, chopped, including
   greens
¼ cup dried apricots, chopped
2 tablespoons Soy Sauce Substitute
   (page 227)
2 tablespoons cold water
1 tablespoon cornstarch

1. In 8-inch square casserole, place steak. Rub all over with garlic and ginger powders and pepper. Let stand 10 minutes.
2. In wok, heat oil over high heat. Add steak and sear on each side 3 minutes. Transfer to platter. Slice thin across the grain. Set aside.
3. To wok, add orange, boiling water, bouillon, scallions, and apricots. Reduce heat to medium and cook 5 minutes, stirring occasionally.
4. Stir in soy sauce.
5. Add steak. Reduce heat to low and simmer 2 minutes.
6. While steak mixture is simmering, in bowl, combine cold water and cornstarch. Stir into steak mixture. Raise heat to medium and continue stirring until mixture thickens.

Per serving: 368 calories; 57.2 mg. sodium; 22.5 gm. carbohydrates; 9.5 gm. fat.

Ground Beef in Hoisin Sauce   SERVES 4

Duck Sauce (page 234) makes an interesting and delicious substitute for the hoisin sauce in this dish with a Shantung flair.

¾ pound ground chuck
1 tablespoon dry red wine
2 teaspoons low-sodium beef
  bouillon
1 teaspoon sesame seed oil
1 onion, chopped
2 cloves garlic, minced
1 leek, chopped, including greens
2 carrots, scraped and cut in
  ½-inch rounds

1 small eggplant, pared and cubed
3 tablespoons Hoisin Sauce
  Substitute (page 228)
⅓ cup water
1½ teaspoons mustard powder
8 snow pea pods, halved diagonally

1. In bowl, combine first 3 ingredients. Cover and refrigerate ½ hour.
2. In wok, heat oil over low heat. Add onion and garlic. Stir-fry 2 to 3 minutes, or until onion is wilted.
3. Add leek and carrots. Stir to blend. Stir-fry 2 minutes.
4. Push vegetables to sides of wok. Add beef mixture. Turn heat to medium and stir-fry until beef loses all pink color.
5. Reduce heat to low. Stir to blend all ingredients in wok. Then add eggplant to top of mixture. Cover and simmer ½ hour.
6. Stir in hoisin sauce. Cover and simmer 5 minutes more.
7. While mixture is cooking, in bowl, combine water and mustard powder. Stir into mixture, blending thoroughly.
8. Place snow pea pods on top of mixture. Cover and simmer 5 minutes more.

Per serving with hoisin sauce: 350 calories; 73.0 mg. sodium; 23.3 gm. carbohydrates; 19.4 gm. fat.
Per serving with duck sauce: 349.6 calories; 67.7 mg. sodium; 23.8 gm. carbohydrates; 19.3 gm. fat.

Spiced Beef with
Cabbage, Pepper, and Squash   SERVES 4

This one-dish eastern meal needs only boiled white rice to make it complete.

¾ pound flank steak, minced
⅛ teaspoon ground coriander
1 star anise
1 teaspoon white vinegar
1 teaspoon peanut (or vegetable) oil
3 cups Chinese or American white cabbage
2 slices ginger root, minced, or ¹⁄₁₆ teaspoon ginger powder

1 cup water
1 cup Meat Stock (page 69)
1 red pepper, sliced thin
1 yellow squash, chopped
1 tablespoon dried cilantro (or parsley)

1. In bowl, combine first 4 ingredients. Stir to blend. Let stand 20 minutes.
2. In wok, heat oil over medium heat. Add beef mixture and stir-fry until beef loses all pink color.
3. Cover beef with cabbage. Add ginger and water. Reduce heat to low. Cover and simmer 45 minutes, or until water is absorbed.
4. Add meat stock, red pepper, and squash. Cover and simmer 20 minutes more.
5. Stir in cilantro. Raise heat to medium. Cook, uncovered, 5 minutes more, or until mixture bubbles around the edges. Discard star anise.

Per serving: 216 calories; 86.9 mg. sodium; 7.8 gm. carbohydrates; 7.7 gm. fat.

Stir-Fried Beef and Vegetables

SERVES 8

Shanghai in origin, wonderfully tasteful, and perfect with Curried Fish Soup (page 77).

1½ pounds flank steak, sliced thin
2 tablespoons dry sherry
2 tablespoons Soy Sauce Substitute (page 227), divided
1 teaspoon white vinegar
1 teaspoon lemon juice
2 tablespoons vegetable oil, divided
1 onion, minced
2 slices ginger root, minced, or ⅟₁₆ teaspoon ginger powder
2 cloves garlic, minced
1 can (8 ounces) bamboo shoots, sliced
2 tomatoes, chopped

3 tablespoons Sweet Bean Sauce (page 236)
1 cup Meat Stock (page 69)
1 teaspoon low-sodium beef bouillon
¼ cup cold water
1½ tablespoons cornstarch
3 scallions, chopped, including greens

1. In 8-inch square casserole, combine meat, sherry, 1 tablespoon soy sauce, vinegar, and lemon juice. Let stand ½ hour. Drain, reserving marinade.
2. In wok, heat 1 tablespoon oil over low heat. Add onion, ginger, garlic, and meat. Raise heat to medium and stir-fry 1 minute.
3. Push meat mixture to sides of wok. To well created in center, add remaining oil. Add bamboo shoots and tomatoes. Stir-fry 1 minute.
4. Stir in sweet bean sauce, blending thoroughly.
5. Add meat stock and bouillon. Reduce heat to low and simmer 5 minutes.
6. While meat is simmering, in bowl, combine water and cornstarch. Stir into wok mixture.
7. Add scallions. Raise heat to medium and cook, stirring constantly, until mixture thickens.
8. Stir in remaining tablespoon soy sauce.

Per serving: 267.6 calories; 65.4 mg. sodium; 15.0 gm. carbohydrates; 10.5 gm. fat.

Lemon Lamb   SERVES 8

This dish with the gentle flavors of Fukien is sure to become your favorite recipe for leg of lamb. It deserves special companions like Snow Pea Pods and Bamboo Shoots (page 200).

1 3-pound leg of lamb
⅓ cup Soy Sauce Substitute (page 227)
2 tablespoons dry sherry
2 tablespoons dried cilantro (or parsley)

⅛ teaspoon ground coriander
⅛ teaspoon ginger powder
Black pepper to taste
½ cup lemon juice

1. In roasting pan, place lamb. Add all remaining ingredients. Cover and refrigerate overnight, turning occasionally.
2. Preheat oven to 375°.
3. Roast lamb ½ hour, basting occasionally with marinade.
4. Turn lamb. Reduce heat to 325°. Roast 2 hours more, or until lamb is fork tender, basting occasionally. Transfer to platter. Let cool 10 minutes.
5. Skim fat off pan gravy. Serve defatted lemon sauce on the side.

Per serving: 343 calories; 132.0 mg. sodium; 2.2 gm. carbohydrates; 13.6 gm. fat.

Sweet and Hot Lamb in Green Peppers

SERVES 4

The northern Muslim influence is very much in evidence in this delicious dish.

½ pound ground lamb
1/16 teaspoon ground cinnamon
1 tablespoon low-sodium beef
  bouillon
1 leek, chopped, including greens
½ teaspoon paprika
Black pepper to taste
½ can (4 ounces) bamboo shoots,
  chopped

1 cup watercress, chopped
3 tablespoons Hoisin Sauce
  Substitute (page 228)
4 small green peppers, cored and
  seeded
1 cup water

1. In bowl, combine first 6 ingredients, blending thoroughly.
2. In wok, cook lamb mixture in own juices over high heat 1 minute, stirring constantly. Drain. Transfer to bowl.
3. Add bamboo shoots, watercress, and hoisin sauce, blending thoroughly.
4. Stuff peppers with lamb mixture.
5. Preheat oven to 350°.
6. In 8-inch square casserole, place peppers. (If necessary, cut a small piece off the bottom of each pepper so it will sit flat in the casserole.)
7. Pour water into casserole. Bake ½ hour, or until peppers are fork tender, adding more water, if necessary, to prevent sticking.

Per serving: 244 calories; 84.2 mg. sodium; 25.1 gm. carbohydrates; 7.8 gm. fat.

Sweet Lamb with Vegetables

SERVES 4

Another typically northern dish.

½ pound lamb, cubed
2 tablespoons sesame seed oil,
  divided
2 tablespoons Black Bean Sauce
  (page 232)
1½ tablespoons sugar, divided
2 tablespoons dry sherry, divided
⅓ cup cold water
1 tablespoon cornstarch
2 teaspoons cider vinegar
½ cup boiling water
2 teaspoons low-sodium chicken
  bouillon

1 leek, chopped, including greens
½ pound bean sprouts
1 zucchini, chopped
1/16 teaspoon ground cinnamon
2 scallions, chopped, including
  greens
Black pepper to taste

1. In bowl, combine lamb, 1 tablespoon oil, black bean sauce, ½ table-spoon sugar, and 1 tablespoon sherry. Let stand 20 minutes. Drain, reserving marinade.
2. In second bowl, combine cold water and cornstarch. Set aside.
3. In third bowl, combine remaining sherry and vinegar. Set aside.
4. In fourth bowl, combine boiling water and bouillon. Set aside.
5. In wok, heat remaining oil over medium-low heat. Add lamb, leek, and bean sprouts. Stir-fry 1 minute, or until lamb loses all pink color.
6. Add zucchini and cinnamon. Stir-fry 1 minute more.
7. Stir in scallions and pepper. Then stir in remaining sugar.
8. Add marinade and cornstarch, sherry, and bouillon mixtures. Raise heat to medium-high and stir constantly until mixture thickens.

Per serving: 351.4 calories; 51.6 mg. sodium; 23.7 gm. carbohydrates; 19.8 gm. fat.

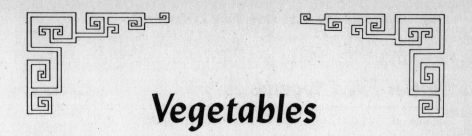

Vegetables

Along with rice, vegetables are the foundation of the Chinese diet because they provide the greatest amount of food for the greatest number of people from the sparse available farmland. The variety and number of Chinese vegetables are not only different in every region but are far more extensive than our own. Since vegetables are an integral part of almost every Chinese dish, this vast selection is a fortuitous deterrent to boredom and makes a healthy diet endlessly pleasurable as well.

Most Chinese vegetables are prepared in a two-step process: first, stir-fried briefly in very hot oil; then, added to a bubbling, seasoned broth and steamed briefly over medium heat. The results are vegetables with a crisp, delectably crunchy texture and a ripe, vibrant color to delight the senses whether hot from the wok or chilled for a cold treat the next day.

The more fragile, leafy vegetables, like spinach and watercress, are flash-fried in seconds, until barely wilted, then seasoned and served immediately so they can be enjoyed at the full height of their flavor.

We tend to think of Chinese vegetables only as ingredients in main dishes, mixed with fish or meat or poultry. The Chinese enjoy them this way, too, but they also relish vegetables as dishes unto themselves. For example, a green, leafy vegetable is served at every meal. Often, a second vegetable dish is served as well; it might feature one vegetable like Sweet and Hot Cabbage (page 193) or a combination such as Bean Curd, Tomatoes, and Mushrooms (page 191).

Only banquets are not favored by these garden-rich dishes, for they are considered too ordinary for special occasions. However, we need not be bound by this tradition. For any way at all, Chinese vegetables are seductive and addictive. Even the fussiest eater will ask for more.

Batter-Fried Vegetables

SERVES 12

A marvelous variety of tastes, expressive of the Szechwan style.

1 zucchini, cut in 1-inch rounds
1 yellow squash, cut in 1-inch
rounds
2 teaspoons sugar
1 teaspoon low-sodium peanut
butter
¼ cup boiling water
1 cup cauliflowerettes
1 cup broccoli flowerettes
¼ teaspoon ground coriander

¼ teaspoon Szechwan Pepper Spice
(page 229)
12 large fresh mushrooms, stems
removed and reserved for future
use
¼ teaspoon ginger powder
2 cups all-purpose flour
2½ cups cold water
3 cups vegetable oil

1. In bowl, combine first 3 ingredients, stirring to blend. Let stand 15 minutes.
2. In second bowl, blend peanut butter and hot water. Stir in cauliflowerettes. Let stand 10 minutes.
3. In third bowl, combine broccoli, coriander, and Szechwan pepper spice. Let stand 10 minutes.
4. In fourth bowl, place mushrooms.
5. In fifth bowl, combine ginger and flour, stirring to blend thoroughly. Slowly stir in water to make a batter, which should be slightly runny.
6. In wok, heat oil over high heat until bubbly.
7. Dip vegetables in batter and fry a few pieces at a time until golden brown all over. Drain.
8. Serve with Duck Sauce (page 234) on the side as a dip.

Per serving: 167.7 calories; 7.0 mg. sodium; 32.6 gm. carbohydrates; 6.4 gm. fat.

Asparagus in Mustard Sauce

SERVES 4

A Cantonese dish that goes well with any main course.

⅓ cup cold water
1½ teaspoons mustard powder
1 teaspoon vegetable oil
1 pound asparagus, trimmed and
cut into 2-inch pieces

½ cup Chicken Stock (page 68),
divided
1 teaspoon sugar
1 teaspoon sesame seeds

1. In bowl, combine first 2 ingredients. Stir until mustard powder is dissolved. Set aside.
2. In wok, heat oil over low heat. Add asparagus and stir-fry 1 minute.
3. Add 2 tablespoons chicken stock and stir-fry 2 minutes more.
4. Stir in sugar. Then raise heat to high and stir in remaining chicken stock and mustard mixture. Cook until mixture bubbles, stirring occasionally.
5. Stir in sesame seeds.

Per serving: 61.8 calories; 6.6 mg. sodium; 7.3 gm. carbohydrates; 2.5 gm. fat.

Asparagus in Oyster Sauce

SERVES 4

The meat stock makes this Cantonese dish extra special. Serve with your favorite dish.

2 teaspoons sesame seed oil
1 pound asparagus, trimmed and
cut into 1½-inch pieces
½ teaspoon sugar
1 tablespoon dry sherry

⅓ cup Meat Stock (page 69)
2 tablespoons Oyster Sauce (page
234)

1. In wok, heat oil over low heat. Add asparagus and stir-fry 1 minute.
2. Stir in sugar. Then stir in sherry.
3. Raise heat to medium. Add meat stock and stir-fry 2 minutes, or until mixture is bubbly around the edges.
4. Stir in oyster sauce, blending thoroughly.

Per serving: 64.4 calories; 7.5 mg. sodium; 7.5 gm. carbohydrates; 3.1 gm. fat.

Bamboo Shoots
in Mushroom Sauce

SERVES 4

The distinct flavor of bamboo shoots in this Cantonese dish is wonderful with fish or meat. See for yourself with Braised Fish and Peanuts (page 109) or Hot and Spicy Pork with Oysters (page 171).

¼ cup dried oyster mushrooms*
12 dried black mushrooms*
1 cup boiling water
1 teaspoon sesame seed oil
1 slice ginger root, minced, or pinch
   of ginger powder
1 clove garlic, minced

2 scallions, minced, including
   greens
1 cup Meat Stock (page 69)
Black pepper to taste
1 can (8 ounces) bamboo shoots,
   sliced

1. In bowl, combine first 3 ingredients. Let stand 20 minutes. Drain, reserving ¼ cup liquid. Slice black mushrooms.
2. In wok, heat oil over low heat. Add ginger and garlic. Stir-fry 1 minute, or until garlic is golden.
3. Add scallions and stir-fry 30 seconds.
4. Add meat stock and pepper. Stir to blend. Raise heat to high and bring to a boil.
5. Reduce heat to medium-low. Add mushrooms and reserved liquid plus bamboo shoots. Cover and cook 3 to 5 minutes, or until mixture thickens.

Per serving: 60.6 calories; 15.0 mg. sodium; 8.8 gm. carbohydrates; 2.2 gm. fat.

* If not available, substitute a total of 12 large fresh mushrooms, sliced, and omit water.

Bean Curd and Peppers

SERVES 4

Another sampling of the Cantonese tradition.

1 tablespoon vegetable oil
1 square bean curd, sliced
1 green pepper, sliced
1 red pepper, sliced
1 clove garlic, minced

1 teaspoon dry sherry
1 teaspoon low-sodium beef
    bouillon
¼ teaspoon mustard powder
⅓ cup boiling water

1. In wok, heat oil over medium heat. Reduce heat to low. Add bean curd and stir-fry 30 seconds.
2. Add green and red peppers plus garlic and stir-fry 30 seconds.
3. Stir in sherry, bouillon, and mustard powder.
4. Raise heat to high and stir in boiling water. Stir-fry 1 minute more.

Per serving: 86.6 calories; 23.5 mg. sodium; 7.1 gm. carbohydrates; 4.2 gm. fat.

Bean Curd,
Tomatoes, and Mushrooms

SERVES 4

Try serving this northern-style dish with Lemon Chicken (page 141).

8 large dried mushrooms*
1 cup boiling water
1 teaspoon vegetable oil
2 scallions, chopped, including
    greens
1 clove garlic, minced
2 slices ginger root, minced, or ¹⁄₁₆
    teaspoon ginger powder

1 tablespoon low-sodium beef
    bouillon
1 large square bean curd, cubed
1 tablespoon dry sherry
1 teaspoon white vinegar
1 tomato, chopped
2 teaspoons sesame seed oil

1. In bowl, combine first 2 ingredients. Let stand ½ hour. Then drain, reserving liquid, and chop mushrooms.
2. In wok, heat vegetable oil over low heat. Add scallions, garlic, and ginger. Stir-fry 30 seconds.
3. Stir bouillon into reserved mushroom liquid. Pour into wok. Raise heat to high. When mixture bubbles, add mushrooms and bean curd.
4. Reduce heat to low. Stir in sherry, vinegar, and tomato. Cover and simmer 15 minutes, or until liquid is almost absorbed.
5. Stir in sesame seed oil.

Per serving: 96.9 calories; 18.4 mg. sodium; 7.1 gm. carbohydrates; 4.7 gm. fat.

* If not available, substitute 8 large fresh mushrooms, sliced.

Peanut-Chili Bean Sprouts   SERVES 8

Absolutely delicious. Serve this Szechwan goody with Braised Steak in Oyster Sauce (page 178).

½ cup boiling water
½ teaspoon Chili Powder (page 231)
3 tablespoons low-sodium peanut butter

1 pound bean sprouts
1 teaspoon dry sherry
2 cucumbers, scraped, seeded, and chopped

1. In bowl, combine first 3 ingredients. Stir until peanut butter is thoroughly blended.
2. In wok, turn heat to low. Add bean sprouts and peanut butter mixture. Stir-fry 2 minutes.
3. Add sherry. Stir-fry 2 minutes more.
4. Stir in cucumber. Cover and simmer 3 minutes.

Per serving: 147.6 calories; 11.1 mg. sodium; 10.1 gm. carbohydrates; 5.8 gm. fat.

Broccoli and Minced Shrimp   SERVES 4

Mildly Szechwan and every bite delicious.

1 tablespoon vegetable oil
2 cups broccoli flowerettes
¼ teaspoon Szechwan Pepper Spice (page 229)
¼ pound small shrimp, shelled, deveined, and minced

1 tablespoon dry sherry
⅓ cup Meat Stock (page 69) or Fish Stock (page 67)

1. In wok, heat oil over low heat. Add broccoli and stir-fry 30 seconds.
2. Add Szechwan pepper spice and stir-fry 2 minutes more.
3. Add shrimp and sherry. Stir to blend.
4. Add meat stock. Raise heat to high and stir-fry until shrimp turn pink —about 30 seconds.

Per serving: 83.4 calories; 50.7 mg. sodium; 4.7 gm. carbohydrates; 4.3 gm. fat.

Broccoli in Garlic Sauce *Good* SERVES 8

This Cantonese delight is simple yet simply delicious. Try it with Braised Shrimp with Leek (page 133).

1 tablespoon sesame seed oil
3 cups broccoli flowerettes
6 cloves garlic, minced
¼ cup boiling water
1 teaspoon low-sodium chicken
  bouillon

1 tablespoon dry sherry
¼ cup unsalted cashews, crushed
  (optional)

1. In wok, heat oil over low heat. Add broccoli and garlic. Stir-fry 2 minutes.
2. Raise heat to high. Add water, bouillon, and sherry. Stir-fry until liquid is absorbed.
3. Add cashews, if desired, and stir to blend.

Per serving with cashews: 79.5 calories; 9.1 mg. sodium; 5.3 gm. carbohydrates; 5.4 gm. fat.
Per serving without cashews: 39.5 calories; 8.03 mg. sodium; 2.04 gm. carbohydrates; 3.3 gm. fat.

Excellent

Sweet and Hot Cabbage SERVES 4

Cabbage has never tasted so good. A marvelous Szechwan accent for Stir-Fried Chicken Legs with Soy Sauce Peaches (pages 146–47).

1 tablespoon Chili Oil (page 230)
4 cups Chinese or American white
  cabbage, shredded
2 tablespoons cider vinegar
1 star anise

Dash of Five Spice-Powder (page
  228)
¼ cup dry sherry
2 teaspoons low-sodium chicken
  bouillon

1. In wok, heat oil over high heat. Add cabbage and stir-fry 2 minutes.
2. Stir in cider vinegar, star anise, and five-spice powder. Stir to blend.
3. Raise heat to medium. Stir in sherry and bouillon. Stir-fry 2 minutes more. Discard star anise.

Per serving: 81.1 calories; 26.6 mg. sodium; 8.3 gm. carbohydrates; 4.4 gm. fat.

Cabbage in Oyster Sauce SERVES 4

As a wonderful variation for this Szechwan dish substitute 2 cans (8 ounces each) of drained, low-sodium corn niblets for the cabbage.

2 cups Chinese or American white cabbage, shredded
3 tablespoons Soy Sauce Substitute (page 227)

2 scallions, chopped, including greens
2 teaspoons Chili Oil (page 230)
¾ cup Oyster Sauce (page 234)

1. In bowl, combine first 2 ingredients. Toss to blend. Let stand 15 minutes.
2. Add scallions. Toss to blend.
3. In wok, heat oil over low heat. Add cabbage mixture. Stir-fry 2 minutes. Cover and simmer 2 minutes more.
4. Stir in oyster sauce. Cover and simmer 10 minutes more, stirring occasionally.

Per serving with cabbage: 66.6 calories; 33.5 mg. sodium; 6.1 gm. carbohydrates; 4.3 gm. fat.
Per serving with corn: 85.4 calories; 23.2 mg. sodium; 10.8 gm. carbohydrates; 4.4 gm. fat.

Carrot and Eggplant Chili SERVES 8

Temper this hot Hunan combination with the subtle taste of Flounder in Silk (page 115).

2 cups Chicken Stock (page 68) or Meat Stock (page 69)
2 large carrots, scraped and cut in 1-inch rounds

1 teaspoon sugar
1 small eggplant, peeled and cubed
1/16 teaspoon ginger powder
1 tablespoon Chili Paste (page 230)

1. In wok, combine first 2 ingredients. Turn heat to high and bring to a boil. Reduce heat to low. Cover and simmer ½ hour.
2. Stir in sugar. Add eggplant. Raise heat to high and bring to a second boil.
3. Reduce heat to medium. Stir in ginger powder and chili paste. Cover and simmer 20 minutes more.

Per serving with chicken stock: 53.1 calories; 20.8 mg. sodium; 7.5 gm. carbohydrates; 1.1 gm. fat.
Per serving with meat stock: 46.6 calories; 18.0 mg. sodium; 7.1 gm. carbohydrates; 0.8 gm. fat.

good

Honeyed Carrots and Watercress SERVES 4

This dish will add a special touch to any meal.

1 tablespoon honey, or 1
  tablespoon sugar
⅓ cup boiling water
2 teaspoons cider vinegar
2 large carrots, scraped and cut in
  1-inch rounds, steamed

2 cups watercress, chopped
Black pepper to taste
¹⁄₁₆ teaspoon ginger powder

1. In bowl, combine first 3 ingredients, stirring to blend.
2. In wok, over medium heat, combine honey mixture and carrots. Stir-fry 1 minute.
3. Add remaining ingredients, stirring to blend thoroughly. Stir-fry 1 minute more.

Per serving with honey: 62.7 calories; 69.3 mg. sodium; 13.0 gm. carbohydrates; 0.4 gm. fat.
Per serving with sugar: 65.6 calories; 69.2 mg. sodium; 10.9 gm. carbohydrates; 0.4 gm. fat.

Carrots and Ginger Apple SERVES 4

This unusual dish from the North is equally good with fish, meat, or poultry.

2 large carrots, scraped and cut in
  ¼-inch rounds
2 cups Meat Stock (page 69)
2 teaspoons sesame seed oil
3 slices ginger root, minced, or ¹⁄₁₆
  teaspoon ginger powder
1 leek, chopped, including greens

¹⁄₁₆ teaspoon Szechwan Pepper
  Spice (page 229)
2 apples (any kind), pared, cored,
  and diced
2 scallions, chopped, including
  greens

1. In saucepan, combine first 2 ingredients. Bring to a boil and continue boiling 5 minutes. Reduce heat to low. Cover and simmer 20 minutes, or until carrots are cooked but still slightly firm.
2. In wok, heat oil over low heat. Add ginger and leek and stir-fry 1 minute.
3. Stir in Szechwan pepper spice and apples. Stir-fry 1 minute more.
4. Stir in scallions and carrot mixture. Cook 1 minute more.

Per serving: 148.2 calories; 36.2 mg. sodium; 28.5 gm. carbohydrates; 4.4 gm. fat.

Curried Cauliflower and Peppers SERVES 4

The heritage of Yunnan and Kweichou is spicily evident here. Try this dish with Duck in Citrus Sauce (page 69).

2 tablespoons vegetable oil
2 cups cauliflowerettes
1 slice ginger root, minced, or pinch of ginger powder
½ green pepper, sliced
½ red pepper, sliced

2 tablespoons Soy Sauce Substitute (page 227)
¾ cup Chicken Stock (page 68)
1½ teaspoons Curry Powder (page 232)

1. In wok, heat oil over medium heat. Add cauliflowerettes and ginger and stir-fry 30 seconds.
2. Stir in green and red peppers plus soy sauce. Stir-fry 30 seconds more.
3. Add chicken stock and bring mixture to a slow boil.
4. Reduce heat to low. Stir in curry powder. Cover and simmer 10 minutes, or until liquid is almost absorbed.

Per serving: 111.5 calories: 25.4 mg. sodium: 6.7 gm. carbohydrates; 8.4 gm. fat.

Sweet and Sour Corn SERVES 4

Very much like a relish with a Cantonese twist. Serve hot with Squid and Mushrooms (page 135), or chilled with Chicken and Snow Pea Pod Salad (page 93).

2 cans (8 ounces each) low-sodium corn niblets, including liquid
2 teaspoons cider vinegar
Black pepper to taste
1/16 teaspoon garlic powder
1/16 teaspoon ginger powder
½ cup Chicken Stock (page 68)

1 cucumber, scraped, seeded and chopped
1 tablespoon honey
2 scallions, chopped, including greens

1. In wok, combine first 5 ingredients. Turn heat to medium and bring to a slow boil, stirring occasionally.
2. Add chicken stock and cucumber, and bring to a second boil.
3. Stir in honey and scallions. Reduce heat to low and simmer 10 minutes, stirring occasionally.
4. Serve hot or chilled.

Per serving: 83.6 calories; 24.9 mg. sodium; 22.3 gm. carbohydrates; 1.1 gm. fat.

Eggplant with
Cashews in Duck Sauce
SERVES 4

Eggplant takes on a royal grandeur in this dish from the Peking cuisine.

1 small eggplant, peeled and cubed
1 cup Meat Stock (page 69)
1 leek, chopped, including greens
Black pepper to taste

¼ cup unsalted cashews, crushed
3 tablespoons Duck Sauce (page 234)

1. In wok, combine first 4 ingredients. Stir to blend. Turn heat to low. Cover and simmer ½ hour.
2. Stir in remaining ingredients. Stir to blend thoroughly. Cover and simmer 15 minutes more.

Per serving: 151.5 calories; 12.0 mg. sodium; 19.2 gm. carbohydrates; 7.8 gm. fat.

Glazed Green Beans
SERVES 4

This dish is perhaps more eastern than anything else, but the preparation method is common throughout China.

¼ cup cold water
1 tablespoon cornstarch
1 pound green beans, cut diagonally in 2-inch pieces
1½ cups Meat Stock (page 69), divided

Black pepper to taste
1 tablespoon sesame seed oil
2 teaspoons sugar
1 teaspoon low-sodium beef bouillon

1. In bowl, combine water and cornstarch, stirring until cornstarch is dissolved. Set aside.
2. In wok, combine green beans and ¾ cup meat stock. Turn heat to low. Cover and simmer 10 minutes, or until liquid is almost absorbed.
3. Raise heat to high. Stir in remaining ingredients except cornstarch and cook until mixture starts to boil.
4. Stir in cornstarch and cook 1 minute more, or until sauce thickens.

Per serving: 115 calories; 19.2 mg. sodium; 17.9 gm. carbohydrates; 5.1 gm. fat.

Green Beans with Pork Bits
SERVES 4

In this dish with a northern touch, ground beef can be substituted for the pork for a totally different flavor. Braised Shrimp Bamboo (page 131) is an excellent main-course selection.

4 tablespoons Soy Sauce Substitute
(page 227)
½ teaspoon mustard powder
1 tablespoon low-sodium ketchup
1 teaspoon sesame seed oil
1 tablespoon vegetable oil
1 pound green beans, cut
diagonally in 1-inch pieces

½ teaspoon orange peel, minced,
or ⅛ teaspoon orange peel
powder
4 fresh mushrooms, chopped
¼ pound ground pork

1. In bowl, combine first 2 ingredients, stirring until mustard is dissolved. Stir in ketchup and sesame seed oil. Set aside.
2. In wok, heat vegetable oil over low heat. Add green beans and stir to coat well. Stir-fry 2 minutes.
3. Add orange peel and mushrooms. Stir-fry 2 minutes more, adding enough soy mixture to keep vegetables from sticking.
4. Push vegetables to sides of wok. Add pork and stir-fry until it loses all pink color.
5. Raise heat to high. Add remaining soy mixture and stir to blend all ingredients.

Per serving with pork: 166.1 calories; 54.3 mg. sodium; 9.9 gm. carbohydrates; 9.9 gm. fat.
Per serving with beef: 175 calories; 47.7 mg. sodium; 9.9 gm. carbohydrates; 11.6 gm. fat.

Braised Leeks in Soy Sauce
SERVES 4

Leeks are favorites in the North, and slow cooking is often used. We have adapted this elegant dish by adding the slightly more pungent onion to balance the sweet-tasting leeks.

4 small leeks, trimmed
4 tablespoons Soy Sauce Substitute
(page 227)
1 small onion, minced

1 cup Chicken Stock (page 68)
½ teaspoon sesame seed oil or
Chili Oil (page 230)
½ teaspoon sugar

1. In 8-inch square dish, combine first 3 ingredients. Let stand 15 minutes, turning leeks occasionally.

2. In wok, over medium heat, bring chicken stock to a slow boil.
3. Add leek mixture and bring to a second boil.
4. Reduce heat to low. Cover and cook 20 minutes, or until stock is almost evaporated.
5. Stir in oil and sugar, stirring until sugar is dissolved.

Per serving: 59.3 calories; 16.5 mg. sodium; 9.6 gm. carbohydrates; 2.0 gm. fat.

Mushrooms in Soy Sauce   SERVES 4

Using soy sauce rather than salt to season green vegetables is unusual because the soy sauce ruins the fresh, clear color. But for mushrooms, that is not an issue, and this eastern dish is the happy result.

12 large dried black mushrooms*
1½ cups boiling water
½ teaspoon vegetable oil
4 fresh mushrooms, sliced
2 scallions, chopped, including greens

4 tablespoons Soy Sauce Substitute (page 227)
1 teaspoon low-sodium beef bouillon
1 teaspoon cornstarch

1. In bowl, combine first 2 ingredients. Let stand ½ hour. Drain mushrooms. Reserve half the liquid.
2. In wok, heat oil over low heat. Add fresh mushrooms. Stir to coat with oil.
3. Add dried mushrooms, ½ cup of the reserved liquid, scallions, and soy sauce. Cover and simmer 20 minutes.
4. Stir in bouillon. Cover and simmer 5 minutes more.
5. While mixture is cooking, combine remaining ¼ cup of reserved liquid with cornstarch, stirring until cornstarch is dissolved. Stir into mushroom mixture and cook, uncovered, 1 minute more, or until sauce thickens.

Per serving: 42 calories; 15.5 mg. sodium; 5.7 gm. carbohydrates; 1.5 gm. fat.

* If not available, substitute 12 large fresh mushrooms, sliced.

Snow Pea Pods and Bamboo Shoots   SERVES 4

Any vegetable can be substituted for the snow pea pods and bamboo shoots in this traditional recipe common to all regions.

1 teaspoon vegetable oil
20 snow pea pods
½ can (4 ounces) bamboo shoots, sliced
¼ teaspoon ginger root, minced, or pinch of ginger powder

1 tablespoon dry sherry
1 tablespoon Soy Sauce Substitute (page 227)

1. In wok, heat oil over low heat. Add snow pea pods, bamboo shoots, and ginger. Stir-fry 1 minute.
2. Stir in sherry and soy sauce. Stir-fry 1 minute more.

Per serving: 35 calories; 1.6 mg. sodium; 4.5 gm. carbohydrates; 1.5 gm. fat.

Stir-Fried Snow Pea Pods   SERVES 4

The orientation is Cantonese. The appeal is universal. This dish is terrific with any fish, meat, or poultry.

1 tablespoon vegetable oil
20 snow pea pods, halved diagonally
½ can (4 ounces) water chestnuts, minced
4 fresh mushrooms, sliced

⅓ cup Chicken Stock (page 68)
1 tablespoon cornstarch
1 teaspoon low-sodium chicken bouillon

1. In wok, heat oil over low heat. Add snow pea pods, water chestnuts, and mushrooms. Stir-fry 2 minutes.
2. In bowl, combine chicken stock and cornstarch, stirring until cornstarch is dissolved. Add to vegetables. Raise heat to medium and stir to blend.
3. Stir in bouillon and continue stirring until mixture thickens.

Per serving: 91.8 calories; 12.3 mg. sodium; 12.0 gm. carbohydrates; 4.4 gm. fat.

Braised Peppers and Almonds SERVES 4

This eastern-style dish can be varied by adding ½ pound cubed pork to Step 1, or 1 large square of sliced bean curd to Step 2.

1 tablespoon vegetable oil
1 green pepper, sliced
1 red pepper, sliced
1 teaspoon sugar
¼ cup unsalted slivered almonds

1 teaspoon low-sodium beef
  bouillon
1 tablespoon Soy Sauce Substitute
  (page 227)

1. In wok, heat oil over low heat. Add green and red peppers. Stir-fry 2 minutes.
2. Stir in sugar. Then add almonds and stir-fry 2 minutes more.
3. Stir in remaining ingredients. Stir-fry 30 seconds.

Per serving plain: 154.9 calories; 23.1 mg. sodium; 10.7 gm. carbohydrates; 12.1 gm. fat.
Per serving with pork: 300.1 calories; 63.1 mg. sodium; 10.7 gm. carbohydrates; 20.2 gm. fat.
Per serving with bean curd: 175.5 calories; 25.1 mg. sodium; 10.7 gm. carbohydrates; 12.1 gm. fat.

Piquant Tomatoes and Cucumbers SERVES 4

A northern dish that elevates two everyday vegetables to sublime taste.

2 teaspoons vegetable oil
2 slices ginger root, minced, or ¹⁄₁₆
  teaspoon ginger powder
1 clove garlic, minced
1 onion, minced
1 tablespoon orange peel, minced,
  or ¼ teaspoon orange peel
  powder
2 large tomatoes, chopped
1 cucumber, scraped, seeded, and
  chopped

1 tablespoon dry sherry
1 tablespoon Soy Sauce Substitute
  (page 227)
1 teaspoon low-sodium chicken
  bouillon
¼ cup boiling water
2 scallions, chopped, including
  greens

1. In wok, heat oil over medium heat. Add ginger, garlic, and onion. Stir-fry 1 minute.
2. Add orange peel, tomatoes, and cucumber. Stir-fry 1 minute more.
3. Stir in remaining ingredients, blending thoroughly, and stir-fry 1 minute more.

Per serving: 110.2 calories; 26.7 mg. sodium; 14.7 gm. carbohydrates; 3.2 gm. fat.

Flash-Fried Watercress and Bean Curd
SERVES 4

The alternating sweet and pungent flavors of this Cantonese dish make it very special indeed. It will accent any main dish you serve.

¼ cup warm water
1½ teaspoons sugar
1 teaspoon mustard powder
2 teaspoons sesame seed oil
1 large square bean curd, cubed
¼ cup unsalted slivered almonds
2 cloves garlic, minced

⅛ teaspoon ground coriander
3 cups watercress, chopped
2 tablespoons Soy Sauce Substitute (page 227)
1 tablespoon dried cilantro (or parsley)

1. In bowl, combine first 3 ingredients, stirring until sugar and mustard powder are completely blended. Set aside.
2. In wok, heat oil over low heat. Add bean curd, almonds, and garlic. Stir-fry 2 minutes, or until garlic is slightly browned.
3. Raise heat to high. Add sugar mixture, coriander, watercress, soy sauce, and cilantro. Stir-fry 1 minute.

Per serving: 161.5 calories; 45.9 mg. sodium; 7.8 gm. carbohydrates; 10.7 gm. fat.

Braised Zucchini in Six-Fruit Sauce
SERVES 4

Shantung cuisine offers no better dish than this, which is exquisite with fish, meat, or poultry.

2 small zucchini, quartered and cut into spears
2 tablespoons Soy Sauce Substitute (page 227)
2 teaspoons vegetable oil
2 slices ginger root, or ⅛ teaspoon ginger powder

2 cloves garlic, minced
¼ cup Chicken Stock (page 28)
2 tablespoons Six-Fruit Sauce (page 242)
2 scallions, minced, including greens

1. In 9-inch square dish, combine zucchini and soy sauce. Stir to blend.
2. In wok, heat oil over low heat. Add ginger and garlic. Stir-fry 2 minutes.
3. Add zucchini mixture. Stir-fry 2 minutes more.
4. Raise heat to high and add chicken stock. Bring to a boil.
5. Reduce heat to medium. Stir in fruit sauce and scallions. Stir-fry until zucchini is completely glazed.

Per serving: 55.3 calories; 6.1 mg. sodium; 6.2 gm. carbohydrates; 3.0 gm. fat.

Fried Zucchini and Onions   SERVES 8

This dish glows with Szechwan heat.

1 cup all-purpose flour (or rice
  flour)
1 cup cold water
½ cup boiling water
2 teaspoons low-sodium chicken
  bouillon
Black pepper to taste

¼ teaspoon hot pepper flakes
2 cups vegetable oil
4 zucchini, cut in ½-inch rounds
3 onions, sliced in ½-inch rounds
3 tablespoons white vinegar

1. In bowl, combine first 2 ingredients, stirring until water is completely
   absorbed.
2. In second bowl, combine boiling water, bouillon, pepper, and hot pepper flakes, stirring until bouillon is dissolved. Let stand 20 minutes.
3. Stir bouillon mixture into flour mixture to make a batter, which should
   be slightly runny.
4. In wok, heat oil over high heat until bubbly.
5. Dip vegetables in batter and deep-fry a few pieces at a time until golden
   brown all over. Drain.
6. Sprinkle vinegar over vegetables and serve immediately.

Per serving: 190 calories; 8.0 mg. sodium; 34.9 gm. carbohydrates; 6.4 gm. fat.

Zucchini and Walnuts   SERVES 8

The cinnamon is the dash that gives this northern-style dish its beautiful distinction. Pork and Almonds (page 170) is a worthy companion.

1 tablespoon vegetable oil
2 large zucchini (or yellow squash), quartered and cut into thin spears
1 onion, minced
1 clove garlic, minced
2 tablespoons dry sherry
3 tablespoons Soy Sauce Substitute (page 227)

1 tablespoon unsalted walnuts, crushed
2 tablespoons unsalted walnuts, chopped
Dash of ground cinnamon

1. In wok, heat oil over low heat. Add zucchini, onion, and garlic. Stir-fry 2 minutes, or until onion is wilted.
2. Raise heat to medium. Add sherry, soy sauce, and crushed walnuts. Stir-fry 2 minutes more.
3. Add chopped walnuts. Stir in cinnamon.

Per serving: 83 calories; 12.3 mg. sodium; 15.6 gm. carbohydrates; 11.6 gm. fat.

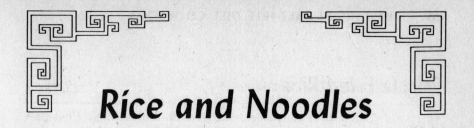

Rice and Noodles

When dinner is about to be served, the Chinese announce, "Rice is ready." More than anything else, that expression signifies the importance of rice to the Chinese diet. In fact, rice is the mainstay of all Chinese people, except those of the northern regions where the arid climate is unsuitable for its growth.

The North, however, is ideal for wheat, whose silky, yellow grains are ultimately transformed into spring rolls, steamed buns, moist egg dumplings, airy pancake confections, and the internationally popular egg roll. From the North, too, come the super-long strands of egg and cellophane noodles, symbolic of long life and, for that reason, served at birthday parties throughout China.

Noodles are never served plain, but are always bathed in a savory sauce and accented with bits of meat, fish, poultry, or vegetables, as in the recipe for Saucy Noodles with Vegetables (page 220). Rice, on the other hand, though delicious when sparked with herbs, spices, or flecks of food, is most often served plain.

Rice is to China what bread is to Western cultures—the staff of life. Indeed, rice, which is served at every meal and provides the bulk of the Chinese diet, is one of the most nutritious foods. It contains most of the required basic nutrients, is low in fat and calories, provides a good level of carbohydrates for energy, and is very low in sodium.

In fact, before the widespread availability of low-sodium foods, people with serious salt-related problems—especially hypertensives—were placed on the Duke rice diet, under the supervision of doctors and nutritionists at Duke University. It might have been boring, but it was also very healthy.

Certainly rice has served the Chinese well for generations. In the Chinese home, rice is never wasted. Children learn very young not to leave so much as one precious pearl in their rice bowls. Even the crust in rice pots is used in soups or porridge, or is deep-fried for snacks. Rice is left over only by design, so it can be chilled in preparation for fried rice, for example.

Only the Chinese bring so much imagination and taste to these basic foods. You will see for yourself when you try dishes like Saucy Noodles with Vegetables (page 220) or Szechwan Fried Rice (page 208) in this chapter.

Simple Fried Rice

SERVES 4

There is nothing simple about the delicious taste of this classic Cantonese specialty, adapted with our own soy sauce and low-sodium beef bouillon.

2 cups cooked cold rice
1½ tablespoons vegetable oil, divided
Black pepper to taste
¹⁄₁₆ teaspoon garlic powder
Dash of ginger powder
1½ tablespoons low-sodium beef bouillon

6 tablespoons Soy Sauce Substitute (page 227), divided
2 eggs, lightly beaten
8 scallions, chopped, including greens

1. In wok, place rice. Turn heat to medium. Stir-fry 2 minutes, breaking up rice.
2. Add 1 tablespoon oil, pepper, and garlic and ginger powders. Stir-fry 2 minutes more.
3. Add bouillon and 2 tablespoons soy sauce. Stir-fry 2 minutes more.
4. Push rice to sides of wok. To well created in the center, add remaining ½ tablespoon oil. Add eggs and stir-fry until eggs start to set. Blend into rice mixture.
5. Push rice mixture to sides of wok. To well created in center, add 2 tablespoons soy sauce and scallions. Stir-fry 1 minute.
6. Add remaining 2 tablespoons soy sauce. Turn heat to high and stir-fry 1 minute more.

Per serving: 255.5 calories; 52.0 mg. sodium; 34.1 gm. carbohydrates; 9.7 gm. fat.

Fried Rice and Oysters

SERVES 8

This Cantonese treat is a fabulous side dish with any main course.

2 cups Chinese or American white
  cabbage, shredded
1½ teaspoons sugar
½ cup Chicken Stock (page 68)
4 cups cooked cold rice
1 tablespoon vegetable oil
Black pepper to taste
1 tablespoon dry sherry
1 tablespoon low-sodium beef
  bouillon

4 tablespoons Soy Sauce Substitute
  (page 227)
2 pints shucked oysters, chopped,
  including liquid
2 scallions, minced, including
  greens

1. In bowl, combine first 3 ingredients. Toss to blend. Let stand 10 minutes. Drain, reserving liquid.
2. In wok, place rice. Turn heat to medium and stir-fry 1 minute, breaking up rice.
3. Push rice to sides of wok. To well created in center, add oil. When hot, add cabbage and stir-fry 2 minutes.
4. Blend cabbage and rice. Add pepper and sherry. Stir to blend.
5. Turn heat to high. Add the bouillon and half the reserved cabbage liquid. Stir-fry until liquid is absorbed.
6. Add remaining cabbage liquid and stir-fry until liquid is absorbed.
7. Add remaining ingredients. Stir-fry 1 minute more.

Per serving: 226.5 calories; 82.2 mg. sodium; 34.8 gm. carbohydrates; 4.4 gm. fat.

Szechwan Fried Rice

SERVES 4

Oh, so good with Duck Salad with Pears (page 94).

2 tablespoons sesame seed oil, divided
8 scallions, chopped, including greens, divided
2 cloves garlic, minced
2 slices ginger root, minced, or ⅙ teaspoon ginger powder
1 fresh chili pepper, seeded and minced, or dash of hot pepper flakes
½ cup boiling water
4 teaspoons low-sodium beef bouillon

1 teaspoon white vinegar
2 tablespoons cold water
1½ teaspoons mustard powder
12 snow pea pods, cut in thirds, diagonally
4 fresh mushrooms, sliced
2 tablespoons Hoisin Sauce Substitute (page 228)
2 cups cooked rice
⅙ teaspoon Szechwan peppercorns, crushed

1. In wok, heat 1 tablespoon oil over low heat. Add half the scallions, garlic, ginger, and chili pepper. Cook 1 minute, stirring occasionally.
2. In bowl, combine boiling water, bouillon, and vinegar. Set aside.
3. In second bowl, combine cold water and mustard powder, blending well. Set aside.
4. To wok, add snow pea pods and mushrooms. Stir to blend.
5. Add hoisin sauce. Stir-fry 2 minutes. Transfer mixture to platter.
6. To wok, add rice, Szechwan pepper, and bouillon mixture. Stir to blend well.
7. Add mustard mixture. Stir to blend well.
8. Add remaining scallions. Cover and simmer 5 minutes.
9. Stir in vegetable mixture. Cover and simmer 5 minutes more, or until liquid is absorbed.

Per serving: 234.7 calories; 20.3 mg. sodium; 35.8 gm. carbohydrates; 8.7 gm. fat.

Rice Patties (Go Ba)

SERVES 8

Rice patties, enjoyed in every region throughout China, are light and crispy—perfect for snacks as well as for soups or salad toppings. When deep-fried, they become crunchy and delicious to munch on. They provide the "sizzle" in Shrimp and Pork Go Ba (page 76).

2 cups white rice   **3 cups water**

1. In saucepan, combine ingredients. Turn heat to high and bring to a boil. Reduce heat to low. Cover and simmer 15 minutes, or until liquid is almost absorbed.
2. Transfer rice to large skillet or baking sheet. Spread rice until it covers the surface. If using a skillet, turn heat to low and let dry-cook 1 hour, or until edges turn lightly brown and the rice can be removed in one piece. (If using a baking sheet, dry-bake in 200° oven 1 hour, or until edges are lightly brown and the rice can be lifted out in one piece.)
3. Transfer rice patty to platter. Let stand overnight to thoroughly dry out.
4. Cut rice patty into 2-inch squares (save all broken pieces). Store in tightly covered jar up to 3 months.

   Note: To deep-fry, use 2 cups of oil, heated until crackling hot. Fry only a few pieces at a time, right before serving, until puffy and lightly browned.

Per serving plain: 155.6 calories; 2.2 mg. sodium; 34.5 gm. carbohydrates; 0.2 gm. fat.
Per serving deep-fried: 202.9 calories; 2.2 mg. sodium; 34.5 gm. carbohydrates; 10.8 gm. fat.

Rice Curry Imperial

SERVES 4

Yunnan and Kweichou introduced curry to China, but now the entire country claims it for its own. You will understand why when you sample this unusual and wonderful meal-in-one. It is also a great way to perk up leftovers—just substitute like amounts for the chicken and shrimp, but add them when you add the stock in Step 5.

2 tablespoons white (or red) wine vinegar
2 tablespoons Soy Sauce Substitute (page 227)
1 tablespoon dry sherry
1 tablespoon Curry Powder (page 232)
2 scallions, chopped, including greens
1 tablespoon vegetable oil
1 onion, chopped
2 cloves garlic, minced

1 green pepper, chopped
1 half chicken breast, skinned, boned, and cubed
½ can (4 ounces) bamboo shoots, sliced
⅓ pound small shrimp, shelled, deveined, and halved lengthwise
8 fresh mushrooms, sliced
⅔ cup Chicken Stock (page 68), divided
2 cups cooked rice

1. In bowl, combine first 5 ingredients. Let stand 20 minutes.
2. In wok, heat oil over low heat. Add onion and garlic. Stir-fry 2 minutes.
3. Add green pepper and chicken. Stir-fry 1 minute, or until chicken is white all over.
4. Push chicken mixture to sides of wok. Raise heat to medium. Add bamboo shoots, shrimp, mushrooms, and 3 tablespoons chicken stock. Stir-fry 1 minute, or until shrimp are pink all over. Transfer mixture to bowl.
5. To wok, add remaining chicken stock and rice. Cook until liquid is absorbed, stirring occasionally.
6. Add chicken and shrimp mixture. Pour on marinade. Reduce heat to low. Cover and simmer 5 minutes, stirring occasionally.

Per serving: 285.4 calories; 94.6 mg. sodium; 41.3 gm. carbohydrates; 5.8 gm. fat.

Hoisin Rice in Four

SERVES 4

A little bit of Shanghai creates a lot of taste. When you add Szechwan Beef (page 174) to the menu, the rest is sure to please.

½ cup boiling water
1 teaspoon low-sodium chicken
  bouillon
4 dried black mushrooms*
2 tomatoes, chopped
1 leek, chopped, including greens
⅓ Chinese Barbecued Pork (or
  Beef) recipe (page 175)
¹⁄₁₆ teaspoon ginger powder

¹⁄₁₆ teaspoon garlic powder
Black pepper to taste
1 teaspoon orange peel, minced, or
  ⅛ teaspoon orange peel powder
2 tablespoons Hoisin Sauce
  Substitute (page 228)
2 cups cooked rice
½ cup Chicken Stock (page 68)

1. In bowl, combine first 2 ingredients, stirring to dissolve bouillon. Add mushrooms. Let stand ½ hour. Drain, reserving liquid. Chop mushrooms.
2. In second bowl, combine tomatoes, leek, barbecued pork, ginger and garlic powders, pepper, orange peel, and hoisin sauce. Stir to blend thoroughly. Let stand 10 minutes.
3. In saucepan, combine rice, tomato-meat mixture, mushrooms, and reserved mushroom liquid. Turn heat to low. Cover and simmer 10 minutes, stirring occasionally.
4. Add chicken stock. Cover and simmer 15 minutss more, or until liquid is absorbed, stirring occasionally.

Per serving with pork: 197.2 calories; 22.3 mg. sodium; 38.5 gm. carbohydrates; 1.6 gm. fat.
Per serving with beef: 195.7 calories; 22.2 mg. sodium; 38.5 gm. carbohydrates; 1.6 gm. fat.

* If not available, substitute 4 large fresh mushrooms, sliced.

Rice and Mixed Vegetables SERVES 8

The simplicity of this dish is matched by its savory flavor. Chinese Pepper Steak (page 179) is a lovely accompaniment.

2¾ cups Chicken Stock (page 68)
1½ cups white rice
Dash of Five-Spice Powder (page 228)
1 carrot, scraped and cut in ⅛-inch rounds
½ can (4 ounces) bamboo shoots, sliced, including liquid
½ cup boiling water

2 teaspoons low-sodium beef bouillon
1 teaspoon white vinegar
½ teaspoon mustard powder
2 broccoli stalks, cut in ⅛-inch rounds
1 leek, chopped, including greens
1½ tablespoons sesame seed oil

1. In saucepan, over medium heat, bring chicken stock to a slow boil.
2. Reduce heat to low. Add rice, five-spice powder, carrot, and bamboo shoots plus liquid. Cover and simmer 10 minutes.
3. While rice is cooking, in bowl, combine boiling water, bouillon, and vinegar. Stir until bouillon is dissolved. Let cool 10 minutes. Then stir in mustard powder, blending thoroughly.
4. Pour mustard mixture into rice mixture. Do not stir. Spoon broccoli and leek over all. Cover and simmer 10 minutes more, or until liquid is absorbed.
5. Stir in sesame seed oil.

Per serving: 202.2 calories; 27.6 mg. sodium; 32.7 gm. carbohydrates; 4.5 gm. fat.

Many-Flavored Fried Rice

SERVES 8

A truly exotic dish, inspired by the imaginative flair of the Cantonese. To complete the meal, serve with Five-Spice Chicken (page 154).

2 tablespoons vegetable oil, divided
1 onion, minced
2 cloves garlic, minced
2 slices ginger root, minced, or ⅟₁₆ teaspoon ginger powder
2 half chicken breasts, skinned, boned, and cubed
¼ pound pork, shredded
8 large shrimp, skinned, deveined, and chopped

4 cups cooked cold rice
Black pepper to taste
¼ cup boiling water
8 dried apricots, chopped
1 can (8 ounces), dietetic pineapple, chopped, including liquid
4 tablespoons Soy Sauce Substitute (page 227)
1 green pepper, chopped

1. In wok, heat ½ tablespoon oil over low heat. Add onion, garlic, and ginger root. Stir-fry 1 minute.
2. Add ½ tablespoon oil. Add chicken and pork. Stir-fry 1 minute, or until chicken turns white all over.
3. Add ½ tablespoon oil. Add shrimp. Stir-fry until shrimp turn pink all over.
4. Push mixture to sides of wok. To well created in center, add remaining ½ tablespoon oil. Add rice and stir-fry 2 minutes, breaking up rice.
5. Add black pepper and stir-fry 1 minute more.
6. Turn heat to high. Add remaining ingredients. Stir to blend thoroughly.
7. Reduce heat to low. Cover and simmer 15 minutes, or until liquid is absorbed.

Per serving: 275.1 calories; 76.9 mg. sodium; 39.4 gm. carbohydrates; 7.1 gm. fat.

Mandarin Rice with Peppers

SERVES 4

Totally unique. If northern chefs did not serve a dish like this to the Imperial Family, they should have.

¾ cup water
6 tablespoons Soy Sauce Substitute (page 227)
1 tablespoon dry sherry
1 can (11 ounces) mandarin oranges, drained and chopped, liquid reserved

1 teaspoon low-sodium chicken bouillon
⅛ teaspoon lemon peel powder
Dash of ginger powder
⅔ cup white rice
½ red pepper, sliced thin
½ green pepper, sliced thin

1. In saucepan, combine first 3 ingredients plus reserved mandarin oranges liquid, bouillon, lemon peel powder, and ginger powder. Turn heat to medium and bring to a slow boil.
2. Reduce heat to low. Add rice and mandarin oranges. Cover and simmer 10 minutes.
3. Place red and green peppers on top of rice. Cover and simmer 10 minutes more, or until liquid is absorbed.

Per serving: 112.5 calories; 20.5 mg. sodium; 23.6 gm. carbohydrates; 1.3 gm. fat.

Fish Congee with Cashews

SERVES 4

Americans call it congee; the Chinese, jook or hsi-fan, which means thin rice, although in the North, the primary ingredient is millet or barley. It is served for breakfast or lunch, as a nourishing snack, or as a late supper. It has countless variations. This exotic delicacy is quite simply the creamy gruel or porridge that is savored throughout China.

⅓ cup long-grain white rice*
4 cups water
1 zucchini, chopped
¼ pound flounder fillets, cut in thin strips
¼ pound red snapper fillets, cut in thin strips
1 tablespoon low-sodium chicken bouillon
½ tablespoon low-sodium beef bouillon

1 teaspoon dry sherry
1/16 teaspoon ground coriander
Black pepper to taste
2 scallions, minced, including greens
2 teaspoons dried cilantro (or parsley)
¼ cup unsalted cashews, chopped

1. In saucepan, combine first 2 ingredients. Turn heat to high and bring to a boil. Reduce heat to medium and cook 5 minutes.
2. Stir rice. Reduce heat to low. Cover and simmer 50 minutes.
3. Add zucchini. Cover and simmer 10 minutes more.
4. Add remaining ingredients. Stir to blend. Cover and simmer 8 minutes, or until fish turns white.

Per serving: 210.1 calories; 51.1 mg. sodium; 20.1 gm. carbohydrates; 8.0 gm. fat.

* Because of the amount of water in this recipe, it is essential to use long-grain rice.

Chinese Chicken and Rice   SERVES 4

A marvelous, easy meal-in-a-wok—all with Cantonese flair.

1 cup boiling water
8 dried black mushrooms*
1 tablespoon low-sodium chicken bouillon
1 tablespoon dry sherry
3 tablespoons Soy Sauce Substitute (page 227)

Black pepper to taste
1½ cups cooked rice
2 half chicken breasts, skinned, boned, and cubed
¼ cup unsalted walnuts, crushed

1. In bowl, combine first 3 ingredients. Let stand ½ hour. Drain, reserving liquid. Chop mushrooms. Set aside.
2. In second bowl, combine reserved mushroom liquid, sherry, soy sauce, and pepper. Stir to blend. Set aside.
3. In wok, place rice. Top with chicken, walnuts, and mushrooms. Pour sherry mixture over all. Turn heat to low. Cover and simmer 20 minutes, or until liquid is absorbed.
4. Toss to blend. Serve with Duck Sauce (page 234).

Per serving: 273 calories; 40.8 mg. sodium; 26.7 gm. carbohydrates; 11.6 gm. fat.

* If not available, substitute 8 large fresh mushrooms, sliced.

Fried Noodles

SERVES 4

These crunchy, browned noodles, loved throughout China, are delicious plain, as a side dish, or served with any topping of your choice for a soul-satisfying main course. May we suggest Braised Shrimp with Leek (page 133).

½ pound egg noodles
2 teaspoons low-sodium chicken
  bouillon
⅓ cup boiling water

3 tablespoons vegetable oil, divided
2 tablespoons Soy Sauce Substitute
  (page 227), divided

1. On platter, spread noodles. Sprinkle with bouillon and boiling water. Let stand 1 hour, or until noodles are dry.
2. In wok, heat half the oil over medium-low heat. Add noodles and flatten into a pancake. Fry 1 minute.
3. Add 1 tablespoon soy sauce and fry 2 minutes more, or until bottom is brown and crisp.
4. Turn noodle pancake. Dribble remaining oil around sides of wok. Fry 1 minute.
5. Add remaining soy sauce and fry 2 minutes more, or until bottom is brown and crisp.

Per serving: 315.2 calories; 5.7 mg. sodium; 44.5 gm. carbohydrates; 12.5 gm. fat.

Spicy Noodles in Orange Sauce   SERVES 4

This dish is purely northern, purely wonderful, and needs no accompanying distraction.

4 tablespoons lime juice
1 tablespoon cornstarch
½ pound bay scallops, sliced
2 tablespoons vegetable oil, divided
1 onion, minced
2 cloves garlic, minced
¼ pound pork, julienned
2 chili peppers, minced, or ¹⁄₁₆ teaspoon hot pepper flakes
½ cup Fish Stock (page 67)
2 tablespoons sugar
2 tablespoons orange peel, minced, or 1½ teaspoons orange peel powder

1 tablespoon low-sodium beef bouillon
2 tablespoons low-sodium tomato paste
1 tablespoon Soy Sauce Substitute (page 227)
¼ cup orange juice
2 scallions, chopped, including greens
½ pound vermicelli, boiled 7 minutes*

1. In bowl, combine first 2 ingredients, blending well. Add scallops and toss to coat thoroughly. Cover and refrigerate 1½ hours.
2. In wok, heat 1 tablespoon oil over low heat. Add onion and garlic. Stir-fry 1 minute.
3. Add pork and chili peppers. Stir-fry 1 minute more, or until pork loses all pink color. Transfer to bowl.
4. In saucepan, combine fish stock, sugar, orange peel, bouillon, and tomato paste. Turn heat to low and simmer 10 minutes, stirring often.
5. Add soy sauce and orange juice. Simmer 5 minutes more. Let cool 10 minutes. Cover and refrigerate 1 hour.
6. In wok, heat remaining tablespoon oil over medium heat. Add scallop mixture and stir-fry until scallops are lightly browned all over.
7. Add pork mixture and ¼ cup fish stock mixture. Stir-fry 1 minute.
8. Add scallions and ¼ cup fish stock mixture. Stir-fry 2 minutes more.
9. Add vermicelli and remaining fish stock mixture. Stir-fry 2 minutes more, or until mixture starts to bubble around the edges.

Per serving: 510.4 calories; 202.6 mg. sodium; 70.6 gm. carbohydrates; 14.2 gm. fat.

* Do not add salt to boiling water.

Beef Lo Mein

SERVES 4

Noodles originated in the North, but Lo Mein, which means mixing noodles, had its beginnings in Canton. This very popular dish is just as good with pork or chicken.

2 tablespoons peanut oil, divided
1 onion, chopped
1 clove garlic, minced
1 cup Chinese or American white cabbage, shredded
4 fresh mushrooms, sliced
1 tablespoon dry sherry
¼ pound Chinese Barbecued Beef (page 175), shredded

¼ pound bean sprouts
2 tablespoons Soy Sauce Substitute (page 227)
½ can (4 ounces) bamboo shoots, sliced
6 ounces cellophane noodles (or vermicelli), cooked 10 minutes*

1. In wok, heat 1 tablespoon oil over low heat. Add onion and garlic. Stir-fry 1 minute.
2. Add cabbage and mushrooms. Stir-fry 2 minutes.
3. Add sherry and stir-fry 2 minutes more.
4. Push cabbage mixture to sides of wok. Add remaining oil. Add barbecued beef and bean sprouts. Stir-fry 2 minutes.
5. Add remaining ingredients and stir-fry 3 minutes more.

Per serving with beef: 348.5 calories; 35.9 mg. sodium; 62.5 gm. carbohydrates; 11.7 gm. fat.
Per serving with pork: 363.8 calories; 37.6 mg. sodium; 62.5 gm. carbohydrates; 13.9 gm. fat.
Per serving with chicken: 325.5 calories; 31.6 mg. sodium; 62.5 gm. carbohydrates; 10.5 gm. fat.

* Do not add salt to boiling water.

Shrimp Lo Mein

SERVES 4

As Cantonese as Beef Lo Mein (page 218) and just as delicious.

½ pound small shrimp, shelled, deveined, and chopped
1 teaspoon dry sherry
1 teaspoon lemon juice
1 teaspoon cornstarch
½ pound vermicelli, boiled al dente*
3 tablespoons Soy Sauce Substitute (page 227), divided
1 tablespoon vegetable oil
1 onion, sliced
2 slices ginger root, minced, or ¹⁄₁₆ teaspoon ginger powder

1 can (8 ounces) water chestnuts, chopped
½ pound green beans, chopped
½ teaspoon sugar
4 fresh mushrooms, sliced
2 scallions, chopped, including greens
1 teaspoon low-sodium beef bouillon
Black pepper to taste

1. In bowl, combine first 4 ingredients. Cover and refrigerate ½ hour.
2. In second bowl, combine vermicelli and soy sauce. Toss to blend thoroughly.
3. In wok, heat oil over low heat. Add onion and ginger. Stir-fry 1 minute, or until onion is wilted.
4. Add water chestnuts. Stir-fry 30 seconds more.
5. Add green beans and sugar. Stir-fry 1 minute more.
6. Stir in mushrooms, scallions, and vermicelli mixture. Stir-fry 3 minutes.
7. Push vermicelli mixture to sides of wok. To well created in center, add shrimp mixture. Stir-fry 1 minute, or until shrimp turn pink all over.
8. Stir in bouillon and pepper. Stir-fry 1 minute more.

Per serving: 391.1 calories; 106.3 mg. sodium; 68.0 gm. carbohydrates; 6.0 gm. fat.

* Do not add salt to boiling water.

Saucy Noodles with Vegetables SERVES 4

Very much like an eastern dish that generally includes pork and chicken, and uses chicken soup instead of the lobster sauce we have chosen. But any way at all, this is a wonderful, filling, but light main dish. It can be both stretched and enhanced by adding 1 pint shucked oysters plus liquid after Step 5, then simmering 30 seconds.

4 cups Lobster Sauce (page 239)
1 can (8 ounces) bamboo shoots, sliced
1 large carrot, scraped and cut in ¼-inch rounds
1 tablespoon dry sherry
3 tablespoons Soy Sauce Substitute (page 227)
Black pepper to taste

1 red pepper, sliced
1 teaspoon cider vinegar
2 cups broccoli flowerettes
¼ cup cold water
2 tablespoons cornstarch
½ teaspoon mustard powder
1 egg, lightly beaten
6 ounces cellophane noodles (or vermicelli), boiled al dente*

1. In wok, combine first 3 ingredients. Turn heat to medium and bring to a slow boil.
2. Stir in sherry, soy sauce, and black pepper. Bring to a second boil.
3. Reduce heat to low. Add red pepper, vinegar, and broccoli. Cook 5 minutes, stirring occasionally.
4. While sauce is cooking, in bowl combine water, cornstarch, and mustard powder. Stir into sauce and stir constantly until sauce thickens.
5. Gradually add egg in a slow stream, stirring constantly.
6. In large bowl, place noodles. Pour sauce over all.

Per serving plain: 333.7 calories; 74.2 mg. sodium; 60.2 gm. carbohydrates; 7.0 gm. fat.
Per serving with oysters: 390.3 calories; 136.8 mg. sodium; 63.2 gm. carbohydrates; 8.6 gm. fat.

* Do not add salt to boiling water.

Peanutty Noodles with Chicken   SERVES 4

More pointedly western and absolutely delicious. Try it with Broccoli and Minced Shrimp (page 192).

⅓ cup boiling water
2 tablespoons low-sodium peanut
  butter
Dash of hot pepper flakes
2 teaspoons low-sodium beef
  bouillon
4 teaspoons peanut oil, divided
2 scallions, chopped, including
  greens
2 cloves garlic, minced
1 half chicken breast, skinned,
  boned, and shredded

½ can (4 ounces) water chestnuts,
  chopped
1 red pepper, sliced thin
12 snow pea pods, cut in thirds
  diagonally
6 ounces vermicelli, cooked 7
  minutes*
1 teaspoon red wine vinegar
½ teaspoon sugar

1. In bowl, combine first 4 ingredients. Stir until peanut butter is completely blended. Set aside.
2. In wok, heat 1 tablespoon oil over low heat. Add scallions, garlic, chicken, water chestnuts, and red pepper. Stir-fry 2 minutes, or until chicken turns white.
3. Add pea pods and stir-fry 30 seconds. Transfer mixture to platter.
4. To wok, add remaining tablespoon oil. Add noodles and stir-fry 2 minutes.
5. Add vinegar and sugar. Stir-fry 2 minutes more.
6. Add peanut butter mixture, vegetables, and chicken. Turn heat to medium and cook 2 minutes, stirring often.

Per serving: 332.3 calories; 38.4 mg. sodium; 47.4 gm. carbohydrates; 10.6 gm. fat.

* Do not add salt to boiling water.

Noodles with Sesame Paste Sauce   SERVES 4

A wonderful representation of the West's penchant for contrasting flavors, this one pairs pungent chili ketchup with the subtle tingle of Szechwan peppercorns, and sweet sesame seed paste with "salty" soy sauce.

2 cups Meat Stock (page 69)
1 tablespoon low-sodium chili
  ketchup
2 tablespoons Soy Sauce Substitute
  (page 227)
4 slices ginger root, or 1/16 teaspoon
  ginger powder
1 star anise
1 tablespoon dry sherry
1/8 teaspoon garlic powder

1 teaspoon paprika
4 scallions, minced, including
  greens
1/16 teaspoon Szechwan
  peppercorns, crushed
2 tablespoons sesame seed paste
1/2 pound noodles, boiled al dente*
1/4 cup unsalted peanuts (or
  almonds), crushed

1. In saucepan, combine all but last 2 ingredients. Turn heat to medium and bring to a slow boil. Reduce heat to low and simmer 1/2 hour. Discard ginger root and star anise.
2. In large bowl, combine sauce plus noodles. Toss to blend thoroughly.
3. Sprinkle nuts on top.

Per serving with peanuts: 373.6 calories; 17.4 mg. sodium; 53.6 gm. carbohydrates; 12.8 gm. fat.
Per serving with almonds: 375.9 calories; 17.3 mg. sodium; 53.4 gm. carbohydrates; 13.6 gm. fat.

* Do not add salt to boiling water.

Noodles with Seafood SERVES 8

Save this special meal in the northern tradition for a worthy occasion. For balance, serve with Sweet and Hot Chicken Mushroom Soup (page 72).

1 cup Chicken Stock (page 68)
1 cup Meat Stock (page 69)
¾ teaspoon paprika
¼ teaspoon garlic powder
1 1-pound lobster, cut into 1-inch pieces
¼ pound cleaned squid, cut into 1-inch pieces
2½ tablespoons all-purpose flour
½ pound shrimp, shelled, deveined, and halved lengthwise
2 slices ginger root, minced, or ¹⁄₁₆ teaspoon ginger powder

3 tablespoons sesame seed oil, divided
1 onion, minced
2 cloves garlic, minced
2 cups broccoli flowerettes
2 tablespoons cider vinegar
1 pound cellophane noodles (or vermicelli), boiled 5 minutes*
¼ cup Oyster Sauce (page 234)
1½ tablespoons cornstarch
4 scallions, chopped, including greens

1. In saucepan, combine first 4 ingredients. Turn heat to medium and bring to a slow boil. Reduce heat to low and simmer ½ hour, or until liquid is reduced by half. Pour into bowl. Cover and refrigerate overnight.
2. In bowl, combine lobster, squid, and flour.
3. In second bowl, combine shrimp and ginger.
4. In wok, heat 1 tablespoon oil over low heat. Add onion and garlic and stir-fry 30 seconds.
5. Add broccoli and stir-fry 30 seconds more. Transfer to platter.
6. To wok, add remaining oil. Add lobster and squid mixture plus shrimp mixture. Stir-fry 30 seconds.
7. Add vinegar. Stir-fry 1 minute more. Transfer to platter.
8. To wok, add noodles. Stir-fry 1 minute.
9. Add chicken and meat stock mixture. Turn heat to medium and bring to a slow boil.
10. While sauce is cooking, in bowl, combine oyster sauce and cornstarch. Stir into wok mixture.
11. Add vegetable and seafood mixture plus scallions. Cook 7 minutes more, stirring often, until mixture thickens.

Per serving: 371.8 calories; 88.2 mg. sodium; 56.4 gm. carbohydrates; 7.9 gm. fat.

* Do not add salt to boiling water.

Noodles with Almond Chicken
SERVES 8

Szechwan overtones mark this memorable one-dish meal.

8 dried black mushrooms*
1 cup boiling water
2 tablespoons cornstarch
2 tablespoons sesame seed oil,
    divided
1 leek, chopped, including greens
2 teaspoons lemon peel, minced, or
    ½ teaspoon lemon peel powder
4 half chicken breasts, skinned,
    boned, and cubed
1 tablespoon white vinegar

2 cups Chinese or American white
    cabbage, shredded
1 teaspoon sugar
¼ cup unsalted slivered almonds
¾ pound vermicelli, cooked 7
    minutes†
1 cup Chicken Stock (page 68)
1 tablespoon low-sodium beef
    bouillon

1. In bowl, combine first 2 ingredients. Let stand ½ hour. Drain, reserving half the liquid. Cut each mushroom in half. Set aside.
2. In second bowl, combine reserved liquid and cornstarch, stirring until cornstarch is dissolved. Set aside.
3. In wok, heat 1 tablespoon oil over medium heat. Add leek, lemon peel, and chicken. Stir-fry 1 minute, or until chicken turns white all over. Transfer to platter.
4. To wok, add vinegar, cabbage, and sugar. Stir to blend. Reduce heat to low. Cover and simmer 5 minutes, stirring occasionally. Transfer to platter.
5. To wok, add remaining tablespoon oil plus almonds and noodles. Raise heat to medium and stir-fry 3 minutes.
6. Add chicken mixture, cabbage, mushrooms, chicken stock, and bouillon. Stir to blend.
7. Add cornstarch mixture and cook until sauce thickens, stirring often.

Per serving: 336.7 calories; 55.6 mg. sodium; 42.5 gm. carbohydrates; 10.2 gm. fat.

* If not available, substitute 8 large fresh mushrooms, sliced.
† Do not add salt to boiling water.

Noodles of Land and Sea

SERVES 8

A fabulous and unusual one-dish meal, combining the best of all regions.

2 tablespoons sesame seed oil,
   divided
2 slices ginger root, minced, or ¹⁄₁₆
   teaspoon ginger powder
2 cloves garlic, minced
1 leek, chopped, including greens
1 half chicken breast, skinned,
   boned, and cubed
¼ pound Chinese Barbecued Pork
   (page 175), cut in matchstick
   strips
¼ pound small shrimp, shelled,
   deveined, and chopped

2 tablespoons dry sherry, divided
1 can (8 ounces) water chestnuts,
   chopped
1 small eggplant, peeled and cubed
4 tablespoons Hoisin Sauce
   Substitue (page 228)
4 fresh mushrooms, sliced
1 cup Chicken Stock (page 68)
1 cup Meat Stock (page 69)
¾ pound vermicelli, boiled 5
   minutes*

1. In wok, heat 1 tablespoon oil over medium heat. Add ginger, garlic, and leek. Stir-fry 30 seconds.
2. Add chicken and barbecued pork. Stir-fry 1 minute, or until chicken is white all over. Remove to 8-inch square casserole.
3. To wok, add shrimp, 1 tablespoon sherry, water chestnuts, and eggplant. Stir-fry 1 minute, or until shrimp turn pink. Remove to casserole.
4. Preheat oven to 350°.
5. Stir all remaining ingredients into casserole. Bake, uncovered, 15 minutes, or until mixture is set.

Per serving: 223.6 calories; 48.2 mg. sodium; 30.2 gm. carbohydrates; 5.9 gm. fat.

* Do not add salt to boiling water.

Beefy Noodles in Chili Sauce   SERVES 4

A hearty and robust dish in the Szechwan tradition.

¼ pound flank steak
2 tablespoons red wine vinegar
1 tablespoon Chili Oil (page 230)
3 tablespoons Soy Sauce Substitute (page 227)
2 tablespoons dry sherry
1 leek, chopped, including greens
¹⁄₁₆ teaspoon ground Szechwan peppercorns
1 star anise
2 carrots, scraped, cut in ¼-inch rounds and steamed

½ can (4 ounces) bamboo shoots, sliced
6 ounces cellophane noodles (or vermicelli), boiled al dente*
½ cup Meat Stock (page 69)
1 tablespoon low-sodium chili ketchup
Dash of ginger powder
1 teaspoon sesame seed oil

1. In bowl, combine first 3 ingredients. Cover and refrigerate at least 4 hours, turning steak occasionally.
2. In wok, place steak mixture. Turn heat to high. Sear steak on both sides.
3. Add soy sauce, sherry, leek, pepper, star anise, carrots, and bamboo shoots. Fry steak 2 minutes more, stirring often.
4. Remove wok from heat. Transfer mixture to platter and slice steak thin. Discard star anise.
5. Return wok to high heat. Add noodles and stir-fry 1 minute. .
6. Add meat stock, chili ketchup, and ginger powder. Stir-fry 2 minutes.
7. Add vegetable and steak mixture plus sesame seed oil. Stir-fry 2 minutes more.

Per serving: 322 calories; 50.6 mg. sodium; 45.3 gm. carbohydrates; 8.2 gm. fat.

* Do not add salt to boiling water.

Sauces and Seasonings

The Chinese have numerous sauces in their repertoire—some subtle, some hot, some pungent and sharp—to tease or taunt the tongue. We have adopted many of them for our own table.

However, whereas we use condiments like Duck Sauce (page 234) as side-dish toppings or dips, the Chinese do not. In line with their art of blending and balancing flavors to create harmony, Chinese chefs add the appropriate sauce during the cooking process so it can lend its special flavor to a given dish, making it wonderfully unique.

You can do likewise, using the sauces in this chapter to transform the simplest dish.

In addition, the following pages provide you with low-sodium recipes for the seasonings called for in this book that are not easily found in super-markets or health food stores.

Soy Sauce Substitute

MAKES 2 CUPS

Here is our rendition of the most basic staple in Chinese cooking. Although it will not taste the same straight from the jar, it will admirably provide that special soy sauce taste in cooking.

1½ cups boiling water
4 tablespoons low-sodium beef
  bouillon
⅟₁₆ teaspoon black pepper

1 tablespoon dark molasses
4 tablespoons cider vinegar
1 teaspoon sesame seed oil

1. In bowl, combine all ingredients, stirring to blend thoroughly. Pour into jars. Cover and seal tightly.
2. May be refrigerated indefinitely. Shake well before using.

Per recipe: 299.2 calories; 129.3 mg. sodium; 35.8 gm. carbohydrates; 17.0 gm. fat.
Per cup: 149.6 calories; 64.7 mg. sodium; 17.9 gm. carbohydrates; 8.5 gm. fat.
Per tablespoon: 9.4 calories; 4.0 mg. sodium; 1.1 gm. carbohydrates; 0.5 gm. fat.

Hoisin Sauce Substitute

MAKES 2¼ CUPS

One of the most popular Chinese sauces, used nationwide although it originated in Peking. Our version has a thinner consistency than the original, but we think you will like it every bit as much.

2 cups Soy Sauce Substitute (page 227)
2 cloves garlic, blanched and mashed
2 dried red peppers, crumbled, or ¹⁄₁₆ teaspoon hot pepper flakes

2 tablespoons low-sodium chili ketchup
2 tablespoons boiling water
2 teaspoons orange peel powder
2 teaspoons sesame seed oil

1. In bowl, combine first 4 ingredients, blending thoroughly.
2. In second bowl, combine remaining ingredients. Let stand 15 minutes. Pour into soy sauce mixture, blending thoroughly.
3. Pour mixture into jars. Cover and refrigerate. Will keep indefinitely.
4. Serve as a dip, or use as a sauce for fish and seafood, meat and poultry.

Per recipe: 437.3 calories; 147.8 mg. sodium; 44.6 gm. carbohydrates; 24.4 gm. fat.
Per cup: 193.6 calories; 65.6 mg. sodium; 19.2 gm. carbohydrates; 11.2 gm. fat.
Per tablespoon: 12.1 calories; 4.1 mg. sodium; 1.2 gm. carbohydrates; 0.7 gm. fat.

Five-Spice Powder

MAKES ⅛ CUP

A sweet ground spice combination, readily available in Chinese markets, blended to both temper and enhance the distinctive flavor of anise. This is a staple throughout China, most often used to season duck and sometimes fish. Spices used include anise or fennel, ginger, nutmeg, cinnamon, cloves, and Szechwan peppercorns. Below is our version.

5 star anise
1 tablespoon Szechwan peppercorns

10 cloves
2 sticks cinnamon
1½ teaspoons ginger powder

1. In blender or food processor, combine first 4 ingredients. Grind to a fine powder.
2. In bowl, combine mixture with ginger powder, stirring to blend thoroughly.
3. Spoon into jar. Cover tightly. Store in cool, dry place. Will keep indefinitely.

Contains only a trace of calories, sodium, carbohydrates, and fat.

Szechwan Pepper Spice

MAKES ⅓ CUP

Substitute aniseed for peppercorns for a uniquely different spice blend. Use to add a nutty, mildly hot flavor to foods.

3 tablespoons Szechwan
  peppercorns
1 teaspoon garlic powder
4 tablespoons low-sodium beef
  bouillon

2 tablespoons unsalted peanuts
  (optional)

1. In wok, combine first 3 ingredients. Turn heat to low and simmer 5 minutes, or until peppercorns start to smoke. Transfer to blender or food processor.
2. Add peanuts, if desired, and grind. Spoon into a jar. Cover tightly. Will keep indefinitely stored in a cool, dark cabinet.

With peanuts. Per recipe: 382.3 calories; 61.4 mg. sodium; 29.9 gm. carbohydrates; 25.9 gm. fat.
Per tablespoon: 73.5 calories; 17.8 mg. sodium; 5.8 gm. carbohydrates; 5.0 gm. fat.
Without peanuts. Per recipe: 216 calories; 60.0 mg. sodium; 24.0 gm. carbohydrates; 12.0 gm. fat.
Per tablespoon: 41.5 calories; 11.5 mg. sodium; 4.6 gm. carbohydrates; 2.3 gm. fat.

VARIATION: *Anise Pepper Spice*—Substitute 3 tablespoons aniseed for the Szechwan peppercorns and proceed as above.

Chili Paste

MAKES ½ CUP

A staple in Szechwan cooking. One teaspoon will add zip to any dish.

1 tablespoon Chili Oil (page 230)
6 fresh chili peppers, seeded and
  chopped, or 1 teaspoon hot
  pepper flakes
1 cup Chicken Stock (page 68)

4 tablespoons sugar
4 tablespoons water
1½ tablespoons cornstarch
2 tablespoons dry sherry

1. In wok, heat oil over low heat. Add chili peppers and stir-fry 2 minutes.
2. Add chicken stock and sugar. Cover and simmer 45 minutes. Let cool 1 hour.
3. Strain through cheesecloth or fine sieve into saucepan. Simmer 5 minutes more.
4. While sauce is simmering, in bowl, combine water and cornstarch, stirring until cornstarch is dissolved. Stir into sauce and simmer until sauce starts to thicken, stirring often.
5. Stir in sherry. Let cool ½ hour. Pour into jars. Cover tightly. Will keep in refrigerator indefinitely.

Per recipe: 583.8 calories; 58.5 mg. sodium; 92.8 gm. carbohydrates; 18.4 gm. fat.
Per tablespoon: 73 calories; 7.3 mg. sodium; 11.6 gm. carbohydrates; 2.3 gm. fat.

Chili Oil

MAKES ¾ CUP

This oil is traditional in Szechwan and Hunan cooking. However, it also adds a wonderful spark to dishes of any region. For variety, substitute sesame seed oil for vegetable oil, or add 1 teaspoon of cayenne or ground Szechwan peppercorns to either oil base. If you don't want to make your own, chili oil is available in all Chinese markets.

¾ cup vegetable oil plus 2
  tablespoons

6 fresh chili peppers, seeded and
  minced, or 2 tablespoons hot
  pepper

1. In wok, heat oil over high heat until sizzling. Reduce heat to low and add chili peppers. Stir-fry 2 minutes.
2. Remove from heat and let stand 1 hour, or until cold. Strain oil through cheesecloth or fine sieve into bottle. Cover tightly and store in cool, dark cabinet. Will keep indefinitely.

Per recipe: 981.6 calories; 1.8 mg sodium; 13.5 gm. carbohydrates; 106.1 gm. fat.
Per tablespoon: 81.8 calories; 0.2 mg. sodium; 1.1 gm. carbohydrates; 8.8 gm. fat.

Chili Powder

MAKES ½ CUP

There are many commercial brands of chili powder available in super-markets. However, since many of these contain salt, here's an easy recipe which will last quite a while.

16 dried red peppers, minced, or
   2 tablespoons hot pepper flakes
1 tablespoon garlic powder
1 tablespoon paprika

2 teaspoons oregano
1 teaspoon ground coriander
8 tablespoons ground cumin

1. In bowl, combine all ingredients, blending thoroughly.
2. Spoon into jars. Cover tightly. Store in dark, cool cabinet. Will keep indefinitely.

Per recipe: 148.6 calories; 57.1 mg. sodium; 36.1 gm. carbohydrates; 0.9 gm. fat.
Per tablespoon: 18.6 calories; 7.1 mg. sodium; 4.5 carbohydrates; 0.1 gm. fat.

Chili Sauce

MAKES 1½ CUPS

The hot of Chili Paste (page 230), followed by a sweet relief. This Szechwan staple is sure to become a favorite of yours as well.

1 tablespoon vegetable (or sesame
   seed) oil
2 cloves garlic, minced
2 slices ginger root, minced, or ⅟16
   teaspoon ginger powder
1 can (6 ounces) low-sodium
   tomato paste
1 cup water
2 tablespoons Soy Sauce Substitute
   (page 227)
1 tablespoon sugar

1 teaspoon orange peel, minced,
   or ⅟16 teaspoon orange peel
   powder
4 scallions, minced, including
   greens
2 tablespoons low-sodium chili
   ketchup
⅟16 teaspoon hot pepper flakes
1 teaspoon paprika
Ground Szechwan peppercorns to
   taste

1. In wok, heat oil over low heat. Add garlic and ginger. Stir-fry 1 minute.
2. Add tomato paste. Stir-fry briefly.
3. Add water. Stir to blend. Simmer 5 minutes.
4. Add all remaining ingredients. Cover and simmer 20 minutes.
5. Pour into jars. Cover tightly. May be refrigerated up to 3 months or frozen indefinitely.

Per recipe: 412.1 calories; 39.3 mg. sodium; 57.8 gm. carbohydrates; 16.5 gm. fat.
Per cup: 274.3 calories; 25.6 mg. sodium; 38.9 gm. carbohydrates; 11.2 gm. fat.
Per tablespoon: 17.1 calories; 1.6 mg. sodium; 2.4 gm. carbohydrates; 0.7 gm. fat.

Curry Powder

MAKES ALMOST ⅓ CUP

Although generic to Indian cuisine, curry powder has found its way via Yunnan and Kweichou into many Chinese dishes—especially those originating in regions appreciative of hot spices, such as Szechwan. Curry powder can be found in the spice section of most supermarkets, but since many commercial blends contain salt, we offer our version below.

6½ teaspoons ground cumin
1 teaspoon ground coriander
1 teaspoon ground cardamom
  (optional)
½ teaspoon ground cinnamon

⅛ teaspoon nutmeg
⅛ teaspoon ginger powder
8 teaspoons turmeric
1/16 teaspoon cayenne pepper

1. In bowl, combine all ingredients. Stir to blend thoroughly.
2. Spoon into jar. Cover tightly. Store in cool, dry place. Will keep indefinitely.

Contains only a trace of calories, sodium, carbohydrates, and fat.

Black Bean Sauce

MAKES 2¼ CUPS

Our version of the sauce that is used in every kind of dish in regions throughout China.

½ pound black beans
4 cups water
2 tablespoons white vinegar
1 tablespoon sesame seed oil

2½ tablespoons low-sodium
  chicken bouillon
6 tablespoons Soy Sauce Substitute
  (page 227)

1. In saucepan, combine first 2 ingredients. Turn heat to medium and bring to a slow boil. Reduce heat to low. Cover and simmer 1½ hours, or until beans soften, adding more water, if necessary, to prevent sticking.
2. Stir in vinegar. Let stand 15 minutes.
3. In wok, heat oil over low heat. Add bean mixture, bouillon, and soy sauce. Simmer 10 minutes, stirring often.
4. Spoon into jars. Cover tightly. Will keep in refrigerator up to 2 months.

Per recipe: 708 calories; 82.7 mg. sodium; 162.3 gm. carbohydrates; 42.6 gm. fat.
Per cup: 314.7 calories; 36.8 mg. sodium; 72.1 gm. carbohydrates; 18.9 gm. fat.
Per tablespoon: 19.7 calories; 2.3 mg. sodium; 4.5 gm. carbohydrates; 1.2 gm. fat.

Brown Sauce

MAKES 1¾ CUPS

A good substitute for Black Bean Sauce (page 232), although the flavor will be subtler. This creation of ours has a Cantonese delicacy and is especially good on chicken and fish.

1 teaspoon vegetable oil
2 cloves garlic, minced
1 large onion, minced
2 cups Chicken Stock (page 68)
2 tablespoons low-sodium chicken
  bouillon

½ teaspoon ground sage
1 teaspoon paprika
2 tablespoons Soy Sauce Substitute
  (page 227)

1. In wok, heat oil over low heat. Add garlic and onion. Stir-fry 1 minute.
2. Add chicken stock. Raise heat to medium and bring to a slow boil. Reduce heat. Cover and simmer ½ hour, stirring occasionally.
3. Stir in bouillon, sage, and paprika. Cover and simmer ½ hour more.
4. Stir in soy sauce. Pour into jars. Cover and refrigerate at least 4 hours, or until liquid gels, before using. Skim off any fat before use. Can be refrigerated up to 2 weeks or frozen indefinitely.

Per recipe: 424.4 calories; 129.4 mg. sodium; 46.0 gm. carbohydrates; 18.8 gm. fat.
Per cup: 242.5 calories; 73.9 mg. sodium; 26.3 gm. carbohydrates; 10.7 gm. fat.
Per tablespoon: 15.2 calories; 4.6 mg. sodium; 1.6 gm. carbohydrates; 0.7 gm. fat.

Dipping Sauce

MAKES ⅞ CUP

This fabulous Cantonese sauce is excellent with any fried food or raw vegetables, Chinese and otherwise.

½ cup white vinegar
6 cloves garlic, sliced
1/16 teaspoon ginger powder
¼ cup Soy Sauce Substitute (page 227)

2 tablespoons sesame seed oil or
  Chili Oil (page 230)
2 scallions, chopped, including
  greens

1. In bowl, combine all ingredients, stirring to blend well. Cover and refrigerate 1 hour before use.
2. Serve with egg rolls, jao-tze, won tons, dumplings, and as a vegetable dip.

Per recipe: 372.5 calories; 26.8 mg. sodium; 25.6 gm. carbohydrates; 31.6 gm. fat.
Per tablespoon: 26.6 calories; 2.0 mg. sodium; 1.8 gm. carbohydrates; 2.3 gm. fat.

Duck Sauce

MAKES 8 CUPS

This American name for plum sauce probably derives from the fact that it was originally served in the United States as an accompaniment to duck. Now, of course, this sweetly pungent condiment is a standard dip sauce for many Chinese dishes, including egg rolls, pork, fish, and vegetables.

3 cans (16 ounces each) purple plums, drained, pitted, and chopped
2 cans (16 ounces each) dietetic apricots, drained, pitted, and chopped
1 can (8 ounces) dietetic peach halves, drained, pitted, and chopped

2 fresh chili peppers, seeded and chopped, or ¹⁄₁₆ teaspoon hot pepper flakes
6 scallions, chopped, including greens
½ cup red wine vinegar
⅔ cup sugar
Black pepper to taste
½ cup water

1. In saucepan, combine all ingredients. Turn heat to low. Cover and simmer 1½ hours, adding more water, if necessary, to keep mixture from sticking.
2. In blender or food processor, puree mixture.
3. Pour mixture into jars. Cover tightly. May be refrigerated up to 6 months.

Per recipe: 1,838.6 calories; 53.6 mg. sodium; 405.9 gm. carbohydrates; 5.0 gm. fat.
Per cup: 229.8 calories; 6.7 mg. sodium; 50.7 gm. carbohydrates; 0.6 gm. fat.
Per tablespoon: 14.4 calories; 0.4 mg. sodium; 3.2 gm. carbohydrates; 0.1 gm. fat.

Oyster Sauce

MAKES 2¾ CUPS

This sauce, traditionally made from salt and oyster extract, is indigenous to all regions. Our version has a thinner consistency but a much richer, meatier flavor thanks to the generous amount of oysters used.

1 pint shucked oysters, liquid reserved
½ teaspoon lemon juice
1½ cups water, divided
1½ tablespoons low-sodium chicken bouillon

2 tablespoons Soy Sauce Substitute (page 227)
Black pepper to taste

1. In wok or large saucepan, combine oysters, lemon juice, and ½ cup of water. Turn heat to high and poach 10 seconds.
2. Pour oysters and water into blender. Grind briefly. Set aside.

3. In wok, combine remaining water and bouillon. Turn heat to medium and bring to a slow boil.
4. Reduce heat to low. Stir in oyster mixture, oyster liquid, soy sauce, and pepper. Simmer 5 minutes, stirring occasionally.
5. Pour mixture into bottles, leaving ½-inch headspace. May be refrigerated up to 1 week or frozen up to 2 months.
   Note: If freezing, it is best to use a freezer tray. The freezer units can each hold about 4 tablespoons of the sauce—perfect since most recipes require only small amounts of the sauce.

Per recipe: 326.5 calories; 280.9 mg. sodium; 23.1 gm. carbohydrates; 11.6 gm. fat.
Per cup: 118.4 calories; 102.4 mg. sodium; 8.0 gm. carbohydrates; 4.8 gm. fat.
Per tablespoon: 7.4 calories; 6.4 mg sodium; 0.5 gm. carbohydrates; 0.3 gm. fat.

Sweet and Sour Sauce
MAKES 2½ CUPS

From Canton, this mainstay can make any dish Oriental. Use this sauce on fish, meat, or poultry. The ingredients can be varied to suit your imagination and taste preference (for example, any fruit can be substituted for the pineapple—or it can be eliminated if you wish).

1 tablespoon cornstarch
3 tablespoons water
1 tablespoon sesame seed oil
1 large onion, minced
3 cloves garlic, minced
⅓ cup low-sodium chili ketchup
⅓ cup orange juice
2½ tablespoons dry sherry
½ cup white vinegar
⅓ cup Soy Sauce Substitute (page 227)
1 can (8 ounces) dietetic pineapple, cut in 1-inch chunks, including juice

1. In bowl, combine first 2 ingredients, stirring to dissolve cornstarch. Set aside.
2. In saucepan, heat oil over low heat. Add onion and garlic and stir-fry 2 minutes.
3. Add ketchup, juice, sherry, vinegar, and soy sauce. Simmer 10 minutes, stirring occasionally.
4. Stir in cornstarch mixture and simmer 5 minutes more, or until mixture starts to thicken. Sauce may be frozen indefinitely or refrigerated up to 2 months at this time.
5. Add pineapple plus its juice 10 minutes before serving, and cook to heat through.
   Note: A green pepper, cut in 1-inch chunks, and 2 carrots, cut in 1-inch rounds and steamed, may also be added at Step 5.

Per recipe: 562.5 calories; 77.7 mg. sodium; 104.6 gm. carbohydrates; 18.0 gm. fat.
Per cup: 225 calories; 31.1 mg. sodium; 41.8 gm. carbohydrates; 7.2 gm. fat.
Per tablespoon: 14.1 calories; 1.9 mg. sodium; 2.6 gm. carbohydrates; 0.5 gm. fat.

Yellow Bean Sauce

MAKES 2 CUPS

Common to all regions. Like Black Bean Sauce (page 232), this sweeter blend should be used sparingly.

½ pound soy beans
4 cups water
4 tablespoons dry sherry
4 tablespoons Soy Sauce Substitute
 (page 227)

½ cup sugar
2 tablespoons sesame seed oil

1. In saucepan, combine first 2 ingredients. Turn heat to medium and bring to a slow boil. Reduce heat to low. Cover and simmer 1½ hours, or until skins open and beans soften, adding more water, if necessary, to prevent sticking.
2. Drain beans through cheesecloth, squeezing out all excess water.
3. In bowl, combine beans, sherry, soy sauce, and sugar. Stir to blend thoroughly. Let stand 20 minutes.
4. In wok, heat bean mixture over low heat 5 minutes, stirring often.
5. Add sesame seed oil and stir-fry until mixture is thoroughly blended.
6. Spoon into jars. Cover tightly. Will keep in refrigerator up to 2 months.

Per recipe: 1,562.4 calories; 41.9 mg. sodium; 262.0 gm. carbohydrates; 34.8 gm. fat.
Per cup: 781.2 calories; 20.9 mg. sodium; 131.1 gm. carbohydrates; 17.4 gm. fat.
Per tablespoon: 48.7 calories; 1.3 mg. sodium; 8.2 gm. carbohydrates; 1.1 gm. fat.

Hot and Spicy Sauce

MAKES 3½ CUPS

An excellent barbecue sauce, with western zest, for all meats and poultry, and a wonderful dip for vegetables.

½ Duck Sauce recipe (page 234)
8 dates, pitted and minced

2½ tablespoons Curry Powder
 (page 232)

1. In saucepan, combine all ingredients. Turn heat to low. Simmer ½ hour, stirring often.
2. Pour mixture into jars. Cover tightly. May be refrigerated up to 6 months.
3. Serve hot or cold.

Per recipe: 1,075.9 calories; 27.4 mg. sodium; 244.7 gm. carbohydrates; 2.8 gm. fat.
Per cup: 307.4 calories; 8.0 mg. sodium; 69.9 gm. carbohydrates; 0.8 gm. fat.
Per tablespoon: 19.2 calories; 0.5 mg. sodium; 4.4 gm. carbohydrates; 0.1 gm. fat.

Chicken Sauce

MAKES 2 CUPS

Wonderful on chicken and anything else. You will love this sauce with an eastern taste.

1 tablespoon sesame seed oil
⅓ cup unsalted walnuts, crushed
3 cups Chicken Stock (page 68)
1 cup boiling water
8 dried black mushrooms*
1 tablespoon cider vinegar

1 teaspoon sugar
4 tablespoons Soy Sauce Substitute
  (page 227)
2 tablespoons cold water
1½ tablespoons cornstarch

1. In wok, heat oil over low heat. Add walnuts and stir-fry 1 minute.
2. Add chicken stock. Raise heat to medium and bring to a slow boil. Reduce heat and simmer ½ hour.
3. While sauce is cooking, in bowl, combine boiling water and mushrooms. Let stand ½ hour. Drain. Chop mushrooms.
4. To sauce, add mushrooms, vinegar, and sugar. Stir to blend. Simmer 10 minutes more.
5. Stir in soy sauce. Simmer 10 minutes more.
6. In bowl, combine cold water and cornstarch, stirring until cornstarch is dissolved.
7. Stir cornstarch mixture into sauce. Simmer 5 minutes more, or until mixture thickens, stirring often.

Per recipe: 1,029.5 calories; 138.7 mg. sodium; 49.6 gm. carbohydrates; 75.6 gm. fat.
Per cup: 515.4 calories; 68.8 mg. sodium; 24.5 gm. carbohydrates; 38.4 gm. fat.
Per tablespoon: 32.2 calories; 4.3 mg. sodium; 1.5 gm. carbohydrates; 2.4 gm. fat.

* If not available, substitute 8 large fresh mushrooms, sliced, and omit boiling water.

Chinese Steak Sauce   MAKES 2 CUPS

This blending of eastern and southern influences is good on any meat.

1 tablespoon peanut oil
1 onion, minced
2 cloves garlic, minced
2 slices ginger root, minced, or 1/16
  teaspoon ginger powder
2 cups Meat Stock (page 69)
1 tablespoon dry sherry

2 tablespoons red wine vinegar
1/2 cup Lobster Sauce (page 239)
  or Oyster Sauce (page 234)
Black pepper to taste
1 tablespoon low-sodium beef
  bouillon

1. In wok, heat oil over low heat. Add onion, garlic, and ginger. Stir-fry 1 minute.
2. Add meat stock. Raise heat to medium and bring to a slow boil. Reduce heat and simmer 1/2 hour.
3. Stir in sherry and vinegar. Simmer 15 minutes more.
4. Stir in remaining ingredients. Simmer 15 minutes more.

With lobster sauce. Per recipe: 391.5 calories; 99.1 mg. sodium; 53.4 gm. carbohydrates; 24.2 gm. fat.
Per cup: 195.3 calories; 49.6 mg. sodium; 27.2 gm. carbohydrates; 12.8 gm. fat.
Per tablespoon: 12.2 calories; 3.1 mg. sodium; 1.7 gm. carbohydrates; 0.8 gm. fat.
With oyster sauce. Per recipe: 427.4 calories; 143.0 mg. sodium; 55.1 gm. carbohydrates; 25.6 gm. fat.
Per cup: 213.7 calories; 72.0 mg. sodium; 27.6 gm. carbohydrates; 12.8 gm. fat.
Per tablespoon: 13.4 calories; 4.5 mg. sodium; 1.7 gm. carbohydrates; 0.8 gm. fat.

Fish Sauce   MAKES 2¼ CUPS

Common to all regions, the following recipe is our version of the very salty Chinese blend of fish extract, water, and salt.

2 cups water
1 pound flounder fillets, cut in
  1-inch chunks
2 tablespoons low-sodium chicken
  bouillon

1 teaspoon low-sodium beef
  bouillon
1 cup Fish Stock (page 67)
1 tablespoon cornstarch

1. In wok, combine first 2 ingredients. Over medium heat, bring to a slow boil. Cover and continue boiling 5 minutes. Remove from heat and let stand 10 minutes.

2. Pour mixture into blender and puree. Return mixture to wok.
3. Add chicken bouillon and, over medium heat, bring mixture to a second boil.
4. Stir in beef bouillon. Reduce heat and simmer, uncovered, 5 minutes.
5. While mixture is simmering, in bowl, combine fish stock and cornstarch, stirring until cornstarch is dissolved.
6. Stir fish stock mixture into sauce. Simmer until sauce thickens, stirring occasionally.
7. Pour sauce into bottles. Seal tightly, leaving ½ inch of headspace. Will keep in refrigerator up to 1 week.
   Note: Stir each time before serving.

Per recipe: 764.2 calories; 514.9 mg. sodium; 40.9 gm. carbohydrates; 17.4 gm. fat.
Per cup: 339.2 calories; 228.8 mg. sodium; 17.6 gm. carbohydrates; 8.0 gm. fat.
Per tablespoon: 21.2 calories; 14.3 mg. sodium; 1.1 gm. carbohydrates; 0.5 gm. fat.

Lobster Sauce
MAKES 2½ CUPS

A creation that offers an alternative to Oyster Sauce (page 234).

Shells from 1 1-pound lobster
5 cups water
1 large onion, minced
Dash of garlic powder
Black pepper to taste

2 tablespoons low-sodium chicken bouillon
1 tablespoon Soy Sauce Substitute (page 227—optional)

1. In wok or Dutch oven, combine first 5 ingredients. Turn heat to medium and bring to a slow boil. Reduce heat to low and simmer 40 minutes, stirring occasionally.
2. Stir in bouillon and soy sauce, if desired. Simmer 10 minutes more.
3. Strain and pour mixture into bottles, leaving ½ inch of headspace. May be refrigerated up to 1 week or frozen up to 3 weeks.
   Note: If freezing, it is best to use a freezer tray. The freezer units can each hold about 4 tablespoons of the sauce—perfect since most recipes require only small amounts of the sauce.

Per recipe: 174.3 calories; 49.0 mg. sodium; 39.2 gm. carbohydrates; 6.8 gm. fat.
Per cup: 69.7 calories; 19.6 mg. sodium; 15.7 gm. carbohydrates; 2.7 gm. fat.
Per tablespoon: 4.4 calories; 1.2 mg. sodium; 1.0 gm. carbohydrates; 0.2 gm. fat.

Shrimp Paste
MAKES 1¼ CUPS

Wonderful with fish and shellfish and a deliciously unique flavoring for meat and poultry as well. The version below has a Cantonese inclination, although every region claims shrimp paste for its own.

1 tablespoon sesame seed (or peanut) oil
4 scallions, chopped, including greens
¼ pound small shrimp, shelled, deveined, and chopped

½ cup Chicken Stock (page 68)
¹⁄₁₆ teaspoon ginger powder
2 teaspoons white vinegar
¼ cup Soy Sauce Substitute (page 227)

1. In wok, heat oil over low heat. Add scallions and shrimp. Stir-fry until shrimp turn pink all over. Transfer to blender or food processor. Grind briefly. Set aside.
2. To wok, add remaining ingredients. Simmer 5 minutes, stirring occasionally.
3. Add shrimp mixture. Stir to blend and simmer 5 minutes more.
4. Pour into jars. Cover tightly. May be refrigerated for 2 to 3 weeks, or frozen up to 1 month.
5. Serve hot or cold as a sauce or dip.

Per recipe: 329.3 calories; 196.9 mg. sodium; 12.0 gm. carbohydrates; 19.3 gm. fat.
Per cup: 264 calories; 156.8 mg. sodium; 9.6 gm. carbohydrates; 16.0 gm. fat.
Per tablespoon: 16.5 calories; 9.8 mg. sodium; 0.6 gm. carbohydrates; 1.0 gm. fat.

Vinegar-Nut Sauce

MAKES 1 CUP

This sauce, derived from the eastern cuisine, adds a wonderful, zesty flavor to fish, meat, poultry, and vegetables—Chinese and otherwise.

¼ cup unsalted walnuts or cashews, chopped
2 slices ginger root, chopped, or ⅟₁₆ teaspoon ginger powder
2 cloves garlic, chopped
4 scallions, chopped, including greens
½ cup Chicken Stock (page 68)

3 tablespoons red wine vinegar
1 teaspoon low-sodium beef bouillon
1½ tablespoons sugar
4 tablespoons water
2½ tablespoons cornstarch
Dash of hot pepper flakes (optional)

1. In blender or food processor, combine first 4 ingredients. Grind fine. Spoon into wok.
2. To wok, add chicken stock. Turn heat to medium and bring to a slow boil. Continue boiling 5 minutes.
3. Reduce heat to low. Stir in vinegar, bouillon, and sugar. Simmer, uncovered, 10 minutes.
4. While sauce is simmering, in bowl, combine water and cornstarch, stirring until cornstarch is dissolved. Stir into sauce.
5. Add hot pepper flakes, if desired, and simmer 5 minutes more, stirring occasionally.

With walnuts. Per recipe: 724.5 calories; 56.9 mg. sodium; 80.0 gm. carbohydrates; 41.4 gm. fat.
Per tablespoon: 45.3 calories; 3.6 mg. sodium; 5.0 gm. carbohydrates; 2.6 gm. fat.
With cashews. Per recipe: 673.1 calories; 64.4 mg. sodium; 87.7 gm. carbohydrates; 30.9 gm. fat.
Per tablespoon: 52 calories; 4.0 mg. sodium; 5.5 gm. carbohydrates; 1.9 gm. fat.

Six-Fruit Sauce

MAKES 12 CUPS

This lovely blend of flavors, common to all regions, can be used as a more piquant alternative to Duck Sauce (page 234).

4 pears, cored and chopped
4 apples, cored and chopped
8 cups water
2 large onions, minced
⅛ teaspoon garlic powder
⅛ teaspoon ginger powder
1 cup prunes, pitted and chopped
1 lemon, seeded and chopped

1 orange, seeded and chopped
1 pint strawberries, hulled and
  halved
½ cup cider vinegar
⅓ cup sugar

1. In saucepan, place first 3 ingredients. Turn heat to medium and bring to a slow boil. Reduce heat, cover, and simmer ½ hour.
2. Add onions, garlic and ginger powders, prunes, lemon, and orange. Cover and simmer 1 hour, stirring occasionally.
3. Add remaining ingredients. Cover and simmer ½ hour more, stirring occasionally.
4. In blender or food processor, puree mixture.
5. Pour mixture into jars. Cover tightly. May be refrigerated up to 2 months.

Per recipe: 1,964.5 calories; 118.0 mg. sodium; 533.6 gm. carbohydrates; 11.7 gm. fat.
Per cup: 234.9 calories; 14.8 mg. sodium; 64.0 gm. carbohydrates; 1.5 gm. fat.
Per tablespoon: 14.6 calories; 0.9 mg. sodium; 3.9 gm. carbohydrates; 0.1 gm. fat.

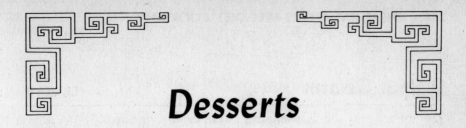

Desserts

Desserts, those sweet delights that deliciously end our meals, have no real place on the Chinese menu. However, that is not to say that the Chinese have no pastrylike delicacies of their own, only that they play a less important role in the Chinese diet.

Sweets like Apricot-Orange Buns (page 252) or Thousand-Layer Cake (page 255) are enjoyed as between-meal snacks or as respites and refreshers between courses at formal banquets.

For everyday dining, after several fried, braised, and simmered dishes, the Chinese prefer to end a meal on a light, refreshing note. A mild soup is often their choice. Otherwise, a luscious array of fruits, specially prepared, more than fills the bill. One bite of Ginger Citrus with Pineapple (page 246) will satisfy even the sweetest tooth.

Whatever dessert you choose, be sure to top off your meal in the Chinese fashion with a tantalizing cup of your favorite tea. One final note: in China it is considered not only polite but a sign of appreciation to belch after a meal.

Almond Gelatin   SERVES 8

Common to all regions, this dessert tastes richer than it really is. The almond flavor makes it special, but try it with your own fruit favorite.

2 packages unflavored gelatin   ¼ cup low-fat milk
3¾ cups boiling water   2 teaspoons almond extract
3½ tablespoons sugar

1. In bowl, combine first 2 ingredients, stirring until gelatin is completely dissolved.
2. Stir in sugar, blending to dissolve.
3. Stir in milk and almond extract.
4. Pour into 6-inch square shallow dish. Refrigerate 5 hours, or until firm.
5. Cut gelatin into small cubes and serve with peaches, pineapple, mandarin oranges, loquats, stewed prunes, or any other fruit of your choice.

Per serving: 50.4 calories; 4.0 mg. sodium; 6.6 gm. carbohydrates; 0.02 gm. fat.

Walnut Gelatin   SERVES 4

The crushed nuts add an interesting texture and subtle flavor.

1 package unflavored gelatin
1 tablespoon sugar
1 cup boiling water
¾ cup cold water

¼ cup low-fat milk
2 teaspoons almond extract
¼ cup unsalted walnuts, crushed

1. In bowl, combine first 2 ingredients. Stir to blend.
2. Stir in boiling water. Continue stirring until gelatin and sugar are dissolved.
3. Stir in cold water, milk, and almond extract.
4. Pour equal amounts of mixture into 4 custard cups. Refrigerate 1 hour.
5. Sprinkle 1 tablespoon of walnuts on top of each gelatin cup. Chill 1 hour more, or until gelatin is set.

Per serving: 132.3 calories; 8.0 mg. sodium; 8.8 gm. carbohydrates; 8.5 gm. fat.

Apples with Strawberries   SERVES 8

A bit of northern flair from Shantung, this is just as good chilled as warm from the oven.

4 apples, cored and halved
1 cup water
½ cup dry sherry

½ pint strawberries, hulled and
    chopped
4 teaspoons sesame seeds

1. Preheat oven to 350°.
2. In 8-inch square casserole, place apples cut side down. Pour water and sherry over all. Bake 40 minutes.
3. Turn apples cut side up. Spoon strawberries into well of each apple half.
4. Sprinkle each apple half with ½ teaspoon sesame seeds.
5. Bake 20 minutes more.

Per serving: 91 calories; 2.0 mg. sodium; 17.1 gm. carbohydrates; 2.0 gm. fat.

Bananas and Loquats   SERVES 8

A Shanghai delicacy, amended here with spices rather than bean paste.

4 firm bananas, peeled and halved
   lengthwise
4 tablespoons lemon juice
1 can (16 ounces) loquats, drained,
   juice reserved
1/16 teaspoon ground cardamom
   (optional)

1/2 tablespoon orange peel powder
2 tablespoons sesame seed oil,
   divided
1/4 cup water
1 teaspoon almond extract

1. On platter, place bananas, cut side up. Sprinkle with lemon juice. Set aside.
2. In bowl, combine loquats, cardamom, if desired, and orange peel powder. Stir to blend.
3. In large skillet, heat 1 tablespoon oil over low heat. Add half the bananas, cut side down, and fry 3 minutes. Turn and fry 2 minutes more. Transfer to platter.
4. Repeat Step 3 with remaining oil and bananas.
5. To wok, add loquat mixture. Turn heat to medium and stir-fry 2 minutes. Spoon over bananas.
6. To wok, add water, almond extract, and loquat juice. Cook until juice starts to bubble around the edges. Pour over bananas and loquats.

Per serving: 121 calories; 1.4 mg. sodium; 28.4 gm. carbohydrates; 4.5 gm. fat.

Coconut Strawberries   SERVES 8

The champagne and nutmeg show the influence of Peking in this splendid and luxurious delicacy.

2 pints strawberries, hulled and
   halved
1 cup champagne

1/16 teaspoon ground nutmeg
2 tablespoons shredded coconut

1. In bowl, combine first 3 ingredients. Spoon into 8 dessert bowls.
2. Garnish with coconut.

Per serving: 72 calories; 2.2 mg. sodium; 9.4 gm. carbohydrates; 1.8 gm. fat.

Ginger Citrus with Pineapple   SERVES 4

The style is eastern. The dessert is just terrific.

2 oranges, peeled and sectioned,
  rind chopped
1 grapefruit, peeled and sectioned,
  rind chopped
2¼ cups water, divided
3 tablespoons sugar

½ teaspoon ginger powder
¼ cup dark raisins*
1 can (8 ounces) dietetic pineapple
  chunks, drained
2 tablespoons shredded coconut
  (optional)

1. In bowl, combine orange and grapefruit sections. Cover with ¼ cup water and refrigerate until ready to use.
2. In saucepan, combine orange and grapefruit rinds and water. Turn heat to medium and bring to a slow boil. Reduce heat and simmer 45 minutes.
3. Stir in sugar, ginger powder, and raisins. Simmer 20 minutes more, stirring often. Let cool 15 minutes.
4. Drain orange and grapefruit sections. Add pineapple. Toss to blend.
5. Pour sauce over fruit. Garnish with coconut, if desired.

Per serving plain: 184.8 calories; 6.2 mg. sodium; 48.0 gm. carbohydrates; 0.4 gm. fat.
Per serving with coconut: 224.8 calories; 6.2 mg. sodium; 51.8 gm. carbohydrates; 3.2 gm. fat.

* Preserved in nonsodium ingredient.

Peaches and Pineapple   SERVES 4

Cantonese in its simplicity; pure Chinese in flavor.

¼ cup dry sherry
Dash of ground cinnamon
Dash of ginger powder
4 peaches, halved and pitted

½ fresh pineapple, cubed, or 1 can
  (8 ounces) dietetic pineapple
  chunks, drained

1. In bowl, combine first 3 ingredients.
2. In 8-inch square casserole, lay peach halves, cut side up.
3. Spoon pineapple over peach halves.
4. Pour sherry mixture over all. Cover and refrigerate at least 1 hour.

Per serving: 76 calories; 2.0 mg. sodium; 20.0 gm. carbohydrates; 0.3 gm. fat.

Pears Baked in Almond Honey

SERVES 8

Every region would be proud to claim this superb dessert as its own, and they all do.

2 tablespoons honey
1 tablespoon lemon juice
1 tablespoon cherry brandy (or any
  fruit liqueur)

1 tablespoon sesame seed oil
4 firm pears, with 1-inch cap cut
  from top and cored
½ teaspoon almond extract

1. Preheat oven to 325°.
2. In bowl, combine first 4 ingredients.
3. In 8-inch square casserole, set pears. Spoon honey mixture evenly into pear centers. Cover with caps. Add enough water to cover bottom of casserole. Stir in almond extract.
4. Place pears on rack in oven 4 inches above a pan filled halfway up with water. Bake 45 minutes, or until pears are fork tender.
5. Cut pears in half. Serve hot or cold.

Per serving: 95 calories; 2.5 mg. sodium; 18.7 gm. carbohydrates; 2.3 gm. fat.

Sherry-Fried Apples

SERVES 12

A specialty for which Peking is justifiably famous. For best results, use a naturally crunchy apple like Delicious or Granny Smith apples.

1 Multi-Purpose Batter recipe (page
  65)
4 tablespoons dry sherry
½ teaspoon ginger powder
½ teaspoon ground cinnamon

2 tablespoons lemon juice
6 apples, pared, cored, and
  quartered
2 cups vegetable oil

1. In bowl, combine batter with sherry, ginger powder, cinnamon, and lemon juice, stirring to blend thoroughly.
2. Coat apples in batter. Set aside.
3. In wok, heat oil over high heat until crackling hot. Gently slip wedges into oil and deep-fry 2 minutes, or until golden brown.
4. With slotted spoon, remove to platter. Serve at once.

Per serving: 173.9 calories; 11.0 mg. sodium; 27.4 gm. carbohydrates; 6.3 gm. fat.

Stewed Fruit in Nut Sauce   SERVES 12

A dish fit for the royal palate and, fittingly, from Peking.

3 oranges, quartered, rind intact
1 lemon, sliced
1 cup prunes, pitted and chopped
6 cups water
1/16 teaspoon clove powder

3 apples, pared, cored, and sliced
2 teaspoons sesame seed oil
1/4 cup unsalted cashews, chopped
1/4 cup unsalted walnuts, chopped

1. In saucepan, combine first 4 ingredients. Turn heat to high and bring to a boil. Reduce heat to low. Cover and simmer 45 minutes.
2. Stir in clove powder and apples. Cover and simmer 15 minutes more.
3. While fruit is cooking, in wok, heat oil over low heat. Add nuts and stir-fry 2 minutes.
4. Stir nuts into fruit mixture. Remove from heat. Let stand 10 minutes.
5. Serve warm or chilled.

Per serving: 168.3 calories; 3.9 mg. sodium; 29.1 gm. carbohydrates; 7.7 gm. fat.

Sesame-Peanut Cookies   SERVES 18
                                  (MAKES 36 COOKIES)

We can thank the Cantonese for this classic treat, to which we have added the peanut center.

1 cup flour
3 teaspoons low-sodium baking
  powder
1/2 cup sugar
1 egg

1 tablespoon sesame seed oil
1 teaspoon vanilla extract
4 tablespoons sesame seeds, divided
1/4 cup unsalted peanuts

1. In bowl, combine first 3 ingredients, stirring to blend thoroughly.
2. Beat in egg, oil, and vanilla to form a smooth batter.
3. Stir in 2 tablespoons sesame seeds.
4. Onto greased baking sheet, drop batter by the teaspoonful, leaving 1 inch between cookies.
5. Preheat oven to 350°.
6. Top each cookie with 1 peanut, lightly pressed into center. Then sprinkle remaining sesame seeds over all.
7. Bake 15 to 20 minutes, or until golden brown.

Per serving: 119.8 calories; 3.8 mg. sodium; 12.2 gm. carboyhdrates; 4.5 gm. fat.

Chinese Rice Pudding

SERVES 16

A classic every region claims. Just a little of this creamy, rich dessert is enough to satisfy, but if you want perfection, garnish with a little shredded coconut.

1½ cups rice
2 cups water
2 tablespoons vegetable oil
2 tablespoons sugar
⅓ cup dates, pitted and chopped

⅓ cup dark raisins*
1 can (16 ounces) lychee nuts, chopped, juice reserved

1. In saucepan, combine first 2 ingredients. Turn heat to high and bring to a boil. Reduce heat to low. Cover and simmer 20 minutes, or until liquid is absorbed.
2. Stir in oil and sugar, blending well.
3. In blender or food processor, puree dates and raisins.
4. In greased 8-inch square casserole, spread half the date-raisin mixture. Top with half the rice. Then top with half the lychee nuts.
5. Repeat Step 4 with remaining date-raisin mixture, rice, and lychee nuts.
6. In 325° oven, place casserole in shallow pan filled halfway with water. Bake 40 minutes.
7. Pour reserved lychee juice over all and bake 10 minutes more, or until pudding is set and lightly browned on top.

Per serving: 146.1 calories; 3.3 mg. sodium; 30.9 gm. carbohydrates; 2.1 gm. fat.

* Preserved in nonsodium ingredient.

Banana Pancakes

SERVES 8

Pancakes originated in the North but are enjoyed now in every region—whether served with a main course or for dessert as they are here. Fresh, slightly overripe strawberries (½ pint) are a lovely substitute for the bananas in the Cantonese version of this popular dessert. Serve with powdered sugar, if desired.

¼ cup flour plus 2 tablespoons
¼ cup water
½ teaspoon vanilla extract
2 tablespoons orange juice
¹⁄₁₆ teaspoon ground cinnamon
2 bananas, mashed

1 egg, lightly beaten
1½ tablespoons unsalted walnuts, crushed fine
2 tablespoons unsalted margarine, divided

1. In bowl, combine first 4 ingredients, blending thoroughly.
2. Stir in cinnamon.
3. Add bananas and egg, beating to blend until smooth.
4. Stir in walnuts.
5. In small 4-inch fry pan, melt ½ tablespoon margarine over medium heat. Pour in ¼ of the batter. Fry 1 minute, or until bottom is lightly browned. Transfer pancake to platter.
6. Repeat Step 5 until margarine and batter are used up.
7. Cut each pancake in half and roll up.

VARIATION: *Strawberry Pancakes*—Substitute ½ pint mashed strawberries for the bananas and proceed as above.

Per serving with bananas: 110 calories; 8.0 mg. sodium; 14.1 gm. carbohydrates; 5.2 gm. fat.
Per serving with strawberries: 94 calories; 8.0 mg. sodium; 9.3 gm. carbohydrates; 5.3 gm. fat.

Fruit and Nut Rolls

SERVES 16

Adopted and adapted throughout China, these sweet, chewy confections are positively addictive.

2 peaches, pitted and chopped (or
  12 dried apricots, chopped)
1 pear, pared, cored, and chopped
8 dates, pitted and chopped
8 prunes, pitted and chopped
⅓ cup unsalted cashews, chopped

1 tablespoon dry sherry
1 tablespoon sugar
8 Egg Roll Skins (page 64)
2 cups vegetable oil
8 teaspoons powdered sugar

1. In bowl, combine first 7 ingredients, blending thoroughly. Place in blender or food processor. Grind well.
2. In center of each egg roll skin, place 1½ tablespoons filling and spread in a thin line down center of skin.
3. Fold skin over filling and pinch edges together. Then fold short ends over and pinch together.
4. In wok, heat oil over high heat until crackling. Add egg rolls seam-side down, a few at a time, and fry until golden brown and crispy. Drain on paper towels. Cut each egg roll in half.
5. Sprinkle powdered sugar over rolls.

Per serving with peaches: 187.7 calories; 5.9 mg. sodium; 24.8 gm. carbohydrates; 5.0 gm. fat.
Per serving with apricots: 193.1 calories; 7.0 mg. sodium; 26.2 gm. carbohydrates; 5.0 gm. fat.

Apricot-Orange Buns

MAKES 16 BUNS

These delicate, light, and lovely morsels make a delicious dessert treat. They may be stuffed with any dried fruit and jam combination, dried fruit alone, or dried fruit and nuts. Just use in the same proportions as the apricot and orange marmalade, respectively. You can find these tempting treats in every region in China.

1 Basic Buns recipe (page 62)   **8 teaspoons orange marmalade***
½ cup dried apricots, minced

1. Follows Steps 1 through 5 for Basic Buns.
2. Turn Basic Buns dough onto floured surface. Knead until springy. Divide into 2 equal parts and shape into an 8-inch log.
3. Cut each log into 8 equal pieces.
4. Flour each piece and roll into a 5-inch circle.
5. Place 1 teaspoon of apricots in center of each circle. Then top with ½ teaspoon of marmalade.
6. Flute edges all around and bring the edges together into a knot.
7. Place buns, knot side down, onto lightly floured board, leaving 2-inch space between each bun. Cover with cloth and let stand in warm place ½ hour.
8. Turn half the buns, knot side up, onto heatproof plate.
9. Place on rack over boiling water. Cover with damp cloth and steam 15 to 20 minutes. Shut off water. Let buns rest 5 minutes. Set aside.
10. Repeat Step 9 with remaining buns.
11. May be refrigerated up to 4 days. Reheat by steaming 15 to 20 minutes.

Per bun: 183.5 calories; 3.5 mg. sodium; 38.8 gm. carbohydrates; 0.6 gm. fat.

* Preserved without sodium or pectin.

Coconut-Apricot Cakes

SERVES 16

Just one bite of these feathery sweets will convince you that steaming cakes should be adopted in the United States. The recipe itself is our version of the cake prepared in every Chinese region.

1½ cups rice flour
½ cup sugar
¾ cup water
2 tablespoons lemon peel powder
2 tablespoons orange peel powder

6 tablespoons vegetable oil, divided
¼ cup shredded coconut
½ cup dried apricots, chopped

1. In bowl, combine first 2 ingredients, blending thoroughly.
2. Stir in water, blending well.
3. Stir in lemon peel and orange peel powders plus 4 tablespoons oil. Stir until smooth.
4. Stir in coconut and apricots, blending thoroughly.
5. Pour batter into greased 8-inch square baking pan. Place on rack over boiling water. Cover and steam 40 minutes. Let cool ½ hour. Then cut into 2-inch square cakes.
6. In skillet, heat 1 tablespoon remaining oil over low heat. Add half the cakes and fry until lightly brown all over.
7. Repeat Step 6 with remaining oil and cakes.

Per serving: 191.5 calories; 2.4 mg. sodium; 31.1 gm. carbohydrates; 7.2 gm. fat.

Lemon Sponge Cake

SERVES 16

Sponge cake is a melt-in-the-mouth low-calorie treat all over the world. The recipe below is the Cantonese variation, and it is truly wonderful.

3 eggs, separated
¾ cup sugar
¼ cup lemon juice
1 tablespoon lemon peel, minced, or 1 teaspoon lemon peel powder

½ teaspoon vanilla extract
1¼ cups all-purpose flour
1 teaspoon low-sodium baking powder

1. In bowl, beat egg whites until light and fluffy.
2. Add sugar, a little at a time, beating until egg whites become stiff.
3. In second bowl, beat egg yolks.
4. Beat in lemon juice, lemon peel, and vanilla.
5. Beat egg yolk mixture into egg white mixture.
6. In third bowl, sift together flour and baking powder.
7. Beat flour mixture into egg mixture, a little at a time.
8. Line 2 8-inch cake pans with waxed paper. Pour batter into pans.
9. Place pans—one at a time—on rack over boiling water. Cover and steam ½ hour, or until toothpick inserted in cake comes out clean.
10. Let cakes cool 20 minutes before slicing.

Per serving: 122.8 calories; 10.9 mg. sodium; 24.4 gm. carbohydrates; 1.0 gm. fat.

Thousand-Layer Cake

Not really a thousand, but every one there is is spectacular—compliments of Peking.

1½ tablespoons orange peel powder
6 cups all-purpose flour
1 package dry yeast
1¼ cups warm water

¼ cup lemon juice
¾ cup sugar
½ cup shortening
¾ cup unsalted walnuts, crushed

1. In bowl, combine first 2 ingredients, stirring to blend well. Set aside.
2. In second bowl, combine yeast, water, and lemon juice, stirring until yeast is dissolved.
3. Stir sugar into flour mixture, blending well. Then stir in yeast mixture, blending thoroughly until smooth dough is formed, adding more warm water if necessary.
4. Cover with damp cloth. Set in warm place and let stand 3 hours, or until double in bulk.
5. Turn dough onto floured board. Divide into 3 equal portions. Roll out each portion into thin rectangle, approximately 6 x 14 inches.
6. Smooth some shortening on one dough strip. Sprinkle with a few walnuts.
7. Place a second dough strip on top of the first. Smooth some shortening on it. Then sprinkle with a few more walnuts.
8. Place the third dough strip on top of the second. Roll out these combined strips into a rectangle, approximately 10 x 24 inches.
9. Smooth some shortening over ⅔ of the rectangle. Sprinkle some walnuts on top.
10. Fold the bare surface ⅓ over. Smooth shortening over it and sprinkle with walnuts. Then fold remaining exposed ⅓ on top.
11. Repeat Steps 8 through 10 twice more, starting with rolling out the dough.
12. Let stand ½ hour.
13. Place dough on damp cloth. Then place—complete with damp cloth —on rack over boiling water. Cover and steam 1 hour. Let cool ½ hour.
14. Cut cake into bars 1 x 2 inches.

Per serving: 244.4 calories; 1.3 mg. sodium; 38.0 gm. carbohydrates; 7.4 gm. fat.

Water Chestnut Cake

SERVES 16

Water chestnuts find their way into every course on a Chinese menu—perhaps because they are supposed to have medicinal powers. In any case, this Cantonese specialty shows them to deliciously sweet advantage.

4 cans (8 ounces each) water
 chestnuts, drained and chopped
½ cup unsalted pecans, crushed
¼ cup shortening
½ cup sugar
¼ cup lemon peel powder

2½ cups water
1 cup water chestnut (or rice) flour
 (or cake flour)
1⅓ cups low-fat milk

1. In blender or food processor, combine first 2 ingredients. Grind.
2. In saucepan, combine water chestnut mixture, shortening, sugar, lemon peel powder, and water. Turn heat to medium and bring to a slow boil, stirring constantly. Reduce heat to low and simmer 5 minutes.
3. While mixture is simmering, in bowl, combine flour and milk, stirring until a pasty mixture is formed, adding more milk if necessary.
4. Gradually stir half the flour mixture into the chestnut mixture. Raise heat to medium and bring to a second boil. Remove from heat. Let cool 5 minutes.
5. Gradually stir in remaining flour mixture, stirring vigorously to form a smooth batter.
6. Pour batter into greased 8-inch square baking pan. Place on rack over boiling water. Cover and steam ½ hour. Let cool ½ hour. Then cut into 2-inch squares.
7. Serve cool or, if desired, reheat by steaming.

Per serving: 184.5 calories; 21.9 mg. sodium; 30.3 gm. carbohydrates; 5.7 gm. fat.

A Chinese Menu
for Entertaining

Everybody loves a good party. And what makes a good party? A friendly, relaxed, and inviting atmosphere, gracious hosts, guests in a festive mood, pleasing drinks, fabulous food.

And one thing more: organization. Good organization and advance preparation will make your party a success and guarantee that you will have as good a time as your company.

The trick is not to panic. Just think of party planning as meal planning on a larger scale. Then do as the Chinese do.

Make a list of all the ingredients, cooking equipment, serving utensils, etc., you will need and have everything ready and waiting ahead of time.

Do not, for your own peace of mind, feel obligated to experiment with something new and wonderful. Instead, rely on dishes you know are winners. You will be confident; your guests delighted.

That aside, play with menu ideas. Aim for variety—in the foods you choose, in the methods of preparation, in the tastes and textures of the finished dishes. Think how boring it would be if all the foods were fried or very spicy. Try to include at least one dish that can be completed, in whole or in part, a day or two before the party.

You will see how easy it can be, for in the end, good party planning comes back to the Chinese philosophy of harmony and balance—yin and yang in all things.

Chinese food is perfect for parties. First of all, it is easy for you because so much can be done in advance. Secondly, the cuisine's numerous cooking methods allow you the luxury of choice and timing. You can pop something into the oven, and just before it is done, stir-fry a second dish on the stove. The result is worry-free, elegant entertaining, with you in complete control.

This chapter will highlight meals for a few guests and for many, and will include brunch, lunch, formal dinners, buffets, and cocktail parties—with preparation tips for each. Some menus will be composed entirely of Chinese dishes; others will be punctuated by Chinese specialties, with suggestions for the other dishes.

You will discover that Chinese food is a never-ending discovery of sensuous and satisfying taste sensations totally unlike any other.

Brunch for 4

Spiced Scallops and Cashews in Tomatoes (page 88)
Peanutty Noodles with Chicken (page 221)
Ginger Citrus with Pineapple (page 246)

Preparation Tips:
1. Prepare Spiced Scallops and Cashews in Tomatoes* the night before, if desired, or 1 hour before serving. Let stand 15 minutes at room temperature before serving.
2. Prepare Ginger Citrus with Pineapple 45 minutes before guests arrive. Refrigerate until ready to serve.
3. Prepare Peanutty Noodles with Chicken 15 minutes before guests arrive.
4. Serve with Mimosas.

* If you are not allowed shellfish, substitute 1 can (7 ounces) low-sodium tuna or 8 ounces leftover flounder.

Brunch for 4

Ginger-Sherry Shrimp (page 55)
with Hoisin Sauce Substitute (page 228)
Sweet and Pungent Chicken (page 138)
2 Cups Boiled White Rice
Coconut Strawberries (page 245)

Preparation Tips:
1. Start to cook rice ½ hour before serving.
2. Prepare Ginger-Sherry Shrimp* 20 minutes before serving. (Hoisin Sauce Substitute should be a staple in your pantry, ready for use.)
3. Start to prepare Sweet and Pungent Chicken 15 minutes before serving.
4. Prepare Coconut Strawberries† immediately before serving.

* If you are not allowed shellfish, substitute 1½ pounds swordfish, cut in 1-inch chunks.
† Use ½ recipe.

Brunch for 4

Basic Buns (page 62)
Scrambled Eggs and Onions
Steak Slices in Oyster Sauce (page 37)
Fresh Pears

Preparation Tips:
1. Prepare Basic Buns up to 4 days in advance. Keep refrigerated and reheat by steaming for 15 to 20 minutes before serving.
2. Start to prepare Steak Slices in Oyster Sauce 1½ hours before serving.
3. Prepare Scrambled Eggs and Onions 10 minutes before serving. Keep warm in chafing dish.
4. Finish cooking Steak Slices in Oyster Sauce.

Brunch for 4

Orange and Grapefruit Slices
Lobster Salad Cantonese (page 88)
Low-Sodium Wheat Toast
Low-Sodium Colby and Cheddar Cheeses

Preparation Tips:
1. Prepare Lobster Salad Cantonese* 1 hour before serving. Keep chilled in refrigerator until ready to serve.
2. Peel and section oranges and grapefruit ½ hour before serving. Keep chilled in refrigerator until ready to serve.
3. Make toast 10 minutes before serving. Wrap in aluminum foil and keep warm in oven until ready to serve.
4. Let cheese stand at room temperature 10 minutes before serving.

* If you are not allowed shellfish, substitute 1 pound of poached flounder, minced.

Brunch for 8

Bean Curd and Shrimp Puffs (page 30)
Chicken Salad of Many Flavors (page 92)
Green Bean and Fruit Salad (page 105)
3 Cups Boiled White Rice
Pears Baked in Almond Honey (page 247)

Preparation Tips:
1. Prepare pears and start to bake 45 minutes before serving.
2. Prepare rice 40 minutes before ready to serve.
3. Boil chicken and let cool ½ hour before serving.
4. Follow Step 1 for Bean Curd and Shrimp Puffs.*
5. Follow Step 1 for Green Bean and Fruit Salad.
6. Continue preparation of Chicken Salad of Many Flavors through Step 3.
7. Finish preparation of Green Bean and Fruit Salad. Let stand until ready to serve.
8. Five minutes before serving, finish preparation of Bean Curd and Shrimp Puffs.
9. Immediately before serving, finish preparation of Chicken Salad of Many Flavors.

* If you are not allowed shellfish, substitute ¼ pound pork, shredded.

Brunch for 8

Chicken Livers Fukien (page 164)
Coconut Chicken Wings (page 37)
Rice and Mixed Vegetables (page 212)
Apricot-Orange Buns (page 252)

Preparation Tips:
1. Prepare Apricot-Orange Buns up to 4 days in advance. Keep refrigerated and reheat by steaming for 15 to 20 minutes before serving.

One-half hour before guests arrive, do the following:

2. Prepare Chicken Livers Fukien through Step 2.
3. Prepare Coconut Chicken Wings through Step 1.
4. Prepare Rice and Mixed Vegetables through Step 2.
5. Continue preparation of Chicken Livers Fukien through Step 5.
6. Continue preparation of Rice and Mixed Vegetables through Step 3.
7. Continue preparation of Chicken Livers Fukien through Step 6.
8. Continue preparation of Rice and Mixed Vegetables through Step 4.
9. Start to broil Coconut Chicken Wings.
10. Finish preparation of Chicken Livers Fukien and Rice and Mixed Vegetables.
11. Finish preparation of Coconut Chicken Wings.

Brunch for 8

Fresh Fruit Cup
Chinese Sweet Bread (page 66)
Salmon with Zucchini in Soy Sauce (page 118)
Hard-Cooked Eggs
Lettuce, Tomato, and Onion Salad
Lemon Sponge Cake (page 254)

Preparation Tips:
1. Prepare Chinese Sweet Bread and Lemon Sponge Cake the day before ready to use. Keep refrigerated. Reheat bread by steaming for 15 to 20 minutes before serving. Lemon Sponge Cake may be reheated the same way or served chilled.
2. Prepare eggs 2 hours before serving. Refrigerate to chill.
3. Prepare platter of lettuce, tomato, and onion 1 hour before guests arrive. Refrigerate to chill.
4. Prepare fresh fruit cup 45 minutes before guests arrive. Refrigerate to chill.
5. Prepare Salmon with Zucchini in Soy Sauce 15 minutes before serving.

Brunch for 8

Orange Juice
Basic Buns (page 62)
Poached Eggs
Watercress-Rolled Pork (page 58)
Yunnan Curried Mushrooms (page 29)

Preparation Tips:
1. Prepare Basic Buns up to 4 days in advance. Keep refrigerated and reheat for 15 to 20 minutes before serving.
2. Prepare Watercress-Rolled Pork through Step 3 the day before ready to use.
3. Finish preparation of Watercress-Rolled Pork 20 minutes before serving.
4. Prepare eggs 10 minutes before serving.
5. Prepare Yunnan Curried Mushrooms 5 minutes before serving.
6. Pour juice into frosted glasses.

Brunch for 16

Egg Roll Filling I (page 47)
with Duck Sauce (page 234)
Crispy Spiced Duck (page 157
Noodles with Seafood (page 223)
Bananas and Loquats (page 245)

Preparation Tips:
1. Prepare Egg Roll Skins as far ahead of time as desired.
2. Prepare Noodles with Seafood through Step 1 the day before ready to use.
3. Prepare Crispy Spiced Duck* through Step 6 the day before ready to use. Cover and refrigerate overnight. Let stand at room temperature ½ hour before carving.
4. Prepare Egg Rolls through Step 4 the day before ready to use. Wrap each individually and refrigerate overnight.

5. Finish preparation of Egg Rolls 15 minutes before serving. Keep warm near oven. (Duck Sauce should be a staple in your pantry, ready for use.)
6. Finish preparation of Noodles with Seafood 10 minutes before serving.
7. Prepare Bananas and Loquats† 10 minutes before serving.

* If you are not allowed duck, substitute chicken.
† Double the recipe.

Brunch for 16

Salmon with Green Beans Mandarin (page 117)
Piquant Tomatoes and Cucumbers (page 201)
Chicken and Shrimp (page 152)
Coconut-Apricot Cakes (page 253)

Preparation Tips:
1. Prepare Basic Buns up to 4 days in advance.
2. Prepare Coconut-Apricot Cakes 2 hours before guests arrive.
3. Prepare Salmon with Green Beans Mandarin through Step 4, 20 minutes before serving.
4. Prepare Piquant Tomatoes and Cucumber* 10 minutes before serving, using skillet.
5. Finish preparation of Salmon with Green Beans Mandarin through Step 7, 7 minutes before serving.
6. Prepare Chicken and Shrimp† 5 minutes before serving, using skillet.
7. Finish preparation of Salmon with Green Beans Mandarin.

* Four times the recipe.
† If you are not allowed shellfish, double the amount of chicken.

Brunch for 16

Low-Sodium Tomato Juice
Beef and Spinach Buns (page 45)
Soft-Cooked Eggs
Swordfish with Hot Sauce (page 121)
Sliced Apples with Grapes

Preparation Tips:
1. Prepare Beef and Spinach Buns through Step 4, 2½ hours before serving.
2. Prepare Basic Buns through Step 5, 3 hours before ready to use.
3. Prepare Swordfish with Hot Sauce through Step 1, 2 hours before guests arrive.
4. Finish preparation of Beef and Spinach Buns 1 hour before guests arrive.
5. Finish preparation of Swordfish with Hot Sauce 15 minutes before serving.
6. Prepare eggs 5 minutes before serving.
7. Slice apples. Place in bowl, along with grapes. Keep refrigerated until ready to use.
8. Pour juice into chilled glasses.

Brunch for 16

Apple Juice
Shrimp in Hot Garlic Sauce (page 56)
Lettuce, Tomato, and Carrot Sticks
with Lemon Wedges
Chicken Salad
Chinese Rice Pudding (page 249)

Preparation Tips:
1. Prepare chicken salad 2 hours before guests arrive. Cover and refrigerate.

2. Prepare Chinese Rice Pudding through Step 5, 1 hour before guests arrive.
3. Prepare platter of lettuce, tomato, and carrot sticks ½ hour before guests arrive. Refrigerate to chill.
4. Finish preparation of Chinese Rice Pudding 1 hour before serving.
5. Prepare Shrimp in Hot Garlic Sauce* 5 minutes before serving.
6. Pour juice into chilled glasses.

* If you are not allowed shellfish, substitute 2 pounds of cod, cut in 1-inch chunks.

Lunch for 4

Sweet and Hot Carrots and Radishes (page 101)
Lemon Chicken (page 141)
Hoisin Rice in Four (page 211)
Stewed Fruit in Nut Sauce (page 248)

Preparation Tips:
1. Prepare Sweet and Hot Carrots and Radishes 2 hours before guests arrive. Keep refrigerated until ready to serve.
2. Prepare Stewed Fruit in Nut Sauce* 1½ hours before guests arrive. Keep refrigerated until ready to serve.
3. Prepare Hoisin Rice in Four through Step 3, 1 hour before serving.
4. Prepare Lemon Chicken through Step 3, ½ hour before serving.
5. Finish preparation of Hoisin Rice in Four.
6. Finish preparation of Lemon Chicken.

* Use ⅓ the recipe. Reserve remainder for future use.

Lunch for 4

Sliced Tomatoes
Squid and Cabbage with Duck Sauce (page 136)
Noodles with Sesame Paste Sauce (page 222)
Fresh Orange Sections

Preparation Tips:
1. Prepare sliced tomatoes and fresh orange sections 1 hour before guests arrive. Refrigerate to chill.
2. Prepare Noodles with Sesame Paste Sauce through Step 1, 40 minutes before serving.
3. Prepare Squid and Cabbage with Duck Sauce ½ hour before serving.
4. Finish preparation of Noodles with Sesame Paste Sauce.

Lunch for 4

Apples with Strawberries (page 244)
Roast Chicken
Watercress, Walnuts, and Red Onion Salad
with Lemon Vinaigrette
Sesame-Peanut Cookies (page 248)

Preparation Tips:
1. Prepare Sesame-Peanut Cookies* the night before ready to use.
2. Prepare watercress, walnuts, and red onion plus lemon vinaigrette 1½ hours before guests arrive. Keep refrigerated until ready to serve.
3. Prepare roast chicken 1 hour before ready to serve.
4. Prepare Apples with Strawberries 45 minutes before ready to serve.

* Serve 2 per person. Reserve remainder for future use.

Lunch for 4

Sweet and Hot Chicken Mushroom Soup (page 72)
Broiled Flounder with Lemon
Carrots and Ginger Apple (page 195)
Saffron Rice with Parsley
Green and Red Grapes

Preparation Tips:
1. Prepare green and red grapes the night before ready to use.
2. Prepare Sweet and Hot Chicken Mushroom Soup through Step 1, 45 minutes before serving.
3. Prepare Carrots and Ginger Apple plus saffron rice with parsley ½ hour before serving.
4. Finish preparation of Sweet and Hot Chicken Mushroom Soup and prepare broiled flounder with lemon 10 minutes before serving.

Lunch for 8

Duck Salad with Pears (page 94)
Steamed Snow Pea Pods
3 Cups Boiled White Rice
Banana Pancakes (page 250)

Preparation Tips:
1. Prepare Duck Salad with Pears* through Step 2 the day before ready to use. Keep refrigerated until ready to use.
2. Finish preparation of Duck Salad with Pears 1½ hours before serving.
3. Prepare rice 40 minutes before serving.
4. Prepare snow pea pods 5 minutes before serving.
5. Prepare Banana Pancakes 15 minutes before serving.

* If you are not allowed duck, substitute chicken.

Lunch for 8

Hot and Sour Soup I (page 70)
Red and Green Shrimp (page 132)
Simple Fried Rice (page 206)
Peaches and Pineapple (page 246)

Preparation Tips:
1. Prepare rice the day before ready to use. Keep refrigerated until ready to use.
2. Prepare Peaches and Pineapple 1½ hours before ready to serve.
3. Prepare Hot and Sour Soup I plus Red and Green Shrimp* through Step 1, 45 minutes before serving.
4. Finish preparation of Simple Fried Rice 10 minutes before ready to serve. Keep warm in chafing dish.
5. Finish preparation of Hot and Sour Soup I plus Red and Green Shrimp 5 minutes before ready to serve.

* If you are not allowed shellfish, substitute 2 whole chicken breasts, skinned, boned, and cubed.

Lunch for 8

Noodles with Almond Chicken (page 224)
Dietetic Lime Gelatin
with Pineapple

Preparation Tips:
1. Prepare gelatin the day before ready to use. Keep refrigerated until ready to use.
2. Prepare Noodles with Almond Chicken* 45 minutes before serving.
3. Serve gelatin topped with 1 can (8 ounces) dietetic crushed pineapple.

* Double the recipe.

Lunch for 8

Tossed Salad Vinaigrette
Mixed Seafood in Hoisin Sauce (page 126)
Parsley Potatoes
Coconut Strawberries (page 245)

Preparation Tips:
1. Prepare salad and vinaigrette 1 hour before serving. Refrigerate both to chill until ready to use.
2. Prepare Mixed Seafood in Hoisin Sauce* through Step 1, 45 minutes before serving.
3. Prepare potatoes ½ hour before serving.
4. Finish preparation of Mixed Seafood in Hoisin Sauce 5 minutes before serving.
5. Prepare Coconut Strawberries immediately before serving.

* If you are not allowed shellfish, substitute 4 whole chicken breasts, or 2 whole chicken breasts and ¾ pound squid. Chicken should be skinned and boned. Both chicken and squid should be cut in 1-inch chunks.

Dinner for 4

Marinated Broccoli Stems and Cauliflower (page 103)
Fruit Steak (page 180)
Carrot and Eggplant Chili (page 194)
2 Cups Boiled White Rice
Walnut Gelatin (page 244)

Preparation Tips:
1. Prepare Marinated Broccoli Stems and Cauliflower plus Walnut Gelatin the night before ready to serve.
2. Prepare Carrot and Eggplant Chili* 1 hour before serving, using saucepan.
3. Prepare rice 45 minutes before serving.
4. Prepare Fruit Steak ½ hour before serving.

* Use ½ the recipe. Reserve the remainder for future use.

Dinner for 4

Watercress and Noodle Salad (page 102)
Garlic Chicken with Snow Pea Pods (page 145)
Braised Peppers and Almonds (page 201)
Fresh Pineapple

Preparation Tips:
1. Core, peel, and cut pineapple into chunks 1 hour before guests arrive. Refrigerate until ready to serve.
2. Prepare Garlic Chicken with Snow Pea Pods through Step 4, ½ hour before guests arrive.
3. Prepare Watercress and Noodle Salad 15 minutes before serving.
4. Continue preparation of Garlic Chicken with Snow Pea Pods through Step 7, 10 minutes before serving.
5. Prepare Braised Peppers and Almonds.
6. Finish preparation of Garlic Chicken with Snow Pea Pods.

Dinner for 4

Sliced Tomatoes
Braised Shrimp with Leek (page 133)
Asparagus in Oyster Sauce (page 189)
Fluffy Mashed Potatoes
Fresh Fruit Bowl

Preparation Tips:
1. Prepare tomatoes and fruit 2 hours before guests arrive. Keep refrigerated until ready to serve.
2. Prepare potatoes 45 minutes before serving.
3. Prepare Braised Shrimp with Leek* 10 minutes before serving.
4. Prepare Asparagus in Oyster Sauce 5 minutes before serving.

* If you are not allowed shellfish, substitute 1 pound of salmon fillets.

Dinner for 4

Puffed Chicken and Tomato Soup (page 72)
Cucumber and Onion Salad (page 104)
Baked Halibut au Gratin
Steamed Green Beans
Paprika Potatoes
Thousand-Layer Cake (page 255)

Preparation Tips:
1. Prepare Thousand-Layer Cake the day before ready to use.
2. Prepare Cucumber and Onion Salad through Step 2, 45 minutes before serving.
3. Prepare potatoes ½ hour before serving.
4. Prepare Puffed Chicken and Tomato Soup 25 minutes before serving.
5. Prepare baked halibut and green beans 20 minutes before serving.
6. Finish preparation of Cucumber and Onion Salad.

Dinner for 8

Ginger Carrot and Peanut Soup (page 81)
Steamed Snapper with Pork Sauce (page 120)
Bamboo Shoots in Mushroom Sauce (page 190)
3 Cups Boiled White Rice
Fruit and Nut Rolls (page 251)

Preparation Tips:
1. Prepare Egg Roll Skins up to 1 month before ready to use.
2. Prepare Fruit and Nut Rolls through Step 2, 2 hours before serving.
3. Prepare Steamed Snapper with Pork Sauce through Step 1, 1 hour before ready to serve.
4. Prepare Bamboo Shoots in Mushroom Sauce through Step 1, ½ hour before serving.
5. Finish preparation of Steamed Snapper with Pork Sauce ½ hour before serving.
6. Prepare rice 25 minutes before serving.
7. Prepare Ginger Carrot and Peanut Soup, using saucepan, 20 minutes before serving.
8. Finish preparation of Bamboo Shoots in Mushroom Sauce 15 minutes before serving.
9. Finish preparation of Fruit and Nut Rolls immediately before ready to use.

Dinner for 8

Poached Bass with Hot Sauce and Vegetables (page 112)
Szechwan Beef (page 174)
Boiled Noodles
Zucchini and Walnuts (page 204)
Ginger Citrus with Pineapple (page 246)

Preparation Tips:
1. Prepare Ginger Citrus with Pineapple through Step 3, 1 hour before serving. Let stand at room temperature.
2. Prepare Poached Bass with Hot Sauce and Vegetables 40 minutes before serving.
3. Prepare noodles 10 minutes before serving.
4. Prepare Szechwan Beef 5 minutes before serving, using skillet.
5. Prepare Zucchini and Walnuts immediately before serving.
6. Finish preparation of Ginger Citrus with Pineapple immediately before serving.

Dinner for 8

Watercress with Cherry Tomatoes
Lemon Lamb (page 184)
Boiled Potatoes with Pearl Onions
Steamed Cauliflower with Nutmeg
Apples with Strawberries (page 244)

Preparation Tips:
1. Prepare Lemon Lamb through Step 1 the day before ready to use. Cover and keep refrigerated, turning occasionally.
2. Finish preparation of Lemon Lamb 2¾ hours before serving.
3. Prepare Apples with Strawberries 1 hour before serving.
4. Prepare potatoes and onions 45 minutes before serving.
5. Prepare watercress with cherry tomatoes ½ hour before serving. Keep refrigerated until ready to use.
6. Prepare cauliflower 10 minutes before ready to serve.

Dinner for 8

Mixed Greens Vinaigrette
Sugar-Sesame Cornish Hens in Lemon Sherry (page 156)
Broccoli in Garlic Sauce (page 193)
Brown Rice
Mixed Low-Sodium Cookies

Preparation Tips:
1. Prepare Sugar-Sesame Cornish Hens in Lemon Sherry through Step 2 at least 3 hours before serving.
2. Prepare salad and vinaigrette 1½ hours before ready to serve. Keep refrigerated until ready to serve.
3. Finish preparation of Sugar-Sesame Cornish Hens in Lemon Sherry 1 hour before serving.
4. Prepare brown rice 40 minutes before serving.
5. Toss salad and dressing immediately before serving.

Buffet for 12

Hot Ribs (page 35)
Broccoli and Minced Shrimp (page 192)
Stir-Fried Chicken Legs with Soy Sauce Peaches (page 146)
Flash-Fried Watercress and Bean Curd (page 202)
4 Cups Boiled White Rice
Lemon Sponge Cake (page 254)

Preparation Tips:
1. Prepare Lemon Sponge Cake the day before ready to use.
2. Prepare Stir-Fried Chicken Legs with Soy Sauce Peaches* through Step 1 40 minutes before serving.
3. Prepare Hot Ribs ½ hour before serving.
4. Prepare rice 20 minutes before serving.
5. Prepare Broccoli and Minced Shrimp†, then Flash-Fried Watercress and

Bean Curd* immediately before serving. Keep both warm in chafing dish.

6. Finish preparation of Stir-Fried Chicken Legs with Soy Sauce Peaches.

* Double the recipe.
† If you are not allowed shellfish, substitute ¼ pound pork, minced.

Buffet for 12

Ginger Squid Salad in Soy Sauce (page 89)
Eggplant with Cashews in Duck Sauce (page 197)
Rice Curry Imperial (page 210)
Stewed Fruit in Nut Sauce (page 248)

Preparation Tips:
1. Prepare Ginger Squid Salad in Soy Sauce* and Stewed Fruit in Nut Sauce the day before ready to use. Keep refrigerated until ready to serve.
2. Prepare Rice Curry Imperial† through Step 5, 1 hour before ready to serve.
3. Prepare Eggplant with Cashews in Duck Sauce‡ 45 minutes before ready to serve.
4. Finish preparation of Rice Curry Imperial 5 minutes before ready to serve.

* Double the recipe.
† Triple the recipe.
‡ Triple the recipe. If you are not allowed duck, substitute chicken.

Buffet for 12

Asparagus au Gratin
Assorted Seafood Salad (page 87)
Baked Potatoes
Thousand-Layer Cake (page 255)

Preparation Tips:
1. Prepare Thousand-Layer Cake the day before ready to use.
2. Prepare Assorted Seafood Salad* through Step 1, 2 hours before ready to serve.
3. Prepare potatoes 1 hour before ready to serve.
4. Prepare asparagus augratin ½ hour before ready to serve.
5. Finish preparation of Assorted Seafood Salad immediately before serving.

* Double the recipe.

Buffet for 12

Crudités
with Hot and Spicy Sauce (page 236)
Cold Sliced Roast Beef
Chinese Sweet Bread (page 66)
Lettuce, Tomatoes, and Onions
Low-Sodium Mayonnaise, Mustard, and Ketchup
Low-Sodium Pickles
Baked Apples

Preparation Tips:
1. Prepare Chinese Sweet Bread 2 to 4 days before ready to use. Reheat by steaming 20 minutes before ready to serve.
2. Prepare Hot and Spicy Sauce and roast beef the day before ready to use. Keep refrigerated until ½ hour before serving. Then bring to room temperature.
3. Prepare apples 45 minutes before ready to serve.
4. Prepare crudités plus lettuce, tomatoes, and onion platter ½ hour before serving. Keep refrigerated until ready to use.

Buffet for 12

Cucumbers and Radishes
with Dipping Sauce (page 233)
Fish and Seafood Soup (page 78)
Szechwan Fried Rice (page 208)
Peaches and Pineapple (page 246)

Preparation Tips:
1. Prepare Fish and Seafood Soup* through Step 1, 2 hours before ready to serve. Keep refrigerated until ready to use.
2. Prepare Peaches and Pineapple 1½ hours before serving.
3. Prepare Dipping Sauce 1 hour before serving.
4. Continue preparation of Fish and Seafood Soup through Step 5, ½ hour before ready to serve, using Dutch oven.
5. Prepare Szechwan Fried Rice† through Step 8, 20 minutes before ready to serve.
6. Prepare cucumbers and radishes 15 minutes before ready to serve.
7. Finish preparation of Fish and Seafood Soup 10 minutes before serving.
8. Finish preparation of Szechwan Fried Rice 5 minutes before serving.

* Double the recipe. If you are not allowed shellfish, substitute 1 pound of haddock, cut in 1-inch chunks, in Step 8.
† Triple the recipe.

Buffet for 16

Cauliflower and Zucchini Crudités
with Six-Fruit Sauce (page 242)
Braised Pork with Orange Rings (page 172)
Asparagus in Mustard Sauce (page 189)
6 Cups Boiled White Rice
Lemon Sponge Cake (page 254)

Preparation Tips:
1. Prepare Six-Fruit Sauce up to 1 week before ready to use. Keep refrigerated until ready to use.
2. Prepare Lemon Sponge Cake the day before ready to use.
3. Prepare Braised Pork with Orange Rings* 1 hour before ready to serve.
4. Prepare cauliflower and zucchini crudités 45 minutes before ready to use. Refrigerate to chill.
5. Prepare rice ½ hour before serving.
6. Prepare Asparagus in Mustard Sauce† 5 minutes before serving.

* Double the recipe.
† Triple the recipe.

Buffet for 16

Carrot and Eggplant Chili (page 194)
Low-Sodium Crackers
Odd-Spiced Duck (page 159)
Mixed Greens
with Low-Sodium French Dressing
Boiled Potatoes
Sesame-Peanut Cookies (page 248)

Preparation Tips:
1. Prepare Sesame-Peanut Cookies the day before ready to use.
2. Prepare Odd-Spiced Duck* 1¾ hours before serving.
3. Prepare Carrot and Eggplant Chili 1 hour before serving.

4. Prepare potatoes 45 minutes before serving.
5. Prepare salad ½ hour before serving. Refrigerate to chill.

* Double the recipe. If you are not allowed duck, substitute chicken.

Buffet for 16

Cantaloupe and Honeydew Balls
Chinese Pepper Steak (page 179)
Fried Rice and Oysters (page 207)
Green Beans in Vinaigrette
Apricot-Orange Buns (page 252)

Preparation Tips:
1. Prepare Apricot-Orange Buns up to 4 days in advance. Keep refrigerated and reheat by steaming for 15 to 20 minutes before serving.
2. Prepare Chinese Pepper Steak* through Step 1 and prepare green beans in vinaigrette the day before ready to use. Keep both refrigerated until ready to use.
3. Prepare melon balls ½ hour before ready to use. Refrigerate to chill.
4. Prepare Fried Rice and Oysters through Step 1, 20 minutes before serving.
5. Continue preparation of Chinese Pepper Steak through Step 5, 10 minutes before serving, using skillet.
6. Finish preparation of Fried Rice and Oysters.
7. Finish preparation of Chinese Pepper Steak.

* Double the recipe.

Buffet for 24

Crudités
with Dilled Low-Sodium Cottage Cheese and Cucumber
Peanutty Chicken and Scallions (page 140)
Potato Salad
Tomato Slices
Coconut Strawberries (page 245)

Preparation Tips:
1. Prepare potato salad the day before ready to use. Keep refrigerated until ready to serve.
2. Prepare cottage cheese, mixed with dill to taste and chopped cucumber, 45 minutes before ready to serve. Refrigerate to chill.
3. Prepare crudités and tomato slices ½ hour before ready to serve. Refrigerate to chill.
4. Prepare Peanutty Chicken and Scallions* 20 minutes before serving.
5. Prepare Coconut Strawberries* immediately before serving.

* Triple the recipe.

Buffet for 24

Ground Beef in Hoisin Sauce (page 181)
Chicken Salad Canton with Peanut Sauce (page 91)
Asparagus in Mustard Sauce (page 189)
Many-Flavored Fried Rice (page 213)
Almond Gelatin (page 243)
with Grapefruit Sections

Preparation Tips:
1. Prepare Almond Gelatin* the night before ready to use. Keep refrigerated until ready to serve.
2. Prepare Chicken Salad Canton with Peanut Sauce* through Step 3 2 hours before ready to serve.
3. Prepare Ground Beef in Hoisin Sauce† through Step 1, 1½ hours before serving. Keep refrigerated until ready to use.

4. Continue preparation of Chicken Salad Canton with Peanut Sauce through Step 5, 1 hour before ready to serve.
5. Continue preparation of Ground Beef in Hoisin Sauce through Step 5 45 minutes before serving.
6. Prepare Many-Flavored Fried Rice† ½ hour before serving.
7. Finish preparation of Chicken Salad Canton with Peanut Sauce 20 minutes before ready to serve.
8. Finish preparation of Ground Beef in Hoisin Sauce 10 minutes before serving.
9. Prepare Asparagus in Mustard Sauce‡ 5 minutes before serving.
10. Garnish Almond Gelatin with grapefruit sections immediately before serving.

* Triple the recipe.
† Double the recipe.
‡ Six times the recipe.

Buffet for 24

Lamb-Filled Jao-Tze (page 60)
Szechwan Vegetable Salad (page 102)
Noodles of Land and Sea (page 225)
Melon with Grapes
Almond Gelatin (page 243)

Preparation Tips:
1. Prepare Jao-Tze Wrappers up to 1 week before ready to use. Keep refrigerated until ready to use.
2. Prepare Almond Gelatin* the day before ready to use. Keep refrigerated until ready to serve.
3. Prepare Szechwan Vegetable Salad* through Step 2, 1½ hours before serving.
4. Prepare melon with grapes 1 hour before serving. Refrigerate to chill.
5. Prepare Noodles of Land and Sea† 40 minutes before serving.
6. Prepare Lamb-Filled Jao-Tze ½ hour before serving, using Dutch oven.
7. Finish preparation of Szechwan Vegetable Salad 20 minutes before serving.

* Triple the recipe.
† Double the recipe.

Buffet for 24

Ground Lamb with Walnuts (page 59)
Zucchini Sticks
Cold Sliced Turkey
Honey Carrots and Watercress (page 195)
Low-Sodium Wheat Bread
Lettuce and Tomatoes
Low-Sodium Mayonnaise and Mustard
Granny Smith Apples with Low-Sodium Cheddar Cheese

Preparation Tips:
1. Prepare turkey the day before ready to use. Cover and refrigerate overnight.
2. Prepare Ground Lamb with Walnuts* through Step 2, 4 hours before serving.
3. Prepare zucchini sticks and lettuce and tomatoes ½ hour before serving time. Refrigerate to chill.
4. Prepare Honeyed Carrots and Watercress* 5 minutes before serving.
5. Finish preparation of Ground Lamb with Walnuts immediately before serving.

* Triple the recipe.

Cocktails for 8

Batter-Fried Vegetables (page 188)
with Duck Sauce (page 234)
Hot and Sour Chicken Wings (page 38)
Shrimp in Black Bean Sauce (page 55)
Lion's Head Miniatures (page 57)

Preparation Tips:
1. Prepare Lion's Head Miniatures 1 hour before ready to serve.

2. Prepare Hot and Sour Chicken Wings through Step 1, 45 minutes before serving. Keep refrigerated until ready to use.
3. Prepare Batter-Fried Vegetables. (Duck Sauce should be a staple in your pantry, ready for use.)
4. Finish preparation of Hot and Sour Chicken Wings and prepare Shrimp in Black Bean Sauce* 10 minutes before serving.

* If you are not allowed shellfish, substitute 3 chicken breasts, skinned, boned, and cubed.

Cocktails for 8

Sherry-Vinegar Baby Spareribs (page 36)
Hot and Sour Soup II (page 71)
Chinese Chicken and Rice (page 215)
Crudités
with Soy Sauce Substitute (page 227)

Preparation Tips:
1. Prepare Chinese Chicken and Rice* through Step 1, 1 hour before ready to serve.
2. Prepare crudités 45 minutes before ready to serve. Refrigerate to chill. (Soy Sauce should be a staple in your pantry, ready to use.)
3. Prepare Sherry-Vinegar Baby Spareribs through Step 2, ½ hour before ready to serve.
4. Prepare Hot and Sour Soup II through Step 1, 25 minutes before ready to serve.
5. Finish preparation of Chinese Chicken and Rice 20 minutes before ready to serve.
6. Finish preparation of Sherry-Vinegar Baby Spareribs 10 minutes before ready to serve.
7. Finish preparation of Hot and Sour Soup II 5 minutes before ready to serve.

* Double the recipe.

Cocktails for 8

Sesame Beef Cubes (page 35)
Sizzling Chicken Wings (page 39)
Scallops in Soy Sauce (page 129)
Raw Cauliflower with Curried Sour Cream Dip

Preparation Tips:
1. Prepare Sesame Beef Cubes* through Step 1 the day before ready to use. Keep refrigerated until ready to use.
2. Prepare cauliflower and mix Curry Powder (see page 232) to taste with sour cream at least 4 hours before serving. Refrigerate to chill.
3. Prepare Scallops in Soy Sauce† through Step 3, 40 minutes before ready to use.
4. Prepare Sizzling Chicken Wings 10 minutes before serving.
5. Finish preparation of Sesame Beef Cubes 7 minutes before serving, using skillet.
6. Finish preparation of Scallops in Soy Sauce 5 minutes before serving.

* Double the recipe.
† If you are not allowed shellfish, substitute 1½ pounds cod, cut in 1-inch chunks.

Cocktails for 8

Beef Lo Mein (page 218)
Baked Mushrooms Topped with Tuna and Cheese
Coconut Chicken Wings (page 37)
Orange Sections Soaked in Dry Sherry

Preparation Tips:
1. Prepare baked mushrooms topped with tuna and cheese at least 2 hours before ready to serve. Refrigerate to chill.
2. Prepare Coconut Chicken Wings through Step 1, 40 minutes before ready to use.

3. Prepare orange sections soaked in dry sherry ½ hour before ready to serve. Skewer with toothpicks and refrigerate to chill.
4. Prepare Beef Lo Mein* 20 minutes before serving.
5. Finish preparation of Coconut Chicken Wings 10 minutes before serving.

* Double the recipe.

Cocktails for 16

Egg Roll Filling I (page 47)
Spiced Beef Cubes (page 34)
Sherried Onion Chicken Wings (page 38)
Crudités
with Sour Cream Dip

Preparation Tips:
1. Prepare Egg Roll Skins as far ahead of time as desired.
2. Prepare Spiced Beef Cubes 2¾ hours before ready to serve, using Dutch oven.
3. Prepare crudités and sour cream dip at least 1½ hours before ready to serve. Refrigerate to chill.
4. Prepare Sherried Onion Chicken Wings through Step 1, 1¼ hours before ready to use.
5. Prepare Egg Roll Filling I through Step 4, 15 minutes before ready to serve.
6. Finish preparation of Sherried Onion Chicken Wings.
7. Finish preparation of Egg Roll Filling I.

Cocktails for 16

Egg Roll Filling II (page 48)
Chinese Barbecued Beef (page 175)
Coconut Chicken Wings (page 37)
Raw Asparagus and Cauliflower
with Mustard-Yogurt Sauce

Preparation Tips:
1. Prepare Egg Roll Skins as far ahead of time as desired.
2. Prepare Chinese Barbecued Beef through Step 2 the day before ready to use.
3. Finish preparation of Chinese Barbecued Beef 2 hours before guests arrive. Keep refrigerated until ready to serve.
4. Prepare mustard-yogurt sauce by mixing 1½ teaspoons mustard in 1 pint lemon yogurt 1 hour before serving. Keep refrigerated until ready to serve.
5. Prepare Coconut Chicken Wings through Step 1, 45 minutes before serving.
6. Prepare asparagus and cauliflower 20 minutes before serving. Refrigerate to chill.
7. Finish preparation of Coconut Chicken Wings 10 minutes before serving.
8. Prepare Egg Roll Filling II 5 minutes before serving.

Cocktails for 24

Chicken Livers Wrapped in Red and Green (page 41)
Crudités
with Sweet and Sour Sauce (page 235)
Noodles of Land and Sea (page 225)
Eggplant Curry Salad (page 106)
with Low-Sodium Sesame Seed Crackers

Preparation Tips:
1. Prepare Sweet and Sour Sauce up to 1 week before ready to use.
2. Prepare crudités 1½ hours before ready to serve. Refrigerate to chill.

3. Prepare Eggplant Curry Salad* through Step 1, 1 hour before ready to serve, using skillet.
4. Prepare Noodles of Land and Sea* 40 minutes before ready to serve.
5. Prepare Chicken Livers Wrapped in Red and Green through Step 1, 25 minutes before ready to serve.
6. Finish preparation of Eggplant Curry Salad 20 minutes before ready to serve.
7. Finish preparation of Chicken Livers Wrapped in Red and Green† 10 minutes before ready to serve.

* Triple the recipe.
† Double the recipe.

Cocktails for 24

Cucumber Stuffed with Chicken Livers (page 40)
Barbecued Chicken Buns (page 42)
Raw Shrimp with Low-Sodium Chili Ketchup
Steak and Tomato Kebobs
Marinated in Oil and Vinegar Dressing

Preparation Tips:
1. Prepare Barbecued Chicken Buns through Step 14 up to 4 days before ready to use. Keep refrigerated until ready to use. Reheat by steaming for 15 to 20 minutes before serving.
2. Refrigerate both raw shrimp† on bed of ice and chili ketchup until ready to serve.
3. Prepare Cucumber Stuffed with Chicken Livers* 1 hour before ready to serve. Keep refrigerated.
4. Prepare steak and tomato kebobs 10 minutes before ready to serve.

* Double the recipe.
† If you are not allowed shellfish, substitute 1 can (7 ounces) low-sodium salmon.

Cocktails for 32

Minced Oysters (page 53)
Low-Sodium Sesame Seed Crackers
Beef and Spinach Buns (page 45)
Shrimp in Hot Garlic Sauce (page 56)
Crudités
with Six-Fruit Sauce (page 242)

Preparation Tips:
1. Prepare Six-Fruit Sauce up to 1 week before ready to use. Keep refrigerated until ready to use.
2. Prepare Basic Buns* through Step 5, 3 hours before ready to use.
3. Prepare Beef and Spinach Buns 2½ hours before serving. Keep refrigerated until ready to use.
4. Prepare crudités 1½ hours before ready to serve. Refrigerate to chill.
5. Finish preparation of Beef and Spinach Buns 20 minutes before ready to serve.
6. Prepare Minced Oysters 10 minutes before ready to serve.
7. Prepare Shrimp in Hot Garlic Sauce† 5 minutes before ready to serve.

* Double the recipe.
† Double the recipe. If you are not allowed shellfish, substitute 2 cans (6½ ounces each) low-sodium tuna and serve as a dip.

Cocktails for 32

Ground Lamb with Walnuts (page 59)
Watercress-Rolled Pork (page 58)
Broiled Chicken Wings
Seasoned with Curry Powder (page 232)
Salmon-Stuffed Cherry Tomatoes
Fresh Pineapple Chunks Dipped in Coconut

Preparation Tips:
1. Prepare Ground Lamb with Walnuts* through Step 2, 4½ hours before ready to serve.
2. Core, peel, and cut pineapple into chunks 2 hours before serving. Dip chunks in coconut and refrigerate to chill.
3. Prepare Watercress-Rolled Pork† 45 minutes before ready to serve.
4. Prepare salmon-stuffed cherry tomatoes and pineapple ½ hour before ready to serve. Refrigerate to chill.
5. Prepare Broiled Chicken Wings Seasoned with Curry Powder 10 minutes before serving.
6. Finish preparation of Ground Lamb with Walnuts immediately before serving.

* Double the recipe.
† Four times the recipe.

A Chinese Diet

Although born of necessity rather than design, the Chinese diet is as close to perfect as any diet could be, especially for the salt-free dieter, believe it or not.

The glorious vegetables coaxed from every nook and cranny of the limited farmland available plus the rice which sprouts along the waterways form the basis of the Chinese diet. These complex carbohydrates not only give the brain its energy but aid the body in metabolizing fat and provide endurance while the slower body-building process reserved for protein takes hold.

The primary source of fat comes from the polyunsaturated oils used in cooking and, to a lesser degree, from meat, fish, and poultry. Fat, too, is important for concentrated energy, and it quite literally greases the way for other nutrients.

Fish, which abound in the lakes, rivers, and sea in and around China, are low in calories, fat, and sodium, but rich in protein and are the main source of that key nutrient at the Chinese table. Meat and poultry, though served in lesser amounts, also provide the protein which gives muscle and tone to the body.

Protein is the smallest portion of a Chinese menu and should be so on everyone's plate, for too much protein drives fluid—and with it, vital nutrients—from the body, leaving it dehydrated and vulnerable to the damage toxic acids can cause. These acids, in turn, can put unnatural and excessive pressure on the body's vital organs and ultimately destroy them.

As you can see and as the Chinese could have told us, the answer once again is balance. Just add up a Chinese diet and that is what you get: a nutritional balance of approximately 50 percent carbohydrate, 30 percent fat, and 20 percent protein—healthy by any dietary and medical standards.

But even the healthiest of diets requires some adjustments for us special dieters. Interestingly enough, whether your problem is salt, carbohydrates, fat, or just plain calories, the dietary requirements we each face have some amazing similarities.

For example, those of us with hypertension, cardiovascular disease, arteriosclerosis, kidney dysfunction, or edema must limit not only our salt intake but fat and calories as well. Those with hypoglycemia or diabetes must monitor and control sugar and/or complex carbohydrate consumption and must also be prudent about fat, salt, and calories.

In short, the goal we all share—although for different reasons—is to avoid weight gain and water retention which could exacerbate our problems. The way to achieve that goal is also the same—that is, by following a balanced and healthy diet with no excesses.

But good intentions can be sorely tried. Probably everyone reading these words has, at one time, been on one diet or another. Stop and think for a minute and remember how boring, how regimented, how bland it was. Remember, too, how tempted you were to cheat or quit altogether.

That is where Chinese food comes in. Once you eliminate the salt, soy sauce, and MSG—ordinarily part of the cuisine—Chinese food is a treat to diet by and inherently low in sodium.

We have already explained how well balanced it is. What should also be obvious is the enormous variety this cuisine offers. That is a very big plus in nurturing your determination and making the diet experience a pleasant transition to a happier, healthier way of life.

Using the recipes in this book, we have prepared a diet based on the following:

1. *Two weeks' duration* because it takes at least this long for your palate both to adjust to the absence of salt and to appreciate new flavors. After the initial two-week period, you can repeat the basic plan with different dishes.
2. *Under 1,200 calories* to show you how much food and satisfaction you can have and still lose weight.

   To determine the proper calorie level for yourself, keep the following points in mind:
   • If you want to maintain your weight, multiply your ideal weight by 13.5 to determine your daily calorie level.
   • If you want to lose weight—or gain it for that matter—just remember that slowly and steadily is the safest, healthiest way to reach and hold on to your goal. That translates to a one-and-a-half-pound gain or loss over a two-week period.

   Add to that the knowledge that 3,500 calories equal one pound. So if you cut out 250 calories per day, you will lose that pound in 14 days; add the same 250 calories, you will gain that pound in the prescribed time.
3. *Under 500 milligrams sodium* to prove how easy it is to live and dine happily and deliciously on a so-called restricted diet.

   If your sodium limits—self-imposed or otherwise—are more liberal, consult a sodium guide (some of which are listed in this book's bibliography) to see what additional options are available to you.

   For example, if you love calves liver or shrimp, enjoy them. Just remember to stay within your limits and not to exceed 1,500 milligrams per day, more than enough sodium for anyone.

   If, like me, you must get by with less than 500 milligrams sodium per day, just replace all shellfish on the menu with meat, poultry, or another fish. Or delete some dairy products. It is just that simple.

Enough advice. Well, maybe just one thing more. Do not let the word "diet" intimidate you. When you think about it, diet is a way of life—*your* way to make you look good and feel good.

The fact that it can also be fun is something you are about to find out for yourself with the Chinese diet.

Note: The menus on the following pages were specifically designed for the saft-free dieter. Thus, if you do use sugar substitutes, please be sure they are not only sugar-free but low-sodium (calcium saccharin or Nutra-sweet) as well.

In addition, much consideration was given to the needs of those with diabetes, which accounts for the carbohydrate snacks throughout the day. (By the way, deliciously healthy, energy-releasing snacking is good for all of us and helps cut down the urge to splurge.) But if you are a diabetic, pass on sugary desserts and, in fact, check this program with your own doctor or nutritionist to see if adjustments are necessary.

DAY ONE

Tips for Day One

Remember, the first day of any diet is the hardest. You feel you are leaving "good" food behind to plunge into a world of weights and measurements, self-consciousness, discipline, and distasteful meals devoid of pleasure. Did I cover all the bases?

Well, there's an old song that tells us to "accentuate the positive and eliminate the negative," so try on these thoughts for size:

1. The first day of anything is the hardest. Remember your first day of school, at overnight camp, on a new job? But once the strangeness wore off and things were familiar, natural, why, you probably started enjoying yourself.

2. Once you do take the plunge, the water will not seem so cold.

3. You will be eating three meals a day—probably for the first time in years. And we do not mean boiled chicken, but delicious, filling meals, including desserts, so you will not feel you are on a diet at all.

4. Go to it. You will find you can have it all: a healthy body, a good-looking body, and good food, too.

	Calories	Sodium (mg.)	Carbo-hydrates (gm.)	Fat (gm.)
BREAKFAST				
½ grapefruit	62.9	1.4	16.4	0.14
1 boiled egg	78.0	55.0	0.4	4.3
1 slice low-sodium bread	89.0	12.5	17.0	1.0
1 teaspoon unsalted margarine	35.0	0.7	0.02	3.9
Coffee or tea	—	—	—	—
1 teaspoon sugar substitute	2.0	0	1.4	0
1 tablespoon low-fat milk	6.3	7.1	0.75	0.1
Total	273.2	76.7	36.0	9.4

	Calories	Sodium (mg.)	Carbo-hydrates (gm.)	Fat (gm.)
LUNCH				
Hot and Sour Soup II* (use flounder)	127.0	70.6	5.7	3.5
1 cup shredded lettuce	18.0	9.0	3.5	0.3
¼ green pepper, chopped	11.0	6.5	2.4	0.1
1½ tablespoons Duck Sauce*	21.6	0.6	4.8	0.2
3 low-sodium crackers	33.0	2.5	4.3	1.5
Coffee or tea	—	—	—	—
1 teaspoon sugar substitute	2.0	0	1.4	0
1 tablespoon low-fat milk	6.3	7.1	0.75	0.1
Total	225.9	96.3	22.9	5.7
SNACK				
1 apple	106.0	2.0	29.0	1.2
½ ounce low-sodium cheddar cheese	56.9	6.0	0.3	4.6
Total	162.9	8.0	29.3	5.8
DINNER				
Curried Chicken with Pineapple*	161.0	31.4	17.3	5.3
1 cup shredded lettuce	18.0	9.0	3.5	0.3
¼ cucumber, sliced	41.0	17.7	2.9	0.1
½ cup boiled white rice	124.6	5.7	27.7	0.1
Lemon Sponge Cake*	122.8	10.9	24.4	1.0
Coffee or tea	—	—	—	—
1 teaspoon sugar substitute	2.0	0	1.4	0
1 tablespoon low-fat milk	6.3	7.1	0.75	0.1
Total	475.7	81.5	77.7	6.9
SNACK				
Almond Gelatin*	50.4	4.0	6.6	0.02
Grand Total	1,188.1	266.5	172.5	27.8

* Asterisked recipes appear in this book. Consult the index.

DAY TWO

Tips for Day Two

Well, you made it through Day One. You are probably surprised at how easy it was and how filling.

If you have leftover Hot and Sour Soup II, store it in a plastic container and refrigerate up to one week. You can use it to replace other menu suggestions of similar composition. For example, Chicken with Vegetable Marinade on Day Two; Sugar-Sesame Cornish Hens in Lemon Sherry on Day Three; Braised Shrimp Bamboo on Day Five; or Assorted Seafood Salad on Day Seven.

As for the Curried Chicken with Pineapple, leftovers can be frozen indefinitely.

Now for the Day Two Menu:

1. If you need to limit your sodium intake to 250 milligrams per day, substitute ½ cup of low-sodium cottage cheese for the yogurt at breakfast.

2. Hang in there. Every day it gets easier.

	Calories	Sodium (mg.)	Carbo- hydrates (gm.)	Fat (gm.)
BREAKFAST				
½ cup plain yogurt	70.9	53.7	5.6	3.9
½ cup strawberries	20.8	0.7	5.5	0.14
1 Steamed Bun*	131.7	1.1	26.9	1.4
Coffee or tea	—	—	—	—
1 teaspoon sugar substitute	2.0	0	1.4	0
1 tablespoon low-fat milk	6.3	7.1	0.75	0.1
Total	231.7	62.6	40.2	5.5
LUNCH				
Chicken with Vegetable Marinade*	189.5	96.0	22.5	4.0
Coffee or tea	—	—	—	—
1 teaspoon sugar substitute	2.0	0	1.4	0
1 tablespoon low-fat milk	6.3	7.1	0.75	0.1
Total	197.8	103.1	24.7	4.1

	Calories	Sodium (mg.)	Carbo-hydrates (gm.)	Fat (gm.)
SNACK				
3 low-sodium crackers	33.0	2.5	4.3	1.5
½ ounce low-sodium Gouda cheese	56.9	6.0	0.3	4.6
Total	89.9	8.5	4.6	6.1
DINNER				
Salmon with Zucchini in Soy Sauce*	247.0	68.0	6.8	14.4
Mandarin Rice with Peppers*	112.5	20.5	23.6	1.3
Pears Baked in Almond Honey*	86.0	2.4	16.1	2.3
Coffee or tea	—	—	—	—
1 teaspoon sugar substitute	2.0	0	1.4	0
1 tablespoon low-fat milk	6.3	7.1	0.75	0.1
Total	453.8	98.0	48.7	18.1
SNACK				
3½ ounces low-sodium tomato juice	19.0	3.0	4.3	0.1
Grand Total	992.2	275.2	122.5	33.9

* See index for recipe page number.

DAY THREE

Tips for Day Three

You must be getting into the swing of things by now. Maybe even feeling a little guilty that it is all so pleasant? Well, don't feel that way. A good diet is not just to lose weight or to deal with special diet needs. It is a way of life and it should be good.

If you have leftover Chicken with Vegetable Marinade you can refrigerate it in a plastic container for up to one week, or use it as a lunch substitute on Day Six or Day Seven, exchanging it for an equal amount of calories.

Day Three is a reward for making it through the first two days. It is effortless cooking and first-class eating.

	Calories	Sodium (mg.)	Carbo-hydrates (gm.)	Fat (gm.)
BREAKFAST				
½ cup puffed wheat	207.0	2.3	44.9	0.9
¼ cup low-fat milk	25.0	28.6	3.0	0.5
1 peach, sliced	43.4	1.1	11.1	0.1
Coffee or tea	—	—	—	—
1 teaspoon sugar substitute	2.0	0	1.4	0
1 tablespoon low-fat milk	6.3	7.1	0.75	0.1
Total	283.7	39.1	61.2	1.6
LUNCH				
Salmon with Zucchini in Soy Sauce*	247.0	68.0	6.8	14.4
½ tomato, sliced	15.7	2.1	3.4	0.1
1 cup shredded lettuce	18.0	9.0	3.5	0.3
Coffee or tea	—	—	—	—
1 teaspoon sugar substitute	2.0	0	1.4	0
1 tablespoon low-fat milk	6.3	7.1	0.75	0.1
Total	289.0	86.2	15.9	14.9

	Calories	Sodium (mg.)	Carbo-hydrates (gm.)	Fat (gm.)
SNACK				
2 low-sodium crackers	22.0	1.7	2.9	1.0
¼ cup low-sodium cottage cheese	45.0	31.0	4.0	1.0
½ pear, cored and sliced	62.0	2.0	15.3	0.4
Total	129.0	34.7	22.2	2.4
DINNER				
Sugar-Sesame Cornish Hens in Lemon Sherry*	173.5	44.5	8.8	7.3
½ cup chopped watercress	9.5	26.0	0.3	0.2
Asparagus in Mustard Sauce*	61.8	6.6	7.3	2.5
½ cup boiled white rice	124.6	5.7	27.7	0.1
Coffee or tea	—	—	—	—
1 teaspoon sugar substitute	2.0	0	1.4	0
1 tablespoon low-fat milk	6.3	7.1	0.75	0.1
Total	377.7	90.0	46.3	10.2
SNACK				
½ cup pineapple	26.0	0.5	6.9	0.1
Grand Total	1,105.4	250.5	152.5	29.2

* See index for recipe page number.

DAY FOUR

Tips for Day Four

You are halfway through the first week. Good for you.

If you still have any Salmon with Zucchini in Soy Sauce, you can serve it for a fast-food dinner on Day Four instead of preparing Spiced Beef with Cabbage, Pepper, and Squash.

By now you deserve a little treat, so arrange for a body massage or facial after your daily workout.

Keep up the good work.

	Calories	Sodium (mg.)	Carbo-hydrates (gm.)	Fat (gm.)
BREAKFAST				
1 orange	98.0	2.0	24.4	0.4
1 poached egg	78.0	55.0	0.4	4.3
1 slice low-sodium bread	89.0	12.5	17.0	1.0
Coffee or tea	—	—	—	—
1 teaspoon sugar substitute	2.0	0	1.4	0
1 tablespoon low-fat milk	6.3	7.1	0.75	0.1
Total	273.3	76.6	44.0	5.8
LUNCH				
Sugar-Sesame Cornish Hens in Lemon Sherry*	173.5	44.5	8.8	7.3
1 cup shredded lettuce	18.0	9.0	3.5	0.3
½ tomato	15.7	2.1	3.4	0.14
2 tablespoons red vinegar	4.0	2.0	1.6	0
1 teaspoon sesame seed oil	42.0	0	0	4.9
Coffee or tea	—	—	—	—
1 teaspoon sugar substitute	2.0	0	1.4	0
1 tablespoon low-fat milk	6.3	7.1	0.75	0.1
Total	261.5	64.7	19.5	12.7

	Calories	Sodium (mg.)	Carbo-hydrates (gm.)	Fat (gm.)
SNACK				
3 low-sodium crackers	33.0	2.5	4.3	1.5
½ ounce low-sodium Swiss cheese	50.7	4.0	0.3	3.9
1 apple, cored and sliced	116.0	2.0	19.0	1.2
Total	199.7	8.5	23.6	6.6
DINNER				
Spiced Beef with Cabbage, Pepper, and Squash*	215.5	86.9	7.8	7.7
½ cup boiled white rice	124.6	5.7	27.7	0.1
Coffee or tea	—	—	—	—
1 teaspoon sugar substitute	2.0	0	1.4	0
1 tablespoon low-fat milk	6.3	7.1	0.75	0.1
Total	348.4	99.7	37.7	7.9
SNACK				
¼ cantaloupe	42.9	17.1	10.7	0.1
Grand Total	1,125.8	266.6	135.5	33.1

* See index for recipe page number.

DAY FIVE

Tips for Day Five

As you start Day Five, your body and taste buds should be experiencing some changes. You might already show some modest weight loss (probably water) from a combination of good nutrition, conserved calories, and low-sodium intake. But weight loss or not, you most certainly feel more energetic, healthier, less bulky, because your body is getting what it needs to do its best for you and is not getting problem foods, like salt, which, in excess, can do serious harm.

In addition, by now your palate should be not just enjoying but actually looking forward to its salt-free meals. Usually, people need one to two weeks to get used to saltless foods. But Chinese food uses so many distinct and pungent ingredients and seasonings—aniseed, garlic, leeks, scallions, sesame seed oil, Szechwan peppercorns, to name a few—that, together with our special sauce substitutes, you will not even notice that salt is gone. Indeed, all you will be adjusting to is the fresh, new taste of pure food. It can be addictive.

As for today, if your doctor does not allow shellfish on your diet, just substitute three ounces of flounder or any other mild fish. The calories will go up slightly, so to compensate, reduce your breakfast raisins* to 1½ tablespoons.

* Preserved in nonsodium ingredient.

	Calories	Sodium (mg.)	Carbo-hydrates (gm.)	Fat (gm.)
BREAKFAST				
3½ ounces apple juice	47.0	1.0	11.9	0.1
½ cup oatmeal	62.9	2.0	11.1	1.1
¼ cup low-fat milk	25.0	28.6	3.0	0.5
2 tablespoons raisins	145.0	14.0	38.7	0.1
Coffee or tea	—	—	—	—
1 teaspoon sugar substitute	2.0	0	1.4	0
1 tablespoon low-fat milk	6.3	7.1	0.75	0.1
Total	288.2	52.7	66.9	1.9

	Calories	Sodium (mg.)	Carbo-hydrates (gm.)	Fat (gm.)
LUNCH				
Three-Color Soup*	91.0	21.5	5.3	2.4
1 slice low-sodium bread	89.0	12.5	17.0	1.0
Coffee or tea	—	—	—	—
1 teaspoon sugar substitute	2.0	0	1.4	0
1 tablespoon low-fat milk	6.3	7.1	0.75	0.1
Total	188.3	41.1	24.5	3.5
SNACK				
Sesame-Peanut Cookie* (1)	59.9	1.9	6.1	2.3
Iced tea with lemon	—	—	—	—
Total	59.9	1.9	6.1	2.3
DINNER				
Braised Shrimp Bamboo*	148.1	89.0	14.4	5.3
1 cup shredded lettuce	18.0	9.0	3.5	0.3
½ tomato, sliced	15.7	2.1	3.4	0.1
2 tablespoons Dipping Sauce*	53.2	4.0	3.6	4.6
Chinese Chicken and Rice*	273.0	40.8	26.7	11.6
Coffee or tea	—	—	—	—
1 teaspoon sugar substitute	2.0	0	1.4	0
1 tablespoon low-fat milk	6.3	7.1	0.75	0.1
Total	482.6	140.9	46.9	21.6
SNACK				
Peaches and Pineapple*	76.0	0.2	20.0	0.26
Grand Total	1,095.0	236.8	164.4	29.6

* See index for recipe page number.

DAY SIX

Tips for Day Six

Day Six: Good health never tasted so good. And by now, you are definitely seeing and feeling results. So, start to be a little daring, a little experimental.

For example, spark up that luncheon tuna with some parsley or freshly squeezed lime juice. Sprinkle cinnamon or grated lemon rind on your yogurt snack. Or forgo that apple half at breakfast and indulge yourself in a lip-smacking smear (or teaspoon) of unsalted margarine on that slice of Chinese Sweet Bread.

In other words, your diet should be flexible in meeting your needs as long as you are on top of keeping it balanced.

	Calories	Sodium (mg.)	Carbo-hydrates (gm.)	Fat (gm.)
BREAKFAST				
½ cup low-sodium cottage cheese	90.0	31.0	4.0	1.0
½ banana	43.0	0.5	11.1	0.1
½ apple	53.0	1.0	15.0	0.6
1 slice Chinese Sweet Bread*	157.7	3.3	28.4	2.8
Coffee or tea	—	—	—	—
1 teaspoon sugar substitute	2.0	0	1.4	0
1 tablespoon low-fat milk	6.3	7.1	0.75	0.1
Total	352.0	42.9	59.7	4.6

	Calories	Sodium (mg.)	Carbo-hydrates (gm.)	Fat (gm.)
LUNCH				
½ can low-sodium tuna	108.0	51.0	0	0.8
Sweet and Sour Corn*	83.6	24.9	22.3	1.1
1 cup shredded lettuce	18.0	9.0	3.5	0.3
Coffee or tea	—	—	—	—
1 teaspoon sugar substitute	2.0	0	1.4	0
1 tablespoon low-fat milk	6.3	7.1	0.75	0.1
Total	217.9	92.0	28.0	2.3
SNACK				
½ cup plain yogurt	70.9	53.7	5.6	3.9
Iced tea with lemon	—	—	—	—
Total	70.9	53.7	5.6	3.9
DINNER				
Garlic Chicken with Snow Pea Pods*	154.3	44.0	12.0	5.1
Hoisin Rice in Four*	195.7	22.2	38.5	1.6
Coffee or tea	—	—	—	—
1 teaspoon sugar substitute	2.0	0	1.4	0
1 tablespoon low-fat milk	6.3	7.1	0.75	0.1
Total	358.3	73.3	52.7	6.8
SNACK				
½ cup strawberries	20.8	0.7	5.5	0.3
Grand Total	1,019.9	262.6	151.5	17.9

* See index for recipe page number.

DAY SEVEN

Tips for Day Seven

Halfway there. You should be proud of yourself.

Any leftover Sweet and Sour Corn can be served as a luncheon side dish in place of the low-sodium crackers. Leftover Garlic Chicken with Snow Pea Pods can be refrigerated up to three days and served cold for an easy dinner on Day Nine instead of Chicken Plus Four.

Enjoy today's goodies. Only one more week to go.

	Calories	Sodium (mg.)	Carbo-hydrates (gm.)	Fat (gm.)
BRUNCH				
½ grapefruit	62.9	1.4	16.4	0.14
Noodles of Land and Sea*	223.6	48.2	30.2	5.9
Coffee or tea	—	—	—	—
1 teaspoon sugar substitute	2.0	0	1.4	0
1 tablespoon low-fat milk	6.3	7.1	0.75	0.1
Total	294.8	56.7	48.8	6.1
LUNCH				
Assorted Seafood Salad* (use snapper)	142.4	72.0	8.4	3.5
3 low-sodium crackers	33.0	2.5	4.3	1.5
Coffee or tea	—	—	—	—
1 teaspoon sugar substitute	2.0	0	1.4	0
1 tablespoon low-fat milk	6.3	7.1	0.75	0.1
Total	183.7	81.6	14.9	5.1
SNACK				
Lemon Sponge Cake*	122.8	10.9	24.4	1.0
½ cup pineapple	26.0	0.5	6.9	0.1
Iced tea with lemon	—	—	—	—
Total	148.8	11.4	31.3	1.1

	Calories	Sodium (mg.)	Carbo-hydrates (gm.)	Fat (gm.)
DINNER				
Stir-Fried Beef and Vegetables*	267.6	65.4	15.0	10.5
1 cup shredded lettuce	18.0	9.0	3.5	0.3
½ cup boiled white rice	124.6	5.7	27.7	0.1
Coffee or tea	—	—	—	—
1 teaspoon sugar substitute	2.0	0	1.4	0
1 tablespoon low-fat milk	6.3	7.1	0.75	0.1
Total	418.5	87.2	48.4	11.0
SNACK				
1 peach	43.4	1.1	11.1	0.1
Grand Total	1,089.2	238.0	154.5	23.3

* See index for recipe page number.

DAY EIGHT

Tips for Day Eight

Just relax. You are in control now.

To reheat the Stir-Fried Beef and Vegetables, add ¼ cup of water and warm over low heat, stirring occasionally.

Also, if you want to spruce up the Chinese Rice Pudding, add a dash of nutmeg and a tablespoon of heavy cream.

	Calories	Sodium (mg.)	Carbo-hydrates (gm.)	Fat (gm.)
BREAKFAST				
½ cup oatmeal	62.9	2.0	11.1	1.1
¼ cup low-fat milk	25.0	28.6	3.0	0.5
½ cup strawberries	20.8	0.7	5.5	0.3
Coffee or tea	—	—	—	—
1 teaspoon sugar substitute	2.0	0	1.4	0
1 tablespoon low-fat milk	6.3	7.1	0.75	0.1
Total	117.0	38.4	21.8	2.0
LUNCH				
Stir-Fried Beef and Vegetables*	267.6	65.4	15.0	10.5
1 cup shredded lettuce	18.0	9.0	3.5	0.3
Coffee or tea	—	—	—	—
1 teaspoon sugar substitute	2.0	0	1.4	0
1 tablespoon low-fat milk	6.3	7.1	0.75	0.1
Total	293.9	81.5	20.7	10.9

	Calories	Sodium (mg.)	Carbo-hydrates (gm.)	Fat (gm.)
SNACK				
3 low-sodium crackers	33.0	2.5	4.3	1.5
½ ounce low-sodium cheddar cheese	56.9	6.0	0.3	4.6
½ apple, cored and sliced	58.0	1.0	14.5	0.6
Total	147.9	9.5	19.1	6.7
DINNER				
Braised Fish and Peanuts* (use cod and snapper)	136.0	93.4	5.7	4.2
Egg Dumplings*	124.0	10.3	22.5	1.4
Braised Zucchini in Six-Fruit Sauce*	55.3	6.1	6.2	3.0
¼ cucumber, sliced	41.0	17.7	2.9	0.1
Coffee or tea	—	—	—	—
1 teaspoon sugar substitute	2.0	0	1.4	0
1 tablespoon low-fat milk	6.3	7.1	0.75	0.1
Total	363.9	134.6	39.5	8.8
SNACK				
Chinese Rice Pudding*	146.1	3.3	30.9	2.1
1 orange	98.0	2.0	12.2	0.2
Total	244.1	5.3	43.1	2.3
Grand Total	1,166.8	269.3	144.2	30.7

* See index for recipe page number.

DAY NINE

Tips for Day Nine

This is a pretty easy day with only dinner to prepare. Everything else is ready-made or, in the case of Braised Fish and Peanuts, a terrific cold leftover.

So you might take a few minutes to think of how sexy you will look at the beach this summer, or to plan that special vacation you have promised yourself as a reward for sticking with it.

	Calories	Sodium (mg.)	Carbo-hydrates (gm.)	Fat (gm.)
BREAKFAST				
½ grapefruit	62.9	1.4	16.4	0.14
½ cup puffed rice	228.0	0.23	51.1	1.1
¼ cup low-fat milk	25.0	28.6	3.0	0.5
Coffee or tea	—	—	—	—
1 teaspoon sugar substitute	2.0	0	1.4	0
1 tablespoon low-fat milk	6.3	7.1	0.75	0.1
Total	324.2	37.3	72.7	1.8
LUNCH				
Braised Fish and Peanuts*	136.0	93.4	5.7	4.2
½ tomato, sliced	15.7	2.1	3.4	0.1
1 cup steamed broccoli	36.6	0.3	6.7	17.1
Coffee or tea	—	—	—	—
1 teaspoon sugar substitute	2.0	0	1.4	0
1 tablespoon low-fat milk	6.3	7.1	0.75	0.1
Total	196.6	102.9	18.0	21.5

	Calories	Sodium (mg.)	Carbo-hydrates (gm.)	Fat (gm.)
SNACK				
3½ ounces low-sodium tomato juice	19.0	3.0	4.3	0.1
½ ounce low-sodium Gouda cheese	56.9	6.0	0.3	4.6
½ cup green grapes	39.4	1.7	9.0	0.6
Total	115.3	10.7	13.6	5.3
DINNER				
Chicken Plus Four*	275.1	36.6	20.7	15.4
½ cup shredded lettuce	9.0	4.5	1.8	0.2
½ cup chopped watercress	9.5	26.0	0.3	0.2
½ zucchini, sliced	17.0	1.0	3.6	0.1
2 tablespoons lemon juice	3.3	0.1	1.3	0.01
½ cup boiled white rice	124.6	5.7	27.7	0.1
1 plum	66.0	2.0	17.8	0
Coffee or tea	—	—	—	—
1 teaspoon sugar substitute	2.0	0	1.4	0
1 tablespoon low-fat milk	6.3	7.1	0.75	0.1
Total	529.0	50.8	79.0	20.1
SNACK				
1 cup low-sodium chicken bouillon	18.0	5.0	2.0	1.0
2 low-sodium crackers	22.0	1.7	2.9	1.0
Total	40.0	6.7	4.9	2.0
Grand Total	1,188.9	240.6	184.6	46.7

* See index for recipe page number.

DAY TEN

Tips for Day Ten

If, by any chance, you have some Chicken Plus Four left over, you can use it for a light lunch in place of Spiced Shrimp and Cashews in Tomatoes. Otherwise, if shellfish are a no-no for you, substitute tuna for the shrimp. Either of the above options will reduce your daily total of sodium. With Chicken Plus Four, you'll save about 20 milligrams, and using tuna (¼ can per serving) will save you about 60 milligrams.

You are at the three-quarter mark on your diet!

	Calories	Sodium (mg.)	Carbo-hydrates (gm.)	Fat (gm.)
BREAKFAST				
1 orange	98.0	2.0	24.4	0.4
1 boiled egg	78.0	55.0	0.4	4.3
1 slice low-sodium bread	89.0	12.5	17.0	1.0
1 teaspoon unsalted margarine	35.0	0.7	0.02	3.9
Coffee or tea	—	—	—	—
1 teaspoon sugar substitute	2.0	0	1.4	0
1 tablespoon low-fat milk	6.3	7.1	0.75	0.1
Total	308.3	77.3	44.0	9.7
LUNCH				
Spiced Shrimp and Cashews in Tomatoes*	139.8	88.9	10.8	5.3
½ cup raw broccoli flowerettes	18.3	8.6	3.4	0.2
Coffee or tea	—	—	—	—
1 teaspoon sugar substitute	2.0	0	1.4	0
1 tablespoon low-fat milk	6.3	7.1	0.75	0.1
Total	166.4	104.6	16.4	5.6

	Calories	Sodium (mg.)	Carbo-hydrates (gm.)	Fat (gm.)
SNACK				
2 low-sodium crackers	22.0	1.7	2.9	1.0
¼ cup low-sodium cottage cheese	45.0	16.5	2.0	0.5
½ banana, sliced	60.7	0.7	15.9	0.1
Total	127.7	18.9	20.8	1.6
DINNER				
Sweet and Hot Lamb in Green Peppers*	248.2	85.2	25.6	8.1
Carrot and Eggplant Chili* (use meat stock)	46.6	18.0	7.1	0.8
1 cup shredded lettuce	18.0	9.0	3.5	0.3
½ cup boiled white rice	124.6	5.7	27.7	0.1
Coffee or tea	—	—	—	—
1 teaspoon sugar substitute	2.0	0	1.4	0
1 tablespoon low-fat milk	6.3	7.1	0.75	0.1
Total	445.7	125.0	66.1	9.4
SNACK				
1 pear	62.0	2.0	15.3	0.4
Grand Total	1,110.1	327.8	162.6	26.7

* See index for recipe page number.

DAY ELEVEN

Tips for Day Eleven

Today is a day for a few modest indulgences—but all within the 1,200-calorie boundary we set. Your menu includes a Basic Bun, Szechwan Fried Rice, and Coconut Strawberries, proving that you really can eat so-called fattening things on a diet. Just one little reminder. If you have to reduce your total sodium, substitute ¼ cup cottage cheese for the yogurt at breakfast.

So live it up. Treat yourself to a relaxing massage and be ready to greet the coming weekend.

	Calories	Sodium (mg.)	Carbo-hydrates (gm.)	Fat (gm.)
BREAKFAST				
½ cup plain yogurt	70.9	53.7	5.6	3.9
½ cup grapes	69.0	3.0	15.7	1.0
1 Basic Bun*	165.1	1.3	34.0	0.5
Coffee or tea	—	—	—	—
1 teaspoon sugar substitute	2.0	0	1.4	0
1 tablespoon low-fat milk	6.3	7.1	0.75	0.1
Total	313.3	65.1	57.5	5.5

	Calories	Sodium (mg.)	Carbo-hydrates (gm.)	Fat (gm.)
LUNCH				
Steamed Chicken in Oyster Sauce*	145.1	68.5	4.3	3.6
1 cup shredded lettuce	18.0	9.0	3.5	0.3
½ tomato, sliced	15.7	2.1	3.4	0.1
2 tablespoons lemon juice	3.3	0.1	1.3	0.01
Coffee or tea	—	—	—	—
1 teaspoon sugar substitute	2.0	0	1.4	0
1 tablespoon low-fat milk	6.3	7.1	0.75	0.1
Total	190.4	86.8	14.7	4.1
SNACK				
Almond Gelatin*	50.4	4.0	6.6	0.02
½ orange	49.0	1.0	12.2	0.2
Iced tea with lemon	—	—	—	—
Total	99.4	5.0	18.8	0.2
DINNER				
Flounder in Silk*	189.0	102.7	10.7	6.8
¼ green pepper, sliced	11.0	6.5	2.4	0.1
¼ cucumber, sliced	41.0	17.7	2.9	0.1
Szechwan Fried Rice*	234.7	20.3	35.8	8.7
Coconut Strawberries*	72.0	2.2	9.4	1.8
Coffee or tea	—	—	—	—
1 teaspoon sugar substitute	2.0	0	1.4	0
1 tablespoon low-fat milk	6.3	7.1	0.75	0.1
Total	556.0	156.5	63.4	17.6
SNACK				
2 low-sodium crackers	22.0	1.7	3.9	2.0
Grand Total	1,181.1	315.1	157.3	22.9

* See index for recipe page number.

DAY TWELVE

Tips for Day Twelve

Feeling good and looking good, you are now coming down the home stretch.

Any leftover Steamed Chicken in Oyster Sauce can be reheated for dinner in place of Sweet Chicken and Mushrooms. Just add ¼ cup hot water and a dash of dry sherry for zip and warm over low heat.

Moreover, if any Flounder in Silk remains, serve it cold for lunch as a substitute for both the Curried Fish Soup and the Beef Strips and Cauliflower in Mustard Sauce.

However, if you must keep your sodium consumption to 250 milligrams daily, the above options will not do it for you. They will simply be an equal exchange. What will work is a new lunch menu: Ginger Squid Salad in Soy Sauce plus one sliced tomato, added to the lettuce and coffee or tea, will bring your sodium comfortably in line, reduce your calories and fat slightly, and have no substantial effect on your carbohydrate level.

So take your choice. You can always have the chicken dish for lunch on Day Thirteen and the flounder for dinner on Day Fourteen. The options are limitless.

	Calories	Sodium (mg.)	Carbo-hydrates (gm.)	Fat (gm.)
BREAKFAST				
½ cup oatmeal	62.9	2.0	11.1	1.1
¼ cup low-fat milk	25.0	28.6	3.0	0.5
½ apple	53.0	1.0	15.0	0.6
½ ounce low-sodium cheddar cheese	56.9	6.0	0.3	4.6
Coffee or tea	—	—	—	—
1 teaspoon sugar substitute	2.0	0	1.4	0
1 tablespoon low-fat milk	6.3	7.1	0.75	0.1
Total	206.1	44.7	31.6	6.9

	Calories	Sodium (mg.)	Carbo-hydrates (gm.)	Fat (gm.)
LUNCH				
Curried Fish Soup*	98.0	60.1	6.5	2.4
Beef Strips and Cauliflower in Mustard Sauce*	203.2	59.6	8.8	10.3
1 cup shredded lettuce	18.0	9.0	3.5	0.3
Coffee or tea	—	—	—	—
1 teaspoon sugar substitute	2.0	0	1.4	0
1 tablespoon low-fat milk	6.3	7.1	0.75	0.1
Total	327.5	135.8	21.0	13.1
SNACK				
1 orange	98.0	2.0	24.4	0.4
Iced tea with lemon	—	—	—	—
Total	98.0	2.0	24.4	0.4
DINNER				
Sweet Chicken and Mushrooms*	157.5	51.4	9.2	8.8
Sweet and Hot Cabbage*	81.1	26.6	8.3	4.4
1 tomato, sliced	31.4	4.2	6.8	0.2
½ cup boiled white rice	124.6	5.7	27.7	0.1
Coffee or tea	—	—	—	—
1 teaspoon sugar substitute	2.0	0	1.4	0
1 tablespoon low-fat milk	6.3	7.1	0.75	0.1
Total	402.9	95.0	54.2	13.6
SNACK				
¼ cantaloupe	42.9	17.1	10.7	0.1
Grand Total	1,077.4	294.6	141.9	34.1

* See index for recipe page number.

DAY THIRTEEN

Tips for Day Thirteen

This is one thirteen that is lucky. It is the last day before the end of your two-week adventure.

Any leftover Curried Fish Soup can be refrigerated and served cold or reheated for a brunch snack on Day Fourteen. The Beef Strips and Cauliflower in Mustard Sauce, as a half-portion, could easily replace the Barbecued Chicken Bun that same morning.

That's all—no problems, a festive dinner to look forward to, and one day to go.

	Calories	Sodium (mg.)	Carbo-hydrates (gm.)	Fat (gm.)
BREAKFAST				
½ cup low-sodium cottage cheese	90.0	31.0	4.0	1.0
3½ ounces pineapple chunks, drained	52.0	1.0	13.7	0.2
1 slice low-sodium bread	89.0	12.5	17.0	1.0
1 teaspoon unsalted margarine	34.3	0.7	0.02	3.9
Coffee or tea	—	—	—	—
1 teaspoon sugar substitute	2.0	0	1.4	0
1 tablespoon low-fat milk	6.3	7.1	0.75	0.1
Total	273.6	52.3	36.9	6.2

	Calories	Sodium (mg.)	(gm.) Carbo-hydrates	Fat (gm.)
LUNCH				
½ can low-sodium tuna	108.0	51.0	0	0.8
Asparagus in Oyster Sauce*	64.4	6.6	7.5	2.5
1 cup shredded lettuce	18.0	9.0	3.5	0.3
½ tomato, sliced	15.7	2.1	3.4	0.1
Coffee or tea	—	—	—	—
1 teaspoon sugar substitute	2.0	0	1.4	0
1 tablespoon low-fat milk	6.3	7.1	0.75	0.1
Total	214.4	75.8	16.6	3.8
SNACK				
1 cup low-sodium chicken bouillon	18.0	5.0	2.0	1.0
2 low-sodium crackers	22.0	1.7	2.9	1.0
1 zucchini, sliced	34.0	2.0	7.2	0.2
Total	74.0	8.7	12.1	2.2
DINNER				
Braised Pork with Orange Rings*	266.1	63.8	6.9	14.4
Rice and Mixed Vegetables*	202.2	27.6	32.7	4.5
Lemon Sponge Cake*	122.8	10.9	24.4	1.0
Coffee or tea	—	—	—	—
1 teaspoon sugar substitute	2.0	0	1.4	0
1 tablespoon low-fat milk	6.3	7.1	0.75	0.1
Total	599.4	109.4	66.2	20.0
SNACK				
½ cup strawberries	20.8	0.7	5.5	0.3
Grand Total	1,182.2	246.9	137.3	32.5

* See index for recipe page number.

DAY FOURTEEN

Tips for Day Fourteen

You made it. Fourteen days. You did not snap at your friends or insult your boss or die of starvation. And no doubt, you *are* a few pounds lighter, a lot more confident, and filled with a vitality you did not know you had.

This newfound energy is mental as well as physical, and will give you the desire to go forward on your own.

Remember, it usually takes three weeks for your body to fully adjust to a new diet. You might not see a major weight drop (two pounds) until then. But there are two things to keep in mind always:

1. A good diet—one that is well balanced, one that will not only take the weight off but keep it off—is a diet that lets you shed pounds slowly and steadily.

2. What you have started is more than a diet. It is a way of life—a healthier, thinner you, better in every way.

Now you know it is in your grasp. The next steps are up to you.

You can start your own meal planning from scratch by following the guidelines in this chapter. Or you can repeat or adapt the first two weeks of this diet until you are comfortable with the concept.

Either way, you now know you can do it! Today, you deserve to splurge a little. Enjoy it and then . . . go get 'em.

	Calories	Sodium (mg.)	Carbo-hydrates (gm.)	Fat (gm.)
BRUNCH				
3½ ounces apple juice	47.0	1.0	11.9	0.1
1 Barbecued Chicken Bun*	146.0	10.3	24.5	2.0
Coffee or tea	—	—	—	—
1 teaspoon sugar substitute	2.0	0	1.4	0
1 tablespoon low-fat milk	6.3	7.1	0.75	0.1
Total	201.3	18.4	38.6	2.2

	Calories	Sodium (mg.)	Carbo-hydrates (gm.)	Fat (gm.)
LUNCH				
Braised Pork with Orange Rings*	266.1	63.8	6.9	14.4
1 cup shredded spinach	18.6	50.7	5.9	0.2
3 tablespoons lemon juice	9.9	0.03	3.3	0.4
Coffee or tea	—	—	—	—
1 teaspoon sugar substitute	2.0	0	1.4	0
1 tablespoon low-fat milk	6.3	7.1	0.75	0.1
Total	302.9	121.6	18.3	15.1
SNACK				
Ginger Carrot and Peanut Soup*	95.0	36.2	2.9	4.9
1 peach	43.4	1.1	11.1	0.1
Total	138.4	37.3	14.0	5.0
DINNER				
Swordfish with Hot Sauce*	184.0	3.3	6.1	9.9
½ tomato, sliced	15.7	2.1	3.4	0.1
Glazed Green Beans*	115.0	19.2	17.9	5.1
½ cup boiled white rice	124.6	5.7	27.7	0.1
Coffee or tea	—	—	—	—
1 teaspoon sugar substitute	2.0	0	1.4	0
1 tablespoon low-fat milk	6.3	7.1	0.75	0.1
Total	447.6	37.4	57.3	15.3
SNACK				
Strawberry Pancakes*	94.0	8.0	9.3	5.3
Grand Total	1,184.2	222.7	137.5	42.9

* See index for recipe page number.

Tables of Nutritional Values

The following tables, based on information from USDA Handbook Number 8, provide an easy reference for nutritional values of all foods used (or suggested) in this book. Specifically included are the calorie, sodium, fat, and carbohydrate content per 100 grams (approximately 3½ ounces).

We ask that you note the following:

1. Nutritional values are based on raw ingredients unless otherwise noted.
2. Zero connotes no presence.
3. A dash connotes trace amounts.

	Calories	Sodium (mg.)	Fat (gm.)	Carbo-hydrates (gm.)
CONDIMENTS				
Honey	304	5.0	0	82.3
Jam	272	12.0	0.1	70.0
Jelly	273	17.0	0.1	70.6
Ketchup				
Chili, low-sodium	56	30.0	0	1.0
Regular, low-sodium	42	20.0	0	1.0
Marmalade	257	14.0	0.1	70.1
Molasses	232	37.0	0	60.0
Peanut butter, low-sodium	630	7.0	52.1	22.0
Sugar				
Regular	385	1.0	0	99.5
Substitute[1]	42	0	0	9.8
Tomato paste, low-sodium	91	10.0	0.4	18.6
Vinegar				
Cider and red	14	1.0	0	5.9
White	12	1.0	0	5.0

[1] Low-sodium as well as sugar-free.

	Calories	Sodium (mg.)	Fat (gm.)	Carbo-hydrates (gm.)
DAIRY				
Cheese				
Cheddar, low-sodium	398	18.0	32.2	2.1
Cottage, low-sodium	106	18.0	4.2	2.9
Gouda, low-sodium	345	35.0	28.0	1.7
Swiss, low-sodium	355	30.0	28.0	1.7
Egg[2]	163	122.0	11.5	0.9
Margarine, unsalted	720	15.0	81.0	0.4
Milk, low-fat	48	145.0	1.0	5.5
Yogurt, plain, low-fat	50	143.0	1.7	5.2
FISH AND SEAFOOD				
Bass				
Sea	93	68.0	1.2	0
Striped	105	—	2.7	0
White	98	68.0	2.3	0
Cod	78	70.0	0.3	0
Flounder	79	78.0	0.8	0
Haddock	79	61.0	0.1	0
Halibut	100	54.0	1.2	0
Lobster[3]	91	210.0	1.9	0.5
Oysters, shucked	66	73.0	1.8	3.4
Perch	91	68.0	0.9	0
Pollack	95	48.0	0.9	0
Red snapper	93	67.0	0.9	0
Salmon				
Raw	217	64.0	13.4	0
Canned, low-sodium	145	70.0	5.9	0
Scallops	81	265.0	0.2	3.3
Scrod	78	70.0	0.3	0
Shrimp	91	140.0	0.8	1.5
Sole	79	78.0	0.8	0
Squid	84	—	0.9	1.5
Swordfish	118	—	4.0	0
Tilefish	79	—	0.5	0
Trout, rainbow	195	50.0	11.4	0
Tuna				
Raw	145	37.0	4.1	0
Canned, low-sodium	108	51.0	0.8	0

[2] One medium egg is approximately 2 ounces.
[3] There are approximately 4 ounces of meat in a one-pound lobster.

	Calories	Sodium (mg.)	Fat (gm.)	Carbo- hydrates (gm.)
FRUIT				
Apple	58	1.0	0.6	14.5
Apricots				
Canned, in juice	54	1.0	0.2	13.6
Dried[4]	260	26.0	0.5	66.5
Banana	85	1.0	0.2	22.2
Coconut, dried	548	—	39.1	53.2
Dates[5]	274	1.0	0.5	72.9
Grapefruit				
Canned, in water	30	4.0	0.1	7.6
Raw	44	1.0	0.1	11.5
Kumquats	65	7.0	0.1	17.1
Lemon	27	5.0	0.3	8.2
Lime	28	2.0	0.2	9.5
Loquats	48	—	0.2	12.4
Lychee nuts, canned in juice	64	3.0	0.3	16.4
Mandarin oranges	46	2.0	0.2	11.6
Orange	49	1.0	0.2	12.2
Peach				
Canned, dietetic	31	2.0	0.1	8.1
Raw	38	1.0	0.1	9.7
Pear				
Canned, dietetic	32	1.0	0.2	8.3
Raw	62	2.0	0.4	15.3
Pineapple				
Canned, in water	39	1.0	0.1	10.2
Raw	52	1.0	0.2	13.7
Plum				
Canned, in water	46	2.0	0.2	11.9
Raw	66	2.0	—	17.8
Prunes[6]	255	8.0	0.6	67.4
Raisins[6]	289	27.0	0.2	77.4
Strawberries[7]	37	1.0	0.5	8.4
Tangerine	46	2.0	0.2	11.6

[4] 1 cup equals 3 ounces.
[5] 1 cup equals 6½ ounces.
[6] 1 cup equals 6 ounces.
[7] 1 cup equals 5½ ounces; 1 pint equals 10½ ounces.

	Calories	Sodium (mg.)	Fat (gm.)	Carbo-hydrates (gm.)
JUICE				
Apple	47	1.0	—	11.9
Grapefruit	42	1.0	0.1	10.2
Lemon	23	1.0	0.1	7.6
Lime	26	1.0	0.1	9.0
Orange	48	1.0	0.2	11.2
Tomato	19	3.0	0.1	4.3
MEAT				
Beef				
Chuck (ground beef)	286	47.0	20.3	0
Flank (London broil)	191	65.0	6.6	0
Sirloin	353	65.0	27.5	0
Lamb				
Leg	192	75.0	7.7	0
Loin	197	75.0	8.6	0
Rib	224	75.0	12.1	0
Shoulder	215	75.0	11.2	0
Liver, chicken	129	70.0	3.7	2.9
Pork				
Loin	254	70.0	14.2	0
Shoulder	244	70.0	14.3	0
Spareribs	440	70.0	38.9	0
NUTS[8]				
Almonds	98	4.0	54.2	19.5
Cashews	561	15.0	45.7	29.3
Peanuts	582	5.0	48.7	20.6
Sesame	582	—	53.4	17.6
Walnuts				
Black	628	3.0	59.3	14.8
English	651	2.0	64.0	15.8
POULTRY				
Chicken[9]				
Fryers	126	58.0	5.1	0
Flesh and skin (whole)	126	58.0	5.1	0
Flesh only (whole)	107	78.0	2.7	0
Breast	110	50.0	2.4	0

[8] ¼ cup equals approximately 2 ounces.
[9] Approximately 60 percent of a whole chicken is actually meat.

	Calories	Sodium (mg.)	Fat (gm.)	Carbo-hydrates (gm.)
POULTRY (continued)				
Drumstick	115	67.0	3.9	0
Thigh	128	67.0	5.6	0
Wing	146	50.0	7.4	0
Roasters				
Flesh and skin (whole)	197	58.0	12.6	0
Flesh only (whole)	131	58.0	4.5	0
Dark meat, without skin	132	67.0	4.7	0
Light meat, without skin	128	50.0	3.2	0
Duck[10]	165	74.0	8.2	0
Rock Cornish Hen[11]	110	50.0	2.4	0
VEGETABLES				
Asparagus	26	2.0	0.2	5.0
Bamboo shoots	27	—	0.3	5.2
Bean sprouts[12]	134	5.0	5.1	13.2
Black beans[13]	118	8.0	1.5	61.2
Broccoli[14]	32	15.0	0.3	5.9
Cabbage[12]				
American	24	20.0	0.2	5.4
Chinese	16	26.0	0.2	2.9
Carrots	42	43.0	0.2	9.7
Cauliflower[12]	27	13.0	0.2	5.2
Cilantro (parsley)	44	45.0	0.6	8.5
Corn				
Canned, low-sodium, plain	57	2.0	0.5	13.6
Canned, low-sodium, creamed	82	2.0	1.1	18.5
Cucumber	48	20.6	0.1	3.4
Eggplant	25	2.0	0.2	5.6
Garlic	137	19.0	0.2	30.8
Green beans	32	7.0	0.2	7.1
Kidney beans[13]	343	10.0	1.5	61.9
Leeks	52	5.0	0.3	11.2
Lettuce[15]	18	9.0	0.3	3.5
Mushrooms[15]	28	15.0	0.3	4.4

[10] Approximately 50 percent of a whole duck is actually meat.
[11] Approximately 40 percent of a whole Rock Cornish Hen is actually meat.
[12] 1 cup equals 4 ounces.
[13] 1 cup equals 6 ounces.
[14] 1 stalk equals 5 ounces.
[15] 1 cup equals 2 ounces.

	Calories	Sodium (mg.)	Fat (gm.)	Carbo-hydrates (gm.)
VEGETABLES (*continued*)				
Onion	38	10.0	0.2	17.4
Peas	84	2.0	0.4	14.4
Peppers				
Bell, green	22	13.0	0.2	4.8
Bell, red	31	25.0	0.3	7.1
Chili, green	37	25.0	0.2	9.1
Chili, red	65	25.0	0.4	15.8
Radishes	17	18.0	0.1	3.6
Rice				
Cooked[16]	109	5.0	0.1	24.2
Raw[13]	363	5.0	0.4	80.4
Scallions	36	5.0	0.2	8.2
Snow pea pods[17]	53	2.0	0.2	12.0
Spaghetti				
Cooked	148	2.0	0.5	30.1
Raw	362	2.0	1.2	75.2
Spinach[18]	26	71.0	0.3	4.3
Tofu (bean curd)	72	7.0	0	—
Tomatoes	22	3.0	0.2	4.7
Water chestnuts	79	20.0	0.2	19.0
Watercress[19]	19	52.0	0.3	0.5
Yellow squash	20	1.0	0.2	4.3
Zucchini	17	1.0	0.1	3.6
WHEAT AND GRAIN				
Bread, low-sodium[20]	241	3.5	2.6	49.3
Crackers, low-sodium[21]	195	4.3	9.0	25.5
Oatmeal, cooked	55	4.0	1.0	9.7
Rice, puffed, salt-free	399	2.0	0.4	89.5
Wheat, puffed, salt-free	363	4.0	1.5	78.5

[16] 1 cup equals 8 ounces.
[17] 1 cup equals 2½ ounces.
[18] 1 cup equals 3½ ounces.
[19] 1 bunch equals 2½ ounces.
[20] One slice equals 1 ounce.
[21] Eleven equal 1 ounce.

	Calories	Sodium (mg.)	Fat (gm.)	Carbo-hydrates (gm.)
MISCELLANY				
Baking powder, low-sodium	83	40.0	—	20.1
Bouillon				
Beef, low-sodium[22]	378	210.0	21.0	42.0
Chicken, low-sodium[23]	378	105.0	21.0	42.0
Cornstarch	362	—	—	87.6
Flour				
All-purpose	365	2.0	1.2	74.5
Rice	368	5.0	2.6	76.8
Gelatin, unflavored[24]	335	2.0	0.1	0
Oil	884	0.0	100.0	0
Wine (dry sherry,				
champagne)	85	5.0	0	4.2
Yeast	282	52.0	1.6	38.9

[22] Content per tablespoon equals 54 calories, 30 milligrams sodium, 3 grams fat, 3 grams carbohydrates.

[23] Content per tablespoon equals 54 calories, 15 milligrams sodium, 3 grams fat, 3 grams carbohydrates.

[24] One package equals 2 tablespoons equals 1 ounce.

Bibliography

American Diabetes Association, Inc., and The American Dietetic Association. *A Guide for Professionals: The Effective Application of "Exchange Lists for Meal Planning,"* 1977.

American Diabetes Association, Inc., and The American Dietetic Association. *Exchange Lists for Meal Planning,* 1976.

American Heart Association. *Cooking Without Your Salt Shaker.* Dallas, Texas: American Heart Association's Communication Division, 1978.

American Heart Association Booklets: *Your 500 Milligrams Sodium Diet, Your 1000 Milligrams Sodium Diet, Your Mild Sodium-Restricted Diet.* Dallas, Texas: American Heart Association, 1957.

Ashley, Richard, and Duggal, Heidi. *Dictionary of Nutrition.* New York: Pocket Books, 1975.

Bieler, Henry G., M.D. *Food Is Your Best Medicine.* New York: Vintage Books, 1975.

Bowen, Angela, M.D. *The Diabetic Gourmet.* New York: Harper & Row, Publishers, 1970, 1980.

Brody, Jane. *Jane Brody's Nutrition Book.* New York: W. W. Norton & Company, Inc., 1981.

Butterfield, Fox. *China: Alive in the Bitter Sea.* New York: Bantam Books, Inc., 1982.

Eisner, Will. *What's in What You Eat.* New York: Bantam Books, Inc., 1983.

Hsuing, Deh-Ta. *Chinese Regional Cooking.* Secaucus, New Jersey: Chartwell Books, Inc., 1979.

James, Janet, and Goulder, Lois. *The Dell Color-Coded Low-Salt-Living Guide.* New York: Dell Publishing, Inc., 1980.

Joslin Clinic. *Diabetic Diet Guide.* Boston, Mass.

Kraus, Barbara. *Calories and Carbohydrates.* Fifth Revised Edition. New York: New American Library, 1983.

Kraus, Barbara. *Sodium Guide to Brand Names and Basic Foods.* Expanded Edition. New York: New American Library, 1983.

Lau, D. C. *Laotzu/Tao Te Ching.* Middlesex, England: Penguin Books, Ltd., 1963.

Lo, Kenneth. *Food the Chinese Way.* New Jersey: Chartwell Books, Inc., 1976.

Middleton, Katharine, and Hess, Mary Abbott. *The Art of Cooking for the Diabetic*. New York: New American Library, 1978.

Ornish, Dean, M.D. *Stress, Diet and Your Heart*. New York: New American Library, 1982.

Rechtschaffen, Joseph S., M.D., and Carola, Robert. *Dr. Rechtschaffen's Diet for Lifetime Weight Control and Better Health*. New York: Random House, Inc., 1980.

Revell, Dorothy. *Cholesterol Control*. Denver, Colorado: Royal Publications, Inc., 1961.

Schell, Merle. *Tasting Good. The International Salt-Free Diet Cookbook*. New York: New American Library, 1981.

Sullivan, Margaret. *The New Carbohydrate Gram Counter*. New York: Dell Publishing, Inc., 1980.

United States Department of Agriculture. Handbook No. 8. U.S. Government Printing Office. Washington, D.C. 20402, 1963.

U.S. Department of Health and Human Services. *Cookbooks for People with Diabetes*. Selected Annotations. NIH Publication No. 81-2177. Bethesda, Maryland 20205: National Diabetes Information Clearinghouse, 1981.

U.S. Department of Health and Human Services. *Diet and Nutrition for People with Diabetes*. Selected Annotations. NIH Publication No. 80-1872. Washington, D.C.: National Diabetes Information Clearinghouse, 1979.

Ware, James R. *The Sayings of Confucius*. New York: New American Library, 1955.

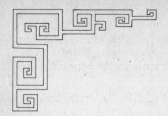
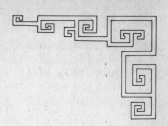

Index

fish and seafood soup, 78
lemon, 128–29
noodles with seafood, 223
salad Cantonese, 88
sauce, 239
  for Chinese steak sauce, 238
seafood casserole Cantonese, 124
Lo mein:
  beef, 218
  chicken, 218
  pork, 218
  shrimp, 219
Loquats, 12–13
  bananas and, 245
Lychees, 13
  Chinese rice pudding, 249

Mandarin chicken, 155
Marinade(s):
  broccoli stems and cauliflower,
    marinated, 103
  vegetable, chicken with, 92
Meats, see Beef; Lamb; Pork
Meat stock, 69
Menus, see Diet, Chinese;
    Entertaining
Minced oysters, 53
Miso, see Black bean sauce
Mixed seafood in hoisin sauce, 126
Mongolian flounder salad, 100
Mongolian lamb salad, 100
Mongolian pork salad, 100
Multi-purpose batter, 65
Mushroom(s):
  batter-fried vegetables, 188
  bean curd, tomatoes, and, 191
  black, see Black mushrooms
  chicken:
    plus four, 149
    and vegetables, glazed, 142
  oyster, see Oyster mushrooms
  sauce, bamboo shoots in, 190
  seafood casserole Cantonese, 124
  soup:
    and corn, 82
    sweet and hot chicken, 72
  in soy sauce, 199
  vegetable buns, sweet, 43
  Yunnan curried, 29
Mustard sauce:
  asparagus in, 189

beef strips and cauliflower in, 97
braised fish in tomato and, 110

Noodle(s), 9, 10, 205, 216–26
  with almond chicken, 224
  beef(y):
    in chili sauce, 226
    in hot peanut sauce, 177
    lo mein, 218
  chicken lo mein, 218
  fried, 216
  of land and sea, 225
  in orange sauce, spicy, 217
  peanutty, with chicken, 221
  salad:
    fried, 101
    watercress and, 102
  with seafood, 223
  with sesame paste sauce, 222
  shrimp lo mein, 219
  soup, seafood and, 80
  with vegetables, saucy, 220
  see also Rice
Nutritional Values, Table of, 323–29

Odd-spiced duck, 159
Onion(s):
  chicken wings, sherried, 38
  salad, cucumber and, 104
  zucchini and, fried, 203
Orange(s):
  buns, apricot, 252
  duck in citrus sauce, 161
  fruit steak, 180
  ginger citrus with pineapple, 246
  Mandarin, salmon with green beans
    and, 117
  Mandarin chicken, 155
  rings, braised pork with, 172
  six-fruit sauce, 242
  stewed fruit in nut sauce, 248
Orange peel, dried, 11, 23
Orange peel powder, 17
Orange sauce:
  scallops in, 130
  spicy noodles in, 217
Oyster(s):
  braised fish and peanuts, 109
  chicken and, 153
  chicken livers and, 163
  fish and seafood soup, 78

Oyster(s) (*cont.*)
fried rice and, 207
minced, 53
noodles with vegetables, saucy, 220
and pork egg rolls, 50
pork with, hot and spicy, 171
puffs, deep-fried, 54
seafood casserole Cantonese, 124
soup, beef, cucumber, and, 74
see also Oyster sauce
Oyster mushrooms, 13
bamboo shoots in mushroom sauce, 190
see also Mushrooms
Oyster sauce, 13, 234
asparagus in, 189
cabbage in, 194
chicken in, steamed, 144–45
for Chinese steak sauce, 238
corn in, 194
steak in, braised, 178
steak slices in, 37

Pancakes:
banana, 250
strawberry, 250
Parsley, 11
Peaches:
duck sauce, 234
duck with pungent fruit sauce, 160
fruit and nut rolls, 251
and pineapple, 246
stir-fried chicken legs with soy sauce, 146–47
Peanut(s):
cookies, sesame, 248
fish and, braised, 109
noodles with sesame paste sauce, 222
sauce:
beef in hot, 177
chicken salad Canton with, 91
soup, ginger carrot and, 81
Peanut butter, 17
beef in hot peanut sauce, 177
peanut-chili bean sprouts, 192
peanutty chicken and scallions, 140
peanutty noodles with chicken, 221

peanutty vegetable buns, 44
sauce, chicken cubes in, 33
Peanut oil, 13
Peanutty chicken and scallions, 140
Peanutty noodles with chicken, 221
Peanutty vegetable buns, 44
Pears:
baked in almond honey, 247
duck:
with pungent fruit sauce, 160
salad with, 94
fruit and nut rolls, 251
six-fruit sauce, 242
Pecans for water chestnut cake, 256
Peppers, *see* Green peppers; Red peppers
Pepper sauce, shrimp in, 134
Perch for seafood casserole Cantonese, 124
Pineapple:
curried chicken with, 144
ginger citrus with, 246
many-flavored fried rice, 213
peaches and, 246
sweet and sour sauce, 235
Piquant tomatoes and cucumber, 251
Plum sauce, *see* Duck sauce
Plums for duck sauce, 234
Poached bass with hot sauce and vegetables, 112
Poaching, 22
Pork, 165, 166–75
balls in hot sauce, 31
barbecued, Chinese, 175
and bean curd, 169
with cabbage, spiced, 167
ground:
green beans with pork bits, 198
lion's head miniatures, 57
and scallop buns, 46
watercress-rolled, 58
hoisin rice in four, 211
and kumquats, 168
lo mein, 218
many-flavored fried rice, 213
meat stock, 69
noodles:
of land and sea, 225
in orange sauce, spicy, 217
with orange rings, braised, 172
and oyster egg rolls, 50

orange:
  scallops in, 130
  spicy noodles in, 217
oyster, 13, 234
  asparagus in, 189
  cabbage in, 194
  chicken in, steamed, 144–45
  corn on, 194
  steak in, braised, 178
  steak slices in, 37
peanut:
  beef in hot, 177
  chicken salad Canton with, 91
peanut butter, chicken cubes in, 33
pepper, shrimp in, 134
pork:
  braised cod in, 113
  steamed shrimp with, 132
  steamed snapper in, 120
pungent fruit, duck with, 160
sesame paste, noodles with, 222
shrimp paste, 240
six-fruit, 242
  braised zucchini in, 202
soy (substitute), 15, 227
  ginger squid salad in, 89
  leeks in, braised, 198–99
  mushrooms in, 199
  peaches, stir-fried chicken legs
    with, 146–47
  salmon with zucchini in, 118
  sherry-, braised duck in, 162
sweet and sour, 235
Szechwan pepper, flounder in, 116
vegetable hot, steamed chicken
    with, 90
vinegar-nut, 241
yellow bean, 236
  chicken in hot, 151
see also Seasonings
Saucy noodles with vegetables, 220
Scallions, peanutty chicken and, 140
Scallop(s):
  and almonds, 130–31
  and cashews in tomatoes, spiced,
    88–89
  and corn soup, 79
  mixed seafood in hoisin sauce, 126
  noodles in orange sauce, spicy,
    217
  in orange sauce, 130

and pork buns, 46
seafood and noodle soup, 80
in soy sauce, 129
Sea bass:
  poached, with hot sauce and
    vegetables, 112
  sweet and sour fish, crispy, 111
Seafood:
  casserole Cantonese, 124
  in hoisin sauce, mixed, 126
  noodles with, 223
  salad, assorted, 87
  soup:
    fish and, 78
    and noodle, 80
  sticks, 125
  twice-cooked, 123
  see also Fish; *individual types of
    seafood*
Seasonings, 229–32
  chili oil, 9, 230
  chili paste, 10, 230
  chili powder, 9, 231
  chili sauce, 231
  curry powder, 11, 23, 232
  five-spice powder, 12, 228
  Szechwan pepper spice, 229
  see also Sauce(s)
Sesame beef cubes, 35
Sesame seed(s), 14
  chicken livers sesame, 163
  -peanut cookies, 248
Sesame seed oil, 14, 23
Sesame seed paste, 14
  sauce, noodles with, 222
Shallow frying, 21–22
Shellfish, *see* Seafood; individual
    shellfish, e.g., Lobster; Shrimp
Sherry(ied), 14
  fried apples, 247
  onion chicken wings, 38
  shrimp, ginger, 55
  -soy sauce, braised duck in, 162
  sugar sesame Cornish hens in
    lemon, 156
  -vinegar baby spareribs, 36
Shredding, 21
Shrimp:
  and beef balls, 32
  in black bean sauce, 55
  braised, bamboo, 131

Spiced shrimp and cashews in
   tomatoes, 89
Spicy fried chicken, 137
Spicy noodles in orange sauce, 217
Spinach and beef buns, 45
Spring roll skins, 15
Squash, yellow:
   batter-fried vegetables, 188
   see also Zucchini
Squid:
   and cabbage with duck sauce, 136
   fish salad with bean curd, 86
   and mushrooms, 135
   noodles with seafood, 223
   salad in soy sauce, ginger, 89
   twice-cooked seafood, 123
Star anise, 15
Steak, *see* Beef
Steamed buns, 63
Steamed chicken in oyster sauce,
   144–45
Steamed chicken with vegetable hot
   sauce salad, 90
Steamed fish with chili ginger sauce,
   108
Steamed shrimp with pork sauce, 132
Steamed snapper with pork sauce,
   120
Steamers, bamboo, 19
Steaming, 22
Stewed fruit in nut sauce, 248
Stir-fried beef and vegetables, 183
Stir-fried chicken legs with soy
   sauce peaches, 146–47
Stir-fried snow pea pods, 200
Stir-frying, 21
Stock, 67–69
   chicken, 68
   fish, 67
   meat, 69
   see also Soups
Strawberries:
   apples with, 244
   coconut, 245
   pancakes, 250
   six-fruit sauce, 242
Striped bass for steamed fish with
   chili ginger sauce, 108
Stuffed chicken of many flavors, 139
Sub gum chicken, 148

Sugar:
   beef salad, 95
   sesame Cornish hens in lemon
      sherry, 156
   and spice tomato soup, 83
Sugar substitutes, 17, 293
Sweet and hot cabbage, 193
Sweet and hot carrots and radishes,
   101
Sweet and hot chicken mushroom
   soup, 72
Sweet and hot lamb in green peppers,
   185
Sweet and pungent chicken, 138
Sweet and sour corn, 196
Sweet and sour fish, crispy, 111
Sweet and sour sauce, 235
Sweet chicken and mushrooms, 147
Sweet lamb with vegetables, 186
Sweet vegetable buns, 43
Swordfish:
   braised fish and peanuts, 109
   with hot sauce, 121
   seafood salad, assorted, 87
Szechwan beef, 174
Szechwan fried rice, 208
Szechwan peppercorns, 15
Szechwan pepper sauce, flounder
   in, 116
Szechwan pepper spice, 15, 229
Szechwan pork with vegetables, 173
Szechwan vegetable salad, 102–03

Table of Nutritional Values, 323–29
Tangerine(s):
   sugar beef salad, 95
   Szechwan vegetable salad, 102–03
Tangerine peel, dried, 11
Thousand-layer cake, 255
Three-color soup, 82–83
Tiger lily buds, 15
Tofu, *see* Bean curd
Tomato(es):
   bean curd, and mushrooms, 191
   beef and vegetables, stir-fried, 183
   and cucumbers, piquant, 201
   and mustard sauce, braised fish in,
      110
   red and green shrimp, 132–33
   scallops and cashews in, spiced,
      88–89

PLUME

A WORLD OF FINE FOODS

(0452)

☐ **THE CLASSIC CUISINE OF VIETNAM by Bach Ngo & Gloria Zimmerman.** Now Western cooks can discover the secrets of Vietnamese cuisine with these 150 distinctive and colorful recipes for both classic and modern dishes from the three gastronomic regions of Vietnam. Surprisingly easy to prepare, these dishes require no special equipment or skill, and most use ingredients that are readily available. (258332—$9.95)

☐ **PASTA AND RICE ITALIAN STYLE by Efrem Funghi Calingaert & Jacquelyn Days Serwer.** With over 250 imaginative and delicious dishes from all over Italy, this outstanding collection is impressive, delightfully different, and certain to tempt your entire family. Includes a guide to wines.
(256186—$7.95)

☐ **NIKKI & DAVID GOLDBECK'S AMERICAN WHOLEFOODS CUISINE.** A complete guide to delicious, high-quality cooking that matches great taste with well-being. These over 1,300 meatless, wholesome recipes from short order to gourmet will please every palate. "Destined to become a classic!" —*Vegetarian Times* (255821—$8.95)

☐ **A MOSTLY FRENCH FOOD PROCESSOR COOKBOOK by Colette Rossant & Jill Harris Herman.** Now the classic recipes previously considered too complex or time-consuming for any but the most expert chef are well within the range of most cooks. "Outstanding . . . adventurous and inspired."—*The New York Times* (254647—$7.95)

☐ **THE LOS ANGELES TIMES CALIFORNIA COOKBOOK.** Here at last is a cookbook that captures the sunny distinctiveness and ethnic diversity of California cuisine. You'll savor this glorious culinary journey through a state where good eating is a way of life, and enjoy the influences of Mexican, Italian, Japanese, Armenian, Indonesian, and many other types of cooking.
(254485—$9.95)

Prices slightly higher in Canada.

To order use coupon on next page.

PLUME

LOOK GOOD AND FEEL GOOD

(0452)